About the Author

Michael Skinner was born in 1933 neai
went to school during World War II. He
the R.A.F., learning Russian in the SECRET CLASSROOMS of the Joint Services Language Course at Cambridge, and the Joint Services School for Linguists at Bodmin in Cornwall. He then read for Honours in Modern and Medieval Languages at Emmanuel College, Cambridge under the late Professor Dame Elizabeth Hill. He spent a career teaching Russian (and French) in secondary and further education, devoting every spare moment to the present topic of Anglo-Russian relations through the Centuries.

WHAT WE DID FOR THE RUSSIANS

and what the Russians did for (some of) us

Michael Skinner

Published in Great Britain by JDS 2008

Printed and distributed by Lulu Press Incorporated

ISBN 978-0-9559760-0-1

Set in Garamond

To my wife Jennifer, with love

Acknowledgement

I would like to thank my son Jonathan, who has given me so much encouragement, and without whom this book would not have been published.

CONTENTS

A note to the Reader xi
Rulers of Russia during the period covered xiv

1 A DROVE OF DISCOVERERS 15

Richard Chancellor (- 1556) 15
Anthony Jenkinson (1530-1609) 19
Daniel Sylvester 20
Sir Jerome Horsey (- 1626) 21
Sir Jerome Bowes (- 1616) 24
Dr Giles Fletcher (c.1548-1611) 24
Sir Alexander Leslie (1568-) 26

2 A GATHERING OF GENERALS 29

James Bruce (1680-) 29
Patrick Gordon (1635-99) 32
Peter Lacy (1678-1751) 35

H.I.M. PETER THE GREAT 36

3 STAGGERING STATISTICS 38

John Perry (1670-1733) 38
John Cook 39

4 AN ASSORTMENT OF ADMIRALS 44

Sir Samuel Greig (1735-88) 44
John Elphinstone (1722-1785) 47

H.I.M. CATHERINE II OF ALL THE RUSSIAS 49

5 A THRONG OF TRAVELLERS 51

John Howard (1726-1815) 51
Samuel Whitbread (1758-1815) 52
An Account of Russia (1768) by G.Macartney 54
John Parkinson 55
John Dundas Cochchrane (1780-1825) 57
Elizabeth Rigby (1809-1893) 58

6 AN INFLUX OF INDUSTRIALISTS 59

Charles Gascoigne (1738-1806) 59
Samuel Bentham (1757-1831) 63
Col. William Upton 64
Matthew Boulton (1728-1809) 65

7 TWO VISITORS 67

Catherine Hamilton 67
George Green 69

8 AN ASSEMBLY OF ARTISTS 70

Charles Cameron (1743-1812) 70
John Field (1782-1837) 73
George Dawe (1796-1829) 75

H.I.M. ALEXANDER I OF ALL THE RUSSIAS 77

9 A MASS OF MEDICS 82

Dr Thomas Dimsdale (1712-1800) 82
Dr John Rogerson (1741-1823) 83
Sir James Wylie (1768-1854) 85
Edward Morton M.B. 88

10 A MINISTRY OF MISSIONARIES 92

Rev Arthur Young (1769-1827) 92
John Paterson (1776-1855) 94
William Allen 98
George Borrow (1803-1881) 99
Rev. Lewis Way (1772-1840) 100
Mrs Mary Holderness 102
Sir George Lefevre (1797-1879) 104

11 EAGER ENGINEERS 106

Sir John Rennie (1794-1874) 106
Capt. G. M. Jones, R.N. 108

12 HOTELS & CLUBS FOR ALL 112

Captain G. Colville Frankland (1797-1876) 112
G. Poulett Cameron (1805-1882) 115
W.R.Wilson (1772-1849) 115
George Augustus Sala (1828-1895) 117
Henry Morley 118

13 A CLUSTER OF CLERGY 122

Rev William Tooke (1744-1820) 122
Rev R.W. Blackmore 125
William Palmer (1811-1879) 127

14 A GAGGLE OF GOVERNESSES 129

Mrs Elizabeth Stephens 129
Miss Kitty Strutton (1811-1891) 131
Miss Hannah Tardsey (1847-) 132
Mrs Elizabeth Franklin (1834-1913) 133
Annette M.B.Meakin (1867-1959) 135
Tatiana Metternich (1915-2006) 137
Kyril Shishmarev 138

15 THE RUSH FOR RAILWAYS 139

George Washington Whistler (1800-49) 139
James Nasmyth (1808-90) 141
Sir Samuel Morton Peto (1809-1889) 142

AN IMAGINARY CONVERSATION BETWEEN TWO RUSSIAN WRITERS:... 144

16 INDUSTRY AGAIN! 146

George Hume 146
Thomas Witlam Atkinson (1799-1861) 149
S.S.Hill 150

17 THE SOCIETY OF SCIENTISTS 151

James Marr (1779-1874) 151

18 STOP THE WAR! 153

Joseph Sturge (1793-1859) 153
Lord Radstock (1833-1913) 154
William T. Stead (1849-1912) 156

19 A LITERARY LOOK 159

Rev Charles L. Dodgson (1832-98) 159
Thomas Budge Shaw 160
W.R.S.Ralston (1828-1889) 162
Edward A. Cazalet (1827-1883) 163
Matthew Edwardes (- 1917) 166
Gordon Craig (1872-1966) 167

20 SPORT - OR SPORT? 168

Herbert Swann (1894-) 168
Sir Archibald Wavell (1883-1950) 169

21 AN OVERALL VIEW 171

Sir John Foster Fraser (1868-1936) 171
Archibald Merrilees 175
Harry de Windt (1856-1933) 176
Miss Kate Marsden (1859-1931) 177
Joseph Wiggins (1832-1905) 178
Algernon Noble 180
Captain M.H.Hayes (1842-1904) 181
Dr Howard Kennard (1872-1916) 182

22 LINGUISTS AND AUTHORS 185

William Gerhardi (1895-1977) 185
William Barnes Steveni (1859-) 186
Stephen Graham (1884-1975) 189
Arthur Ransome (1884-1967) 190
Paul Dukes (1889-1968) 192
William John Birkbeck (1859-1916) 193
Robert Bruce Lockhart (1887-1970) 195
Denis Norman Garstin (1890-1916) 196
Colonel the Hon. Fred H. Cripps (1889-) 198

23 THE TUTOR 200

Sidney Gibbes (1876-1963) 200

Postscript 202
Bibliography 204
Index of Characters 212

A note to the Reader

The book in your hands represents at least two aspects of history so far neglected by the mainstream of published works. The first of these is a description, however incomplete, of the state of Russia in the 16th century, before it was seriously discovered by the West. Admittedly, the Muscovite state had had relations with some Europeans in the years between the withdrawal of the Mongol overlords +/- 1400, until the discovery by Richard Chancellor in 1553.

Take a glance at what Russia was in those days – a land-locked mass, with no warm-water ports, no access to the rest of the world, except by land through countries consistently antagonistic and jealous, mainly Catholic Poland. Bounded on the East by largely unexplored and uncharted Siberia, with its harsh climate and dense forest landscape.

Russia in the 11th century had been quite as advanced as the rest of Europe. Kiev in her golden age had given birth to artists, scholars, saints and soldiers at least equal to those of the West, only to be overrun by the Mongol hordes and enslaved by barbarians for over two centuries. All that Kievan Russia had stood for was demolished, burnt or stolen in the 1240's.

To think that an English adventurer, looking for a route to the East, should land by accident in the Arctic, find his way to Moscow, and survive an interview with one of history's most horrific rulers, Ivan the Terrible, is one of the moments in history which look like chance, or maybe part of the scheme for mankind. The encouragement given out in the earliest meetings was continued through the next century or so. It was clearly in the Russians' interest to keep in with the English – and clearly in the English interest to keep in with the Russians.

The pre-eminent Russian rulers of the next 250 years, Peter the Great, Catherine the Great and Alexander I, all happened by chance (or destiny) to be eager to encourage the British element in all spheres of life: teaching and training the Russians in all manner of ways, military, naval, industrial, commercial, artistic, philanthropic, even religious. We shall be hearing from each of these three famous names in the course of the book.

The second aspect of this collection of testimonies, as it proceeds, is the amount the British element stood to gain from what had started out as a comparatively modest trade in furs, and developed throughout the years into an export market for British goods and expertise. Up to the end of the 18th century the British (with a few exceptions) gave to the Russians more than they gained. But as we reach the 19th century, and the height of the Russian Empire, there is a noticeable trend towards the British gaining from the Russians – in individual cases and in general – in trade and industry. Many entrepreneurs made their fortune.

Because the Industrial Revolution began in Britain, and was exported abroad, modernising and enriching countries which had previously relied on primitive agriculture, (based in the case of Russia on serfdom), the British who took over and organised industry and trade stood to gain as well as give. In the first days it was employment, power, prestige, popularity; later it became serious money. But the most curious aspect of this situation, as the 19th turned into the 20th century, and political campaigning took the Russians over, *as far as one can ascertain*, no British industrialists, traders and other influential parties took any part in the struggle for revolution or counter-revolution. They all kept out of such bother, and concentrated on the task in hand – building up their business and collecting their profit.

The amount of prejudice about Russia has never been really measured – indeed, cannot be measured – and, despite years of campaigning by many organisations to overcome natural insularity and pride on the part of many Britons, much prejudice and ignorance remains to this day. It is as if mystery and darkness – not to say fear – are fated to remain, chiefly through misunderstanding and lack of reliable information. For years the political system in the Soviet Union and Western attitudes to it were the chief culprits. Today, with daily flights in and out of Moscow and St Petersburg, holiday and cruise companies inviting tourists to the very heart of Russia, television and the Internet, there is no excuse for suspicion and ignorance.

The Iron Curtain was nothing new: it had always been there. A few chinks of light were allowed under and around it in the very early years of the 20th century. Apart from that, the most favourable period for British travellers in Russia was the late 18th century, the reign of Catherine the Great. However, such visitors to Russia went there despite the advice of the writers of such books as had appeared. Russian visitors to Britain were eyed with suspicion and fear; after all, they were more often than not fugitives from one form of terror or another. All in all, it is strange and surprising that such a relatively large number of Britons should have found themselves in Russia. Rev R.B.Paul, in his 'Journal of a Tour to Moscow in the Summer of 1836' claims that 'the great anxiety of those of the educated class whom we have met in Russia seems to be to know what was thought of them in England. "We are a people," said one of them, "little known and grievously misrepresented."'

Let us, without too much prejudice, step back a few centuries, and meet some of our ancestors who went to the farthest limit of our continent, and even beyond, and hear how they got on, and what they saw and did. They all speak to us in their own way – some very formally, some less so. Some are interested only in what they themselves achieved; others introduce colleagues or casual acquaintances, Russian or British, giving credit where credit is due. Some, unfortunately, have forgotten the year of their birth, a few do not recall either their birth or death. Some quote from their own reminiscences, others have picked up information from others' writings. Read them all with interest.

Michael Skinner, 2008

Rulers of Russia during the period covered

(All dates are of reigns)

Ivan IV
(the Terrible)
1533-84

Feodor I
1584-98
|
Boris Godunov
1598-1605

(Time of Troubles)

Michael Romanov
1613-45
|
Maria x Alexei x Natalya
            1645-76

Feodor III   Ivan V co-tsar with Peter I   x   (1) Yevdokia   (2) Catherine I
1676-82   1682-96   (the Great)   1725-7
                                     1682-1725

            Anna   Alexei   Elizabeth   Anna
            1730-40 | 1741-62 |
            | | |
Ivan VI   Peter II   Catherine II x Peter III
1740-1   1727-30   (the Great)   1762
                                              1762-96
                                              |
                                              Paul I
                                              1796-1801
                                             /   \
                                    Alexander I   Nicholas I
                                    1801-25   1825-55
                                                   |
                                                   Alexander II
                                                   1855-81
                                                   |
                                                   Alexander III
                                                   1881-94
                                                   |
                                                   Nicholas II
                                                   1894-1917

1 A DROVE OF DISCOVERERS

Richard Chancellor (- 1556)

Allow me to introduce myself – my name is Richard Chancellor – an unusual name, you may say. Actually, my surname dates back to the days when people's trade or profession distinguished them from each other – John Baker, William Turner, etc.

I guess my ancestor was something important, but the fact is I don't know much about my origins or family – nor even the year of my birth (can you believe it?) What I do know is that I was adopted as a boy by another distinguished family, the Sidneys. They were to become well known later because of their son, Sir Philip Sidney, poet, soldier and statesman. He was much younger than I, and only became famous after my death.

I was about 40 when I first achieved fame: sailing to find a north-east passage to China, and ending up in what is now called Russia (the subject of this book). I had had experience of merchant sailing, importing sugar on the ship *Bark Anchor.* This was the time in history when various nations of Europe were getting the itch to explore farther across the world. Sebastian Cabot (1476-1557), son of an Italian navigator, led a Spanish expedition in 1525 to China, which failed in its attempt to find a route. So he returned to England and tried, unsuccessfully, to get permission for another voyage of exploration. By the time King Edward VI granted him a licence, he was too old to lead the expedition himself. So it was Sir Hugh Willoughby who took over command, and appointed me his deputy.

I was somewhat surprised that Sir Hugh was entrusted with this endeavour, seeing that his experience as a seafarer was limited to three years – he was a former cavalry officer. But as you must know, such things are common: it is not always what you know, but who you know!

In addition to the main aim of the voyage (to find a different passage to Cathay, as China was then called), there was a need to find new markets for the export of English cloth (there were so many sheep in England, and the wool trade was not doing too well at that particular time). Another attractive feature of the N-E passage would be freedom from Portuguese interference.

So it was decided to organise three ships: Sir Hugh's was called the *Bona Esperanza* (Good Hope), 120 tons. Apart from the Captain General of the Fleet, as he was known, there were 37 crew members, including carpenters, gunners, quarter-masters and surgeons. Mine was the *Bona Fortuna* (Good Fortune), (was it an omen?), 160 tons, and accordingly had a larger contingent of crew members (49). The third ship was the *Bona Confidentia*, and had a crew of 28 under Cornelius Durforth.

The whole project was financed by a group of London merchants, who were later to call themselves the Muscovy Company, and were influential for centuries to come in holding on to monopolies for trading with Russia. But I digress. In my day, as you probably realise, London was not the huge international centre it is in your century; it was a modest port on the Thames – what you would call the East End.

Go down to Shadwell, near the Rotherhithe Tunnel, and you will find a licensed house called The Prospect of Whitby (probably named after a ship that was at one time moored there). In my day it was called the Devil's Tavern. It was a meeting place for sailors, and it was where we recruited many of our crew members!

I have been told that in the 20th century, when people were beginning to appreciate history and tradition, some well-disposed and highly placed officials managed to persuade the London County Council to commemorate our voyage in ceramic tiles in a small park near the Thames. This was completed in 1922. Four years later they built blocks of affordable houses and flats – among them Willoughby House and (surprise, surprise) Chancellor House. The fact is that Sir Hugh Willoughby deserved recognition, as he was, after all, the leader of the expedition, which set off on May 10, 1553, but why me? You will see why as my story unfolds:

The three ships got separated by storms and we lost touch with each other. We had no radar or telephone in those days! Willoughby struggled with the difficulties of the seaman's calling, which turned out to be insuperable. The leader of the fleet not only had no idea of pilotage; he could not even navigate! After some considerable time the *Esperanza* and the *Confidentia*, quickly losing both hope and confidence, anchored in a little bay at the mouth of the river Varzina, and decided to winter there, although it was only mid-September! I have been told since that their food supplies were almost exhausted, and, as so often happened, scurvy was raging. When the ships were discovered by local hunters early the next spring, they resembled wooden cemeteries. Willoughby himself was sitting in a hut over his log-book, still gripping the pen in his lifeless hand. His notes show that he was still alive in the middle of January 1554.

Did I say my ship was called Good Luck? If you call it good luck to reach land. But what land? Where the river Northern Dvina enters the White Sea, there is now a town called Kholmogori, near where we landed in August. How did we get there? The local fishermen, after the initial shock of confronting such an unusually large ship in their remote corner of the world, welcomed us. I turned on my usual charm and managed to get the locals to provide us with free supplies, while messengers hastened to Moscow. Eventually, orders were received to take us to the tsar. So, on sledges provided by the Kholmogorians, we undertook the lengthy and dangerous journey (it must have been at least 1000 kilometres) through snow, forest and marsh to present our credentials to the ruler. What we did not know was that the man who ruled in Moscow was the one who later became known as Ivan the Terrible!

Well, he did not appear too terrible, but on the contrary was glad to welcome us as customers, and potential providers, taking the place of the so-called Hanseatic League – German trading towns, which had so far had the monopoly of trade in northern Europe, until Ivan had severed links with them.

We dined with the Tsar in the Golden Hall of the Kremlin. Over 100 guests were present. The tables were covered with golden dishes, and 150 servants put on clean livery three times (they needed to!) during the meal, which lasted many hours. I had never seen such incomparable splendour!

In February 1554 we set out on the return journey with an extremely friendly letter of greeting from Ivan to King Edward VI, who had died by the time we reached London, so I gave the letter to Queen Mary. She was delighted with the pioneer work done by all concerned. She granted the Muscovy Company exclusive rights to trade with Russia –

and other countries by way of Russia. The principal imports from Russia were seen to be furs, tallow, wax, timber, flax, tar and hemp. The principal export, as I have already hinted, was English cloth. So you will not be surprised to learn that when I returned to Russia the next year, I took with me some notable London merchants: George Killingworth, a draper, who sold what was known as 'lundish cloth' (London cloth), and purchased flaxen yarn for export at a competitive price. Also with me were George Burton, Arthur Edwards, Richard Gray and Richard Judd, younger son of Sir Andrew Judd, who had been Lord Mayor of London in 1550-1, and was an influential member of the Skinners' Company. (You can guess what they were keen on getting!) Richard Gray set up a rope factory when we got to Kholmogory, and had workmen sent out from England a few years later. Arthur Edwards decided to try his hand at trading with Persia; his death was recorded in 1580 at Astrakhan.

On our return voyage, our four ships were laden with those goods I mentioned before, plus, on my flagship, a more valuable cargo: the Tsar's ambassador, a man called Osip Grigorievich Nepeya, with his retinue of sixteen Russians, and in his pocket a trading agreement between Moscow and London. Unfortunately, we met with unusually bad weather on the way round the north of Norway, and one of our ships was wrecked on the cliffs there. Much nearer home, my ship, this time the *Bonaventura*, came to grief off Scotland; I was drowned, as was my son, whom I had ventured to take with me, most of my crew and seven of the Russians. Now perhaps you can understand that I played quite a big part in setting up Anglo-Russian relations. This is where I must end my story; but not before I tell what I heard later! The Ambassador, who as a Russian landlubber had never in his life seen the sea, swam ashore, saved the Tsar's letter and the inventory of goods, which we should have delivered. In London Nepeya gained an extremely good report, was received by no less than the Lord Mayor of London, and before returning to Russia obtained valuable commercial privileges, and – permission to recruit Englishmen for the Russian service! I wonder whether they took up the challenge? Read on to find out.

Anthony Jenkinson (1530-1609)

I was sorry about poor old Richard, but life must go on, and the track he had carved out between London and Moscow had to be kept open, and trade increased, even if it meant that treacherous sea voyage around the north of Norway and into the frozen wastes of what we now call the White Sea.

I realised that it must have been hard for Richard Chancellor to communicate with Russians; when I went out in 1557 I had the advantage of an Englishman, Robert Best, who had lived in Russia all his life. He was, he told me, descended from Gabriel Best, a Kentish yeoman, who is recorded as emigrating to Russia in 1403 (why?) and whose son Jacob received the rank of boyar (something like a baron in England) and 'the lordship over the town of Serpaisk'. Incidentally, later in history, the family name became russianised into Bestuzhev, and some of them became famous.

In my delegation there were some notable merchants, such as Robert Bunting, with seven cable- and rope-makers, a furrier called Allard, as well as a Mr Leonard Brian, whose mission was to inspect the yew trees in Russia to ascertain whether it was worth exporting them to England. There was an apothecary, two coopers, Henry Lane, an accomplished man, and Christopher Hudson, a London merchant, who, I am afraid to say, sold things to Russians at exorbitant prices over a course of seven years.

The first time I confronted the Tsar, I took Dr Standish with me, and Mr Best helped us out with interpreting. I think Ivan quickly took a liking for my colleague, gave him a horse, a sable coat, and, he told me later, was invited to dine at the Tsar's table at least five times during his stay. I cannot complain, because I dined there on Christmas Day, and at the Epiphany ceremony of Blessing the Waters about ten days later, Ivan recognised me in the crowd, despite the fact that I had dressed in Russian costume, just to be in the spirit of the occasion. He invited me back for a meal once again. Of course, I was somewhat overwhelmed, not least by the splendour of the Kremlin, but also of the plate and jewellery everywhere. Of course, we had to convey gifts from our Monarch to the Tsar, and he reciprocated very generously. The fact is, he was wanting to encourage trade with England.

I am afraid I took advantage of my host to ask permission for myself and my colleagues to set out on an expedition to China. After all, that was what Chancellor's original mission was about. I was rather taken aback when the Tsar agreed to my plan. So I got my party together, left Moscow on 23 April, 1558, sailed down the Oka and the Volga as far as Astrakhan. This city had only been part of Russia for two years; previously it was the capital of a Khanate, and was, and still is, an important fishing centre and port on the Caspian Sea. From there we moved on overland. It was now July, and very hot, but with a caravan of 1000 camels we reached Bokhara, where we were informed that the route to China was discontinued owing to war, so we gave up and returned to Moscow.

In 1567 I was back again in Moscow with a fresh Charter for our Muscovy Company, which included a clause allowing Ivan asylum in England, should his life be endangered. (I guess it was many times!) He offered Queen Elizabeth the same terms. Can you imagine Her Majesty subjecting herself to such an indignity? Ivan told me that the idea of proposing marriage to Queen Elizabeth was suggested to him by one Dr Elisaeus Bomel, a German medic, who had studied at Cambridge, and, after a stormy career in London, was induced by the Russian Ambassador to attend on the Tsar, and so he took his English wife (nee Jane Richards) with him. Apart from his outlandish suggestion about uniting England and Russia by marriage, he also engaged in a Polish conspiracy – always the worst crime in Russia! – Ivan had an excuse to make use of his nickname Terrible, had Bomel tortured and burnt at the stake. The good doctor was also something of an astrologer, so perhaps his supernatural powers came into play – he was about to be buried when they noticed he was still alive! He was thrown into a dungeon, where he died. His wife returned to England.

It was in the summer of 1571 that I was again sent to Russia to appease the tsar, who was furious at his lack of success in his overtures to Queen Elizabeth. Because of famine, plague and war, I was unable to get to Moscow for some months, but when I did meet the ruler, it took me several attempts before I could convince him that there was misunderstanding on both sides. I came back to England in September 1572, and did not undertake any more long voyages, as I was weary and growing old.

Daniel Sylvester

I am the person who carried out a lot of diplomatic journeys between England and Russia in the 1570's. I was lucky enough to have a good working knowledge of Russian, rather rare at the time. Certainly the Tsar needed someone who could speak his language. Queen Elizabeth, as is well known, commanded both Greek and Latin, not to mention French and Italian. Whatever language she wrote to Ivan in, it would need translation, so best to entrust that to an Englishman.

In 1573 I took the message that complained about the ill-treatment of some of the Queen's subjects while in Russia, having caravans plundered, some members even killed. In reply Ivan complained of the conduct of some of the English, and (worse than that) they had taken service with the King of Sweden. This was always a suspicious thing to do! In reply the Queen 'lamented that Englishmen should have conducted themselves so ill in Russia, but hoped that they were such as did not belong to the trading company.' She even suggested that the so-called Englishmen in the Swedish service were probably 'Scotch', and so, were not under her control.

I went back again in the summer of 1576, via Kholmogory, where our people had already set up what was called the English Factory – a headquarters for traders, residents, visitors and seafarers. They even had a tailor, whom I engaged to fit me out with clothes suitable for a royal audience in Moscow. His room was upstairs, and after trying on the new coat, I was just going downstairs, when a terrific flash of lightning struck me on the coat collar, and went down the right side of my body. My boy and my dog both died with me. I have to finish here, but not before reporting what Ivan the Terrible is supposed to have said about my death: 'God's will be done'!

Sir Jerome Horsey (- 1626)

I was the agent of the Muscovy company, and was sent in 1580 to Russia from Queen Elizabeth, but did not expect Tsar Ivan to request military supplies for his war against Poland. But orders is orders, and so the next year I went back with ship-loads of armaments, as well as a doctor, James Roberts, who was to be personal physician to the Tsar. Ivan, still anxious to maintain good relations with England, but thwarted in his plan to marry the Queen, sent his ambassador, Feodor Ivanovich Pisemsky, to discuss and arrange marriage to Lady Mary Hastings, daughter of the Earl of Huntingdon, and a relative of the monarch. Elizabeth found many excuses to let the young lady off this dreadful fate: 'her health was not sufficiently robust to cope with such a journey'; 'she was not beautiful enough for so important a prince'. When it became known that Ivan had murdered his own son…

The episode of the marriage proposals became common knowledge in London, and was for a while the latest joke. In Love's Labour's Lost, Act V, the king of Navarre and his courtiers put on masks, and appear to the assembled company in a garden, 'apparel'd like Muscovites, or Russians,' and later in the scene are described as 'a mess of Russians', 'trim gallants, full of courtship and of state'. When she has unmasked them, Rosaline asks: 'Why look you pale? – Sea-sick, I think, coming from Muscovy.'

Shakespeare certainly did not miss the opportunity to incorporate topical subjects into his plays! Even a witty writer, called Thomas Nashe (1567-1601), in his work 'Have with You to Saffron Walden', could not resist quoting what he had picked up 'in the Russian tongue' *Ponuloi nashe,* have mercy on us. For all their topical jokes, I guess they did not know just how sea-sick some of us got, sailing round the North Cape to Russia. It was always difficult to go by land, especially through Poland, which was constantly at loggerheads with Russia.

In 1584 Ivan at last died, and we were all relieved when his son by his second wife, a young man called Feodor, took over. He asked me to beg Queen Elizabeth to send him an English midwife for his wife's imminent confinement. This request was acceded to, and even improved on: not only a midwife was sent, but a doctor to superintend her! Robert Jacob was recommended as being skilled in female complaints, the Queen herself 'having often benefitted by his advice'. However, the power behind the throne was a boyar called Boris Godunov, the Tsaritsa's brother, who for some reason found the idea of a foreign midwife disagreeable, and the good woman was detained at Vologda, less than half-way to Moscow. There she stayed for a year and then was obliged to return to London, and we never heard any more of her.

Dr Jacob came with me on the next embassy, and the Muscovy Company paid him 100 roubles. On this occasion I took to the Tsar many and varied articles – some of which you will find it difficult to believe: lions, dogs, gilt armour, halberds, pistols, organs, virginals, jewels, gold chains, pearls, white, red and scarlet liveries. Whew! I am sure the pleasure derived from these very desirable presents was the main reason why the Company obtained considerable further advantages for the traders as well as the English residents in Russia.

On my return in 1587 I brought back a new charter, written in Russian. I had over the years picked up quite a lot of the language, and went through the document word for word with the Queen. Her response? 'I could quickly learn it', and turning to the Earl of Essex, she requested him to study Russian 'the famousest and most copious language in the world'.

One of the more successful agents, employed by the so-called English Factory in Moscow, was Sir Francis Cherry, who acquired so good a knowledge of Russian that he was often called to Court as an interpreter, and seems to have been cherished by successive tsars. In 1587 he was given 'a piece of gold stuff and sable furs' by Boris Godunov, which he asked me to convey to England to be made into a dress. But soon afterwards Cherry himself came back to England with a letter from Tsar Feodor to Queen Elizabeth, and seems to have stayed on a bit. Later he started sending ships under various commanders to investigate the existence of walruses at Kola. On the return of one of the vessels with a large quantity of walrus teeth and hides, the island where they were caught was named Cherry Island. Soon after that further islands in the area were named after English kings, princes and nobles. I do not seem to find any trace of these names left!

One little thing that I was very proud of during my time in Russia was writing a Latin grammar book for the son of a high-up man: I wrote the text of the book as best I could in Cyrillic script! Also during the course of my service under Ivan IV I had acquired a Russian Bible, which I brought back to England, and I hear it ended up in the British Library.

By now I would say there were a lot of people high up in the English political and commercial world that got jealous and suspicious of the credit I received for all the useful work I had done in maintaining relations with Russia. The Muscovy Company brought charges amounting to fraud against me, calling me arrogant and extravagant. I was accused of falsifying accounts. By now it was possible to get to Moscow by an overland route via Cologne, so I found it convenient to stay out of England for the next few years. On my last trip in April 1590, the Tsar refused me an audience, so I was obliged to come back. For the next thirty years I settled down to a relatively stress-free life on my estate in Buckinghamshire, though I was a Member of Parliament for various seats in Cornwall.

I left quite a lot of writings about my travels, which were edited long after my death.

Sir Jerome Bowes (- 1616)

My contribution to Anglo-Russian relations was probably less than many of my colleagues, but my experiences could certainly be described as colourful! When I arrived in Moscow in 1583 as ambassador I realised that there would be a certain amount of etiquette to observe, but I did not expect that any ruler would expect me to take off my sword before entering the presence, so I had my boots pulled off and made the Tsar wait till I could go in my night-gown, night-cap and slippers, since I was not allowed to go in as a soldier.

I had been told that Ivan had ordered a man to leap from a window to his certain death, and had been obeyed. I scornfully observed that 'my mistress (the Queen) set more by, and made better use of, the necks of her subjects.'. I flung my gauntlet down in front of the Tsar, and challenged all the nobility to take it up, in defence of their ruler against the Queen.

On another occasion I heard that the French ambassador declined to take off his hat to the Tsar, and Ivan had ordered it to be nailed to his head! So I was ready for anything. Next time I had an audience I kept my hat on: I was threatened with the same treatment as the Frenchman, to which I replied that I did not represent the cowardly king of France, but the invincible Queen of England, 'who does not veil her bonnet nor bare her head to any prince living.' To my amazement, the Tsar commended my bravery and treated me favourably. But it was not to last – Ivan the Terrible died the next year.

Dr Giles Fletcher (c.1548-1611)

I was ambassador to Russia in 1588, having served in the diplomatic corps since leaving Eton and King's, as well as doing a period as an M.P. At the court of the young Tsar Feodor I was treated with indignity, but I did manage to exact some favours from the Lord Protector, Boris Godunov, such as an agreement that members of the English community in Russia should not be put on the whipping block before condemnation. In return, requests were made for refuge in England if the lives of rulers should be in danger. Boris, for all his reputation as a despot, had another side to him, and he frequently evinced a desire to improve his own, and his nation's knowledge.

One of our most highly esteemed scholars was a Cambridge man, Dr John Dee. He had become a Fellow of Trinity College upon its foundation. A mathematician and astrologer, he had been suspected of magic, and was imprisoned by Queen Mary, but was later released, having recommended an auspicious day for Queen Elizabeth's coronation. He travelled abroad and studied all branches of learning. He was in Bohemia when the invitation reached him from the tsar, who offered Dee in return for his company and 'good counsel in divers matters' '2000 pound sterling'. The Lord Protector (Godunov) would give him a thousand 'rubbles' and free provisions 'out of his Majesty's kitchen'. But Dee was too clever to exile himself to any particular country.

However, Dr Mark Ridley, a relative of the Protestant martyr Bishop Nicholas Ridley, spent four years from 1595 in Moscow, during which time he edited his own Russian vocabulary, which is still (I am told) in manuscript at the Bodleian Library, Oxford. A Dr Jessop arranged to go as his replacement, but died before leaving London, so in his place Timothy Willis, an Oxford graduate, set out with great enthusiasm. He suffered the fate common to many talented volunteers: he was kept waiting at the port of entry, and ill fed. When he eventually reached Moscow, he was uncomfortably accommodated. No sooner had he settled into his job than he was expelled for meddling in politics! The Queen received from Moscow an injunction not to send any more people, but later it transpired that Willis's real crime was not bringing any books with him!

Failing in his attempt to attract men of learning, who could perhaps have set up a university in Russia, he undertook to send eighteen youths, including four princes, to the West to improve themselves, and be safe from the internal struggles and threats from impostors to the throne. Of these, four were sent to England to learn the language, and all that goes with it. Mikipher Alphery and his two young brothers were recommended to the care of Mr Joseph Bedell, a merchant of the Muscovy Company, who educated them, and in due course sent them to Oxford. Two of the brothers died of small-pox, and the survivor Mikipher was ordained into the Anglican church, and appointed rector of Woolley, Huntingdonshire. It was said that he was more than once invited back to Russia, where there were supporters anxious to place him on the throne, but he took the easy way out and stayed on in his living, only to be ejected by Cromwell in 1643. He was later reinstated, and died in retirement at Hammersmith at over 80.

Sir Alexander Leslie (1568-   )

I was born in Scotland, and being an aristocrat and a supporter of King James I, was sent as ambassador to Sweden in 1627, then to Russia three years later. This was during the reign of Michael Romanov, who had been placed on the throne at the age of sixteen, but professed to be 'intensely curious about what was happening abroad.' When he first received me at the Kremlin, he asked for news of reigning families in Western Europe, while revealing certain familiarity with western countries.

I had heard that Michael had a fascination for clocks and watches: after all it was recently that one of our fellow-countrymen, Christopher (G)alloway had built the spire over the Spasskie gate into the Kremlin, and adorned it with a striking clock. I understand that the clock was removed a century later, but, as everyone is aware, the original spire still stands.

I was introduced in the first place by an Englishman, Sir Arthur Aston, who had been swaggering around high circles in Russia, calling himself a prince and a Field Marshal. Because he suggested reorganising the Moscovite army, the naïve Michael offered him the title of Voevoda in Chief of the Grand Polk (Commander in Chief of the Great Regiment) at an enormous salary. He bought a house at Kholmogory in 1612. However, at the reception given to Aston and me, we were both presented with furs and clothes in exchange for clocks and watches. Although I was not impressed by the young tsar, who during most of our audience was calmly stuffing his fingers in his nose, he seemed to think well of me – enough to send me as his emissary to Poland, France and Sweden. In 1645 my mission was to hire 5000 Swedish infantry and craftsmen to go to Moscow.

I suppose I was regarded with favour, after the previous embassy had come to grief: Sir Dudley Digges was asked to arrange the terms of a loan, which James I offered Tsar Michael to finance his campaign in Poland. Digges left London in April, 1618, with £20,000, and on reaching Russia, sent his secretary, Finch, to Moscow with half the sum and the letters from the king. The Tsar would hear of no terms, but ordered Finch to hand over the money. Digges returned home with the balance in October.

The chaplain to Digges' embassy was a learned and intelligent Oxonian, Dr Richard James, who also wrote an account of what he observed in Russia, but his manuscript, so I heard, was missing from the Bodleian Library as early as 1697. (It is interesting that the year before that a German, H.W.Ludolf, had published at Oxford his own Grammatica Linguae Russicae. Could Ludolf have had access to James's papers and ?inadvertently removed any one them?) I hear that James's Russian vocabulary is in manuscript still at the Bodleian.

An English doctor, Arthur Dee, was for many years from 1621 very well paid for his practice in Moscow, and also had an estate near the capital, as well as a brick house in the city '60 fathoms long and 40 fathoms wide', which on his retirement he sold to one Simon Digby. Tsar Michael wrote to Charles I for a replacement, suggesting Dr Peter Chamberlayne, but the King replied that a Dr Elmston, a 'native Russian' was on the point of returning from studying medicine in England, and would no doubt agree to act as body-physician to the Tsar.

More interesting, perhaps, was another member of Sir Dudley Digges' suite: John Coplie (also known as John Tradescant) who had come out to follow up his father's discoveries. John the elder, who, as you know, founded the first museum and physic garden in Lambeth, south London, had discovered in northern Russia about two dozen wild species, and recorded that 'the soil of Russia compared with that of Norfolk, the ploughs with those of Essex, and the carts were like those of Staffordshire'. John the younger was to learn something about Russian plants and animals, and kept a detailed Journal of the voyage, as well as a description of life in Russia.

In 1628 an engineer, Captain John Bulmer, had been welcomed to the Kremlin. Bulmer claimed to be looking in Russia for mines which might yield gold, copper, silver or lead. Tsar Michael showed him his clock museum with childlike pride, asked Bulmer to do him a great service: to repair the pendulum of the clock in the Kremlin tower. The captain tried to explain that he was a mining engineer and not a clocksmith, but the naïve Tsar insisted at great length, and finally implored him in tears. Bulmer's book, published in 1649, was entitled 'A note of such Arts and Mysteries as an English Gentleman, a Souldier and a Traveller is able by God's assistance to perform (he having means to perfect the same)'.

In 1645 Michael was succeeded by his son Alexei, who was at least as well-disposed to help from abroad as was his father. Amongst Englishmen who served in Russia during this reign, none was more illustrious than Samuel Collins (1619-1670), son of the vicar of Braintree, Essex. He studied at Cambridge, Padua and Oxford, and was travelling in Holland when he met an envoy of the Russian court, Sir John Hebdon, who was talent-spotting for foreigners to serve the Tsar.

Collins agreed to be appointed Physician to the Tsar in 1660, and held the post for nine years. Although he treated large numbers of nobles, his main patient was, of course, the Tsar, who suffered from extreme obesity. Collins, not surprisingly, wrote about diet and eating, about the properties of tea and coffee. He had to work with the royal apothecary, Robert Tewe, whose son John was very clever at speaking Russian, and acted as Collins' interpreter for most of his stay in Moscow. Collins' book 'The Present State of Russia', published in 1671, is a classic: it comprises a very exacting and detailed account of life in what was, let us admit, an almost unknown country, and may have done much towards attracting interest in Russia in the ensuing years. It was Collins who supplied Robert Boyle with information about the climate in Russia. If Collins was treated with respect, not necessarily so was Dr Wilson, who arrived in Moscow just after the Plague of London, and, I have been told, 'was obliged to undergo several ablutions before being allowed to enter the city of Moscow some months later'!

I married three times, and had three sons, two of whom married Russian ladies. I retired to my estate in Russia.

2 A GATHERING OF GENERALS

James Bruce (1680-)

I am James Bruce, and I was born in Russia. Fact is, my father, William, emigrated there in 1647 – 33 years before I was born. This was a period in history when many foreigners, including 3000 Scots, particularly military men, took up service under Tsar Alexei Michaelovich.

My elder brother, Roman, was born in 1668, became a major-general, and when Peter the Great created the Russian Empire, was made a Count, and has gone down in history as the Third Man in Russia, after Peter himself and Menshikov (the humbly-born Muscovite who became Peter's most powerful collaborator in the reforms). Roman's widow Sarra's contribution to folk-lore was her petition in 1728 for the privilege of manufacturing cement! They had a son, Alexander, whose legacy is greater – supervising the reform of the calendar – which was long overdue! He was to marry in 1745 Princess Ekaterina Dolgorukova, the former bride of Tsar Peter II.

I was born in 1680, and at a tender age entered the Russian army as an ensign, serving in that capacity in the Crimea and at the battle of Azov. At the battle of Narva there was a misunderstanding which deprived me of my rank, but it was restored to me a year later. I became Governor of Novgorod for four years, and in 1704 became Head of the Artillery, which I soon felt the urge to reorganise, to bring it into the modern world!

In 1711 Peter sent me on a mission to Germany to recruit officers and artists for the Russian service. Among those I attracted in this way was my second-cousin Peter Henry Bruce (1692-1757), an architect, whose native tongue was German, his father having been in the service of the Elector of Brandenburg. However, he returned to Scotland in 1724.

In 1718 I was elected a member of the Senate, which Tsar Peter had not long previously set up, as well as President of the School of Mines and Manufactures, being the only non-Russian President out of the nine recently established Colleges. Considering the reliance Peter put on foreign talent, it is surprising that I was alone; but not quite alone: we had a Briton, called Brewer, who was Vice-president of the College of Justice.

Like my father and brother, I was made a Count, with a large sum of money, as well as an estate near Moscow, with 500 houses and many serfs. That was what it was like in those days. I had earned it all: by service to successive sovereigns, including making the Treaty with Sweden at the Congress of Aland, and procuring advantageous terms for the Russians at the Congress of Neustadt. I acted as one of the bridegroom's brothers at the marriage of Peter the Great's daughter Anna Petrovna to the Duke of Holstein.

When Catherine I, Peter's wife, succeeded him in 1725, I was the first knight of the newly instituted Order of St Alexander, and when I retired from Court, I was made a Marshal. From my retirement until my death in April, 1735, I devoted my time to study and humanitarian work. I had written for Peter an abridgement of the rudiments of geometry, which involved translating several elementary English and Dutch works. What I really wanted to do was a geographical description of the Russian nation, but that proved too ambitious a scheme. I corresponded with Leibnitz, the German philosopher, upon the origin of the Russian nation, a study which was curtailed by his death in 1716. I had a fine library and a large collection of coins and minerals, all of which I bequeathed to the Academy of Sciences in St Petersburg.

I like to think I made a contribution to the development of the Russian Empire. If nothing else, a Moscow street was named after me: Brussovski Pereulok (Bruce's Lane)!

The poet Valery Brussov (1873-1924) was among many Russians who claimed descent from my family. And – I nearly forgot - my son James became Governor-general of Moscow later in the 18th century; my daughter Ekaterina Yakovlevna (Katherine daughter of James) married Count Moussin-Pushkin, and had an estate with 14,000 serfs, which was managed by the poet G.R.Derzhavin (1743-1816).

Those who think that Peter the Great built the Russian navy must concede that there were ships afloat in Russia before his reign, but probably only on rivers. The English traders approached Russia via the Arctic. There was no other way until Peter had conquered the Black Sea and Baltic coasts, and given himself warm-water seaports. The story of the young Peter discovering a derelict English boat in a lumber shed, and thereby resolving to build himself a naval force, with the help of the British, may be taken with a large pinch of salt. Nevertheless, it remains a fact that of all the Anglophile tsars in history, he had the most to be grateful to the British for.

Don't forget that Peter was brought up in a Scots household – his mother, Natalia Narishkina, second wife of Tsar Alexei, was herself adopted by Morozov, who was married to a Scot, Mary Hamilton. She, it is said, kept in touch with her homeland, and without doubt the young Peter was familiar with all things Scottish. What surprises me is that on his famous visit to London, Peter made no attempt to go to Scotland. Perhaps time was against him! He and his entourage stayed three months in the capital, partly getting to know King William III, partly working and studying in the dockyards and shipbuilding yards at Deptford. It was notably reported that 'his evenings were generally spent with the Marquis of Carmarthen, with pipes, beer and brandy, at a tavern near Tower Hill, which is still called the "Czar of Muscovy".'

The Marquis, for his kindness in entertaining Peter, was presented with the right to license 'every hogshead of tobacco exported to Russia by an English company, who paid him fifteen thousand pounds for the monopoly, and to charge five shillings for each licence.' Carmarthen's ship, the 'Royal Transport', commanded by Captain Ripley, was responsible for bringing Peter's discoveries to Russia. These included a geographical clock, which Peter bought from its maker, Mr John Earle, 'at the sign of the Dial and Crown, near Essex Street, Strand'. The Tsar chose at least one horse while in England. It appears in pictures of the Battle of Poltava, and was later stuffed with straw and exhibited at the Academy of Sciences. Captain Ripley found his way to Moscow, where he lost his life: his body was found in the river Yauza, near Preobrazhenskoye, with the back of his head beaten in, bruises on his right hand, the silver buttons cut off his coat, and his pockets turned inside out. Needless to say, the 'Royal Transport' became a Russian ship.

Along with Ripley's ship came other vessels, bearing the shipbuilders, engineers and officers, whom Peter had succeeded in attracting, encouraging, bribing or forcing to join him in his new adventure of opening Russia to the West. Peter saw the need for education and training, if the Russians were to succeed. But, unfortunately, the treatment meted out to his proteges, once they were in Russia, is exemplified by the story of Mr Andrew Ferguson (or Farquarson) from Christ Church, Oxford, who with two young assistants, Stephen Gwynne, a Welshman, and Richard Graves, came to Russia at Peter's invitation. Ferguson, originally a professor at Aberdeen, taught mathematics and astronomy, was the author of text-books in Russian, and was responsible for surveying the projected great road from Moscow to St Petersburg. He never received any salary while in Russia, and when he wanted to return to England, was denied a passport! Gwynne became the first mathematics instructor at the Naval Academy in St Petersburg from 1717 onwards, and Graves established the School of Navigation in Moscow. One of them (I forget which) was set upon by rogues and murdered. To all these persons Peter had promised liberal salaries, which were often never paid, and the option of returning home when they chose; but in reality, those few who escaped assassination by some jealous Russian or other were able to find their way back to Britain. What they 'did for the Russians' will probably never be evaluated, but, believe me, Russia was never the same again.

Patrick Gordon (1635-99)

I was born at Auchleuchries, a small estate in Aberdeenshire, and went to school there until the age of 15 when, as a Roman Catholic, I was sent to the Jesuit College at Braunsberg in Prussia. But I did not take to the school way of life, so I decided to leave, but not to go home. There were so many opportunities to have an exciting time, and so after a while I found myself in Poland, where I was amazed and delighted to find so many of my fellow-countrymen. You must realise that those of us who supported the Stuarts were finding it very uncomfortable in Britain, and many Scots fled to Europe to find a more congenial society.

Well, after a few years with the Swedish army in Poland, including a period of imprisonment by the Poles, I joined the Polish cause until the Swedes captured me – I rejoined them. I did like to be on the winning side!

In 1658 in Poland I joined in a plot to assassinate Richard Bradshaw, the English ambassador to Moscow, whom I thought I recognised as the man responsible for the death of Charles I. The plan did not work out, as the ambassador was too well guarded to give us any chance of success. Eventually I decided to enter the Muscovite service myself, and I was welcomed by Tsar Alexei in Moscow. I soon proved my worth by suppressing a revolt in 1662 which was caused by the depreciation of the coinage. I was now riding high, and particularly because I married Catherine, daughter of a German, Colonel Bockhoven, who was also in the tsar's service.

I really felt important when Alexei sent me on a mission to England, where I was honoured with an interview with Charles II. What a privilege – a Stuart restored to the throne of Great Britain!

In 1676 Alexei died, and was succeeded by a weak tsar, Feodor. Not long afterwards I was made a major-general, and then took command of Kiev. When Feodor died, the throne passed to two young boys, Peter and Ivan, with their elder sister Sophia acting as Regent. This was not the most auspicious of times for me, especially as my wife died, leaving me with two sons and two daughters. This did not, however, prevent me from pursuing my career. It was during this time that I met the Swiss Lefort, who was later to become famous for his untiring efforts on behalf of Peter when reforming Russia. Lefort and I became great friends and colleagues.

In 1685 I remarried: Ronaer was of Dutch extraction. We had another son. In that year I obtained leave to visit England. I must say I found Regent Sophia difficult. She was probably unsure of herself trying to handle two younger brothers: Ivan who was a non-entity, and Peter, who, as you know, was only waiting for the chance to show himself what he later became – Peter the Great, first Emperor of Russia, reformer of state institutions and father of the Russian navy. I recognised in him a potential giant, even at the age of 14, when he sent me off on my way with a glass of brandy, and a command 'to return speedily.' Well, I had served his country well, I must admit, and I was intending to continue… However, the woman with the power, either to avoid losing me altogether, or just to be her usual difficult self, retained my family as a pawn.

While back in Britain visiting my old home, I had an interview with James II. You will remember we were fellow Roman Catholics, and he urged me to quit the Russian service and hasten back to England. I was tempted, but all my family were in Russia; I had to get back there. It was not long before I was involved in an expedition against the

Crimean Tartars, as a result of which I was promoted to the rank of General. This did not suit the Orthodox hierarchy, and the Patriarch prophesied disaster so long as the Russian armies were commanded by a heretic such as me! But the regiment was stationed near Moscow, and I soon had a lot more to do with the young Peter. When the struggle for power took place which confirmed Peter as sole ruler, I did a lot to help the young man's cause. It was while Peter was away on his famous tour of Western Europe, I had my hands full attempting to conciliate the Streltsi, (a crack military corps) who were objecting to the westernising influences then prevailing. I tried to negotiate with them, but when reason failed, I felt myself obliged to resort to force. Those who were not executed were kept in confinement until Peter's return, and he dealt with them accordingly!

I really got on well with Peter. As a young man he used to come down to the so-called Nemetskaya Sloboda, or German Suburb of Moscow, and have a drink (or two) with us 'foreigners'. Most of the writers who have commented on this period in Russian history pay tribute to the part played by us in the westernising of Russia. Before Peter the Russians merely drank mead; we introduced spirits – and tobacco – not to mention shaving off beards! Much later in history, Lord Byron wrote this verse about me:

"Then you've General Gordon,
Who girded his sword on
To serve with a Muscovite master;
And help him to polish
A nation so owlish
They thought shaving their beards a disaster."

Most of my life I kept a very full diary of my experiences and travels, even down to the price of every article I bought. Most of it still exists in a Russian government archive, but parts were published in 1859 by Joseph Robertson for the Spalding Club at Aberdeen.

I found myself surrounded by Britons – not only Scots, but Englishmen, and an Irishman, named Butler, who was captain of one of the earliest Russian ships, called the Orel, built at Dedinovo on the Volga. She made her maiden voyage to Nizhni Novgorod, but was immediately needed at Astrakhan, owing to the activities of Stepan Razin, leader of a peasant revolt. On arrival at the scene of battle the ship, which had cost the Government over 9000 roubles, was set on fire, and Butler fled, I am sorry to say. Also at Astrakhan was Thomas

Boyle, an English colonel, who had undertaken to man the ramparts of the town on the land side. When Razin took the town, Boyle fled too! No more is known about either.

I could go on and on about the contribution made by my countrymen to Russia's modernisation; many of them have gone unrecognised. One of them I am particularly indebted to was my namesake Alexei Alexeevich Gordon, who was a Major in my regiment, and who retired to Scotland in 1711. His work 'History of Peter the Great' was published in Aberdeen in 1755. But he did not tell my two favourite stories: when my daughter Mary married Daniel Crawfurd, Tsar Peter honoured us with his presence at the wedding. I am told that when I died, Peter personally closed my eyelids! No one could ask for a greater honour, especially as he arranged for me to be buried in the Roman Catholic church in the German suburb, which I take credit for having built.

Peter Lacy (1678-1751)

Perhaps I am the first Irishman to appear in Russian history. I was born in Co. Limerick, and for the first twenty years or so I served my King (James II). Along with my father and brothers I left Ireland to serve in France, Italy, Hungary and Poland, which is where I first met Peter the Great, who selected me as one of a hundred officers to train Russian troops, and I was appointed captain in Colonel Bruce's infantry regiment. After taking part in action against the Swedes, I was appointed to command the so-called Grand Musketeers, composed of a hundred Russian nobles armed and horsed at their own expense.

My career took off in leaps and bounds: one campaign after another – one promotion after another, until I became a Lieutenant-general in 1720. Three years later I was summoned to take my seat at the council of war, and at the coronation of Tsaritsa Anna (1730) I was required to ride behind the Imperial carriage, throwing gold and silver coins to the people! For my pains I was made a knight of the Alexander Nevsky order, and was appointed commander-in-chief in St Petersburg, Ingria and Novgorod, to which Estonia and Courland were added the year after. I think I can safely claim to have been instrumental in winning the long-drawn out war for Russian dominance over Sweden, and I was greatly involved in many campaigns against Turkey. My second-in-command was a Scotsman, James Keith, who supported me as one would expect from a fellow-Briton: among other events, we had to put down a mutiny in St Petersburg on Easter Sunday, 1742. Russian officers were savagely ill-treating the foreign members of their regiment. It was said afterwards that we had 'saved St Petersburg, and perhaps the Empire.' Later I was credited with having converted the Russians from the worst into some of the best troops in Europe. True, I always tried to set a soldierly example, and showed unremitting care of my troops.

Another Scot, George Ogilvie (1664-1711), having served for forty years in Germany, was hired for service in Russia, where Peter placed him in command at the battle of Narva in 1704. As a result of his successful five-week siege of the city until the Swedish garrison surrendered, he was made a Field Marshal. He was popular with his troops (he abolished among other things the prevalent but foolish practice of night attacks), but not so popular with his officers, perhaps partly through his inability to speak Russian. Even Prince Menshikov, officially his subordinate, found it difficult to accept instructions from Ogilvie. After retreating from Grodno in 1707, he pleaded ill-health and asked to be relieved of his command. His resignation was accepted, his salary paid in full, and he left Russia, only to enter the service of the King of Saxony, where he served for the last four years of his life! Many of my family stayed on in military history: my five daughters all married generals and privy-councillors, and my elder son eventually became a Count of the Holy Roman Empire after a lifetime's service in Saxony. My younger son, Maurice, joined the Austrian army at the age of twelve in the regiment of Count Brown, a relative of ours. He eventually became a Field-marshal and was credited by Frederick the Great with having created his army!

H.I.M. PETER THE GREAT (Reigned 1682-1725)

It is surely no accident that I was the first Peter in Russian history. It was as though my father, Alexei, a man of high principles, humanity and ability, who had presided over a Russia considerably settled after years of trouble and muddle, wanted to celebrate the improvement in our country by naming at any rate one of his children by a novel, classical, international, western name.

As I am sure you will know already, I came to power somewhat by default, as my elder brother, Feodor, was regarded by the influential Patriarch and the nobles as weak and incompetent. But not until 1689, when I was 17, did I attain full authority. Up till then I was watched over by my sister Sophia as regent, but I was relatively free to mix with people of various classes and nationalities. In 17th century Moscow there was the so-called German Suburb (Nemetskaya Sloboda), where many westerners lived and worked. You have met Patrick Gordon, my special friend; there was also Francois Lefort, a Swiss, and a Dutchman called Timmerman. I learnt a variety of arts and skills, and – more importantly – respect for foreign customs and accomplishments. On my famous tour of Europe – including England – I added so much to what I had started, and it gave me not only ideas, but support and encouragement.

My formal education was sadly lacking, but I have always been a man of action rather than words, and if my greatest achievement was the acquisition of warm waters by defeating Sweden, then the second proud legacy was the building of my capital, St Petersburg. In both of these activities I am indebted to foreigners – including Britons – for ideas, leadership, support. The Russians on the whole provided the manpower and little else, except prejudice and disapproval.

I was the first Russian monarch (and the last for over a century) to travel abroad; I was the first to be proclaimed Emperor. I created the Russian navy, and re-organised the army (with help from several Britons). I set up the Academy of Sciences, curtailed the power of the Church, reformed the Russian alphabet. I started the movement for emancipating women – which may have led the way to the part played by more than one Empress, starting with my own wife, Catherine I.

If you think, as many do, that I was cruel and masterful, I will tell you that I had to be – to achieve my ambition of being Peter the Great.

3 STAGGERING STATISTICS

John Perry (1670-1733)

After a short career as a lieutenant in the Royal Navy, I met Peter the Great when he visited London in 1698, and was offered a ten-year contract as a hydraulic engineer in Russia. I worked on the canal projects to link the Volga to the Don, (a scheme which had been started with some success as early as 1560) and St Petersburg to the Volga. I designed the docks at Poltava, which Peter had wrested from the Swedes in 1709.

I, like many others of my compatriots, found it difficult to obtain my salary, but eventually managed after some scheming to find my way home to England, where I spent the rest of my life on such works as draining the Lincolnshire fens. I wrote a book 'The State of Russia under the present Tsar' which was published in 1716.

During my period of service in Russia, I was amazed at the number of British shipbuilders there were, notably Mr Cozens, who was employed for eight years, and Mr Nye eleven years, chiefly on the river Don. There were three yards on this river: Mr Cozens was paid £500 per annum, his under-master £100. Their three assistants were: Robert Davenport, who later went to St Petersburg and became a Master Builder himself in 1719, and then on three years later to Revel; Francis Kitchen; and William Snelgrove, of whom I know no more. Mr Nye received £250 salary, and the help of an Under-Master, Henry Johnson and an assistant, William Gardner. The Tsar himself ran a ship-yard on the Don, with Russian assistants. Naturally there were Russian workmen in all these yards, but what is clear is that most of the top jobs were in the hands of the British. The mast-makers and other artificers were stationed at Stupena, and included Henry Wright, H. Atherley, S.Hopkins, and Baggs. Anchors were all made at Dobrove, about 100 miles from Voronezh: the British there were R.Halley, Robert Davies and Thomas Daniel. Smaller ship-building yards were at Olonets on Lake Onega, where Richard Brent operated, assisted by Edward Hill; and at Ladinople, Richard Brown had the help of Messrs Hunt, Evans and Mallard. Brown himself was originally from Chatham, and later became chief constructor at Kronstadt. John Deane met Peter at Deptford and came back with him, becoming supervisor of the dockyard at Voronezh, subsequently serving afloat as a captain, before being dismissed in 1722, or so I am told!

Of course, Peter negotiated with officers of the Royal Navy to join the Russian service; some of them brought their own ship with them, like William Baker, who came over in 1714 with the *Fortune*. Two years later he was in the Arundel, and by 1717 was captain of the *Varakiel*, but was soon dismissed the service. Finch, the captain of the *Arundel*, was dismissed after a year in Russia, having been offered a contract to build ships in England. William Batting, captain of the *Lesela* in 1715, subsequently of the *St Paul*, was heading for Archangel, but because the ship was so rotten, it never got beyond Copenhagen. Batting, however, was later to become Flag Captain to Vice Admiral Thomas Gordon in the *Moskva*, only to be replaced in 1719 by William Hay.

John Delap, an Irishman, became a lieutenant on Peter's own ship, the *Ekaterina* in 1714, but by 1719 he had his own ship, the *Ezekiel*, and contributed to Peter's success by capturing three Swedish ships. Lord Duffus, a Scot, was invited by Peter to come to Russia to escape the consequences of his involvement in plots. He was given the rank of Rear Admiral and a post in the Admiralty, and died, apparently, in about 1730. I could name at least twenty more Britons who served, besides many others unknown to me.

John Cook

When I arrived at Kronstadt, the shipmaster told me I should pay my compliments to the commander of the citadel. You will not be surprised to hear that he was a Scotsman, Admiral Thomas Gordon. So I made my way to the palace, but before I could enter, a man at the door pointed to my dusty shoes and offered to clean them before I should go inside. I offered the man a tip, whereupon a gentleman in the lobby asked me if I thought the master could not pay his servants. This, it transpired, was Admiral Gordon himself!

After this inauspicious start, I went on to St Petersburg, where I lodged at the only British public boarding house in the city, run by another Scot, Mr Frazer. He was a retired Major of the Russian army. During my stay of a few weeks in the capital, I made it my business to contact my compatriots as much as possible; it was not difficult. They heard I was in town, and made a point of seeing me. Mr Ferguson, Professor of Astronomy, came from the Academy to drink tea with me. I dined with Mr Selkirk, surgeon to the Guards, who lived on the north side of the river. Mr Lewis Calderwood lived out of town at Peterhof. He had come to Russia in 1728, and had, when I visited him (1744), recently replaced a German as Household Surgeon to the Tsar.

Lieutenant Alexander Gordon (another of the clan), having done some business in the capital, decided to stay in the house where I was. One evening we were walking together along the Nevski Prospect, which, I am sure you know, is the main riverside street in St Petersburg, when we were set upon by four rogues. We fought them off with our swords. I can only presume that we foreigners presented an unusually smart, prosperous appearance. This was not the only time I fell prey to footpads.

At a hospital in the capital, I helped to treat a sailor, whose skull had been cracked by a falling rocket at a firework display, held to celebrate the capture of Azov from the Turks.

Someone much more interesting was Miss Hadderling, whose father was superintendent over all the sloop-builders; her mother had been a Miss Edwards, daughter of the captain of a Russian naval ship.

In those days a traveller could sail to St Petersburg or Kronstadt and enter the city without either a passport or Russian currency, but to travel to the interior of the Empire, it was necessary to obtain a passport from the British Resident, who, when I was there, was Mr Rowndox (some people thought he was French, and spelt his name Rondeau). I had met another Scots doctor, John Bell (1691-1780), who shared with me the strong desire to see foreign parts, and so had obtained recommendatory letters to Dr Erskine, chief physician and privy councillor to Peter the Great. Dr Bell told me that he was staying with Mr Nye, an English shipbuilder. He had been received by Dr Erskine in a very friendly manner, and he was able to get an early opportunity of visiting parts of Asia, at least those parts bordering on

Russia, having been nominated medical attendant to Volynsky, the Russian ambassador to Persia, with whom he travelled from 1715 to 1718. (He later went to China and Siberia, eventually returning to Scotland in 1746. He wrote his experiences in a posthumously published account, which was among books recommended by Dr Johnson to Boswell.)

Bell supported my application, as well as giving me some commissions to deliver on my way south. I then applied to the Admiralty for money, horses, and any despatches that I could deliver for them in return. The secretary-translator who interviewed me was yet another Gordon, who on this occasion would have no part in the affair, recommending bribery as the most efficacious method in Russia! So I asked to see the Chief Secretary, and was amazed to find he was Russian, and did not understand English; an Admiral called Mushiakoff being on hand, who spoke good English, speeded the matter up.

On the way to Moscow I encountered a company of sailors travelling in carts to Azov, among whom was an English boatswain, called Rannie. We decided to stay together on the journey. During the eighth night of the journey I had a pair of new shoes and buckles stolen from my wagon while I slept in it! When I told Rannie about it, it transpired that he had lost a belt, a coat and a vest. Rannie must have had suspicions as to the thief's identity, and when he found him, I think he would have killed him, were it not for the intervention of the Commander, who seized them both.

At Moscow I delivered Dr Bell's commission to a Mr Tarner, who was kind enough to ask me to stay to supper, and then sent me home in his coach. South of Moscow, at a place called Tavrov, another British surgeon, Mr Burman, was sick and I was asked to help out at the hospital for officers and sailors. You will not be surprised to hear that I met a number of British officers, such as survivors of the battle of Azov: lieutenants Every, Smallman and Luggar; Colonel Johnston, who had many scars on his body, resulting from wars in Russia; Captain Grey, who was born in Prussia of English parents; and finally, General Leslie, who had been attacked by a large body of Tartars while passing through Ukraine with a small body of men.

I decided it was high time I knew some Russian, and applied myself to learning the language. In this task I was helped particularly by one Peter Miln, who had been nine years in Siberia, working as keeper of the books to a Russian industrialist. He told me he was unable to remember his native language! But time and distance were telling on me, and I was missing Miss Hadderling, so I decided to return to St

Petersburg to propose marriage to her. Having been exposed for weeks to wind and weather, I was now so brown that I was almost unrecognisable, even to my own brother who had stayed back in the capital. He kindly offered to go with me on my first visit to see the lady who was to become my wife.

As I probably said previously, I was anxious to travel to Persia, or even beyond. Before I left, I was approached by Messrs Mungo Graeme, Panton, Brown and Van Mirope with a view to allowing them to accompany me. The first of these was originally partner to John Elton, who it seems, had created something of a scandal, having been some years a senior captain in the Russian fleet, but abandoned his duties in 1739 to create a new trade link between Russia and Persia. On arrival in Persia, Elton left Graeme behind to negotiate with the Shah, returned to St Petersburg, where he engaged Mr Finch, the new Resident, to apply to the Tsar for authorisation, which was granted, then left for London, where he persuaded Parliament to pass an Act to the same effect. He went back to Kazan and built ships, independent of the Russian navy. This, as you can imagine, did not go down too well with Arapov, the Russian Resident in Reshd. Eventually, Elton defected to the Shah.

Meanwhile I was in Astrakhan, amazed again at the numbers of British pioneers in that city. At the garrison hospital was a Mr Malloch, a Scots surgeon. The commander, Lieutenant Glassford, was taken ill with a fever, becoming delirious two or three days before he died, and allowed a Russian priest to baptise him. His widow was kept in Astrakhan by the Governor, with her two children, on the pretext that, as their father had embraced the Russian Orthodox faith, the children should be educated in the same religion. With the help of Mr Thomson, the British agent in Astrakhan, I got Mrs Glassford and her children back to St Petersburg, and eventually they were repatriated.

I left my younger brother, William, in the care of Mr Thomson, while I travelled north. On the way I stopped off at the Jerusalem Monastery in Moscow, where I was told by a bishop who had been ten years in the navy, how Admirals Gordon, Paddon, Saunders and others had shown him 'particular marks of their favour', and 'his breast glowed with gratitude, as it were, to a Briton'. While I was in Moscow (1750) there was an extensive fire, which burned down two thousand houses, amongst which was that of Prince Golitzin. What I found most interesting was that almost all his furniture which was lost was very expensive, high quality - and English!

I had every admiration for my dear wife, who had travelled with me and borne four sons, three of whom were still living, and I was anxious they should get safely out of Russia and home to Scotland. But before that, I had one or two little duties to perform at St Petersburg. My professional advice was in demand by Commodore Paddon, who, unfortunately, had cancer in his tongue. And, more cheerfully, I was invited to supper by Vassili Nikitich Tatishchev at his home in Klin. He had recently completed his five-volume 'History of Russia from the Earliest Times'; when he showed me his work, I offered to take it to London to the Royal Society, who, I was sure, would publish it. On passing through Riga, which had fairly recently become a Russian city, again I was amazed at the British presence: the Minister was Guy Dickens; one of the army physicians was a Dr Shilling; one of the regiments was commanded by Count Yuri Yurievich Brown, an Irishman, who went to Russia with Peter and served his adoptive country for sixty years! I also met Mr Wallace, the only remaining Scots shipmaster.

I am proud to record that I published my memoirs of travel in 1770.

4 AN ASSORTMENT OF ADMIRALS

Sir Samuel Greig (1735-88)

I was born at Inverkeithing, Fife. My father was a shipmaster, and I had a spell in the merchant navy before I joined the Royal Navy. Not satisfied with this, I transferred to the Russian service in 1763, and am very glad that I did. My career went in leaps and bounds, thanks to the encouragement I received from the Empress, Catherine the Great. She, as you probably know, being non-Russian by birth, had a preference for foreigners of ability.

I suppose my greatest contribution was towards the victory at Chesma (1770), considered by historians as the beginning of Russian interest in the Mediterranean. Chesma is situated on the western coast of Turkey, a very strategic position near the Dardanelles (entry to the Black Sea). The naval supremo was Alexei Orlov, who commanded three squadrons of warships from Kronstadt, via the English Channel and the Straits of Gibraltar to the Eastern Mediterranean. I was not the only British officer present: have you heard of lieutenant Francis Dennison; of Brayer, Todd and Beakes; of Harland, Carston and Elphinstone; of lieutenants Allen, Andrews and Arscott; of captains John Biggs and James Trevenen? This latter was a somewhat younger man, who was born in Cornwall, trained at Portsmouth, and sailed under Captain Cook on H.M.S. Resolution. During their voyaging in the Pacific, Trevenen was struck by the possibilities of fur trading, and determined to suggest doing so through the ports of Siberia. His scheme was forwarded to St Petersburg by the Russian Ambassador in London, and it so impressed Catherine that she offered him an appointment in her navy. Without permission from the British authorities he came to Russia, where he received the rank of Commander at the age of 27! His trade plan never materialised, owing to the more urgent matter of fighting the Turks and others. He later excelled as captain of the *Rossia* in the Baltic fleet. He married the daughter of John Farquharson, a Scottish business man, and set up home in the Russian capital. Unfortunately, he was mortally wounded at the age of 30 by a cannon ball while fighting the Swedish fleet.

On a somewhat lighter note, I cannot help referring to my colleague Crown, who was an Irishman, and had also been for a time in the Royal Navy. He arrived at St Petersburg during a threat from the Swedish fleet, and was induced to quit his ship to assist the Russians. He later became Commander of the Baltic fleet, despite his modest stature: he was only five feet tall! His wife became well known for her care of the wounded on board her husband's ship during battles. Anecdotes abounded about Admiral Crown: the officers and sailors believed he never slept, since the slightest irregularity was noticed from his flag-ship, even at night. His bluntness and honesty were proverbial, and he gave offence more than once to the Emperor Paul. Nevertheless, at a Court ball in the 1820's, I am told, he was seen by an observer to appear literally 'covered in orders'.

But on that score I cannot complain: in recognition of my contribution to remodelling the navy, I was honoured by Catherine, and given an estate, called Sans Ennui. I was made Governor of Kronstadt, where I reorganised the port and planned a new prison, which was praised by John Howard, when he visited Russia in 1781. I founded a Masonic lodge, the Neptune, intended for sea-going men, both Russian and British, and I had my portrait painted by Ivan Argunov. One of my less pleasant tasks was to travel to Leghorn, in Italy, and bring as a prisoner the Princess Tarakanova, the illegitimate daughter of Empress Elizabeth, and a threat to Empress Catherine. She had fled to Italy, but had been caught up with by Catherine's favourite Alexei Orlov.

I married Sarah Cook, a relative of Captain Cook. I am glad to know that when I died my dear wife received 2000 roubles in pension and a large estate. Of my children, Alexei, born in 1775, was christened after Alexei Orlov; I sent him to school in Edinburgh, and he served several years in the Royal Navy. When he returned to Russia, he was rapidly promoted, but got into hot water with Emperor Paul for remonstrating with him for his severity towards British seamen. However, he was reinstated, became a Vice-Admiral and in the 1820's was commanding the Black Sea fleet! He seems to have been well liked among the

Russians, particularly the St Petersburg society. One incident stands out: my son always had at least six at dinner, and a band of music was in attendance. A certain Captain Jones was invited during his stay in the capital, and Alexei pressed him to stay a day longer, when he would be having 'the horn music' – sixty performers. In the event, the Captain stayed, they had the small band as well as the horns; Captain Jones left it on record that it was a 'lovely concert of Italian airs and songs, followed by 'God save the King' and 'Rule Britannia'.

My other son, Samuel, was a Captain; he married, in 1804, Mary Fairfax, who gave him a son, called Vorontsov, after another famous Russian. (Mary later married William Somerville, and went on to found Somerville College, Oxford.)

While I am talking to you, I think I ought to mention a fellow-Scot, who took a small part in Russian affairs, and of whom I am not too proud. John Paul Jones was born in 1747, the youngest of the children of a gardener and a cook on an estate at Kirkbean, Dumfries. His eldest brother sailed to Virginia to work in the plantations. John was always keen on ships, and at the age of thirteen sailed to find his brother in the New World, but actually joined a slave trading ship. By a stroke of fate the ship he was on was attacked by fever, and he had to assume the role of captain. Henceforth his career was one of smuggler, pirate and sea-dog. He offered his services to the Colonists against England, was involved in the War of Independence, and became an officer in the first U.S.Navy. The name of Paul Jones became legendary as a name to dread in England: they even named a country dance after him, presumably because it involves constantly changing partners! Catherine the Great made overtures to him to take command of one of her ships. As soon as this fact was known to the British officers in the Russian fleet, they sent their resignations in. Jones arrived in St Petersburg (after risking his and others' lives amid the ice floes of the Baltic in winter), spent a fortnight in the capital, then set off to join Prince Potemkin in the south, where he was engaged in war against the Turks. The Empress was flattered at his success in battle, and prepared aristocratic apartments for him. On hearing, however, that he had violated a girl, she took fright, and to reject him from her Court, offered him the command of the Baltic Fleet! I grant that he did carry out his commission successfully, even examining personally every vessel, and making himself ill from a disease caught from exposure to the holds of ships. He was awarded the Order of St Anne, restored to favour at Court, granted leave of absence with pay, and a return ticket to Paris. On the way there, he stopped off at Harwich, where, dressed in Russian uniform, he was not immediately recognised, but when word got around as to who he was, the local populace were not sparing in their denunciation of an enemy of England. In Paris he met the leaders of the Revolution, and hoped to take command of the navy of the French Assembly, but his illness gained ground rapidly, and he died the same year (1790).

John Elphinstone (1722-1785)

If you think that the Russian Empire gained in power and prestige by taking command of the Black Sea, (which most people do), then you will acknowledge the part I and some more of my fellow Scots played in the naval battles for achieving the final defeat of the Turks in that area.

I was attached to the Russian navy as a captain in 1769, and was responsible for commanding the fleet which set off from the Baltic to (!) stir risings against the Turks in Greece. We sailed round Europe and through the Mediterranean to Chios, an island in the Aegean Sea. The Battle of Chesma took a lot of planning, and in that I had much help from Lieutenant Robert Dugdale, who was responsible for the fire-ships that destroyed the Turkish fleet stationed in that port. His Russian crew deserted him, which did not deter him. For his part in the battle he was promoted to Captain; he resigned from the navy in 1788, and I heard no more of him.

Another of my protégés was James Preston, who was dismissed after Chesma, but re-instated in 1788, later becoming an admiral. He died in 1819. His daughter married Mr Barns, an English merchant in Russia.

The Treaty of Kuchuk-Kainardji recognised, among other things, Russian control of the Black sea coast, including the Crimea, and the right to build a church in Istanbul (a huge prestige point with the Russians, embracing as they have always done the Eastern Orthodoxy, which came from Constantinople).

When Anglo-Russian relations became strained in 1778, I was recalled to Britain. My son, Howard (1773-1846) became known to English history as an admiral.

A Briton who did his best for Russia at this time was Sir Charles Knowles (?1697-1777), who was a Rear Admiral in the Royal navy, but resigned on accepting a command in the Russian fleet. Most of his service was administrative, which kept him at St Petersburg and neighbourhood. After the 1774 Peace referred to above, Knowles returned to England, but not before he had been responsible for building several battleships and frigates while in Russia. If you read Rev William Anderson's "Sketches of the History and present State of the Russian Empire" (1815), you learn that 'in consequence of negligence, waste and imposition, the cost of building ships was expensive. Knowles told (Empress) Catherine that he would engage to fetch all the materials needed from Russia, pay the duties upon them, and then deliver from England ships completely equipped, at much less than they cost in her own dockyards'. One cannot help admiring Knowles' entrepreneurial outlook, even if it did achieve more for Knowles than for Russia!

During Knowles' four-year stay in Russia, his private secretary was John Robison (1739-1805), a close friend of both James Watt and Joseph Black, and Professor of Chemistry at Glasgow from 1766. His knowledge of mathematics and Russian led to his appointment in 1772 as Professor of Mathematics at the Naval Cadet Corps in Kronstadt. When he returned to Scotland in 1774 to take up a professorial chair at Edinburgh, he took three cadets to study under him. In 1800 he was elected an Honorary Member of the St Petersburg Academy of Sciences.

Another British officer for whom I have the greatest respect and admiration was Joseph Billings (1763-1806), who spent much of his early life as an able seaman under Captain James Cook on the 'Discovery' and the 'Resolution'. After Cook's death in 1779, Billings seems to have gone on a merchant vessel to St Petersburg. He was induced to join the Russian navy as a lieutenant. He became known to the authorities as an adventurous and capable navigator, and when it was decided, in 1785, to send an expedition to north-east Asia 'to bring to perfection the knowledge of the seas lying between the continent of Siberia and the opposite coast of America', Billings was suggested as a fit man to lead such a party, by Rev William Coxe, who was in Russia at the time, (and whom you will undoubtedly meet ere long). Billings' deputy was the Russian Gavril Saruchev (note the order of priority). It is reported in E.D.Clarke's "Travels in various Countries" (1810) that the expedition was long written on his gravestone in Moscow, where he retired to in 1797:

'Here lieth the body of Commodore Joseph Billings, Knight, of the 3rd class of the order of St Vladimir, born in London, September 5, 1763. He was employed in the last expedition with the renowned

Captain Cook, by the late Empress, Catherine II, to make discoveries in the north part of Siberia and Kamchatka, as far as the Icy Sea. After having served the Emperor of Russia twenty years he married, February 6, 1803, Catherine, daughter of Gen. Boris Vladimirovich von Pestel, and died March, 1806, in the 43rd year of his age'.

We are told that he was long in being authorised to leave, and that Billings began to despair that it would ever take place. So by enlisting the aid of Professor Peter Pallas the German naturalist, who was well in favour with Empress Catherine, he found himself one day at Tsarskoe Selo, in the gardens where Her Majesty took her daily walk. She greeted Pallas, and enquired who the young officer was that accompanied him.

"The person whom your Majesty was pleased to appoint to lead the expedition."

"And what delays his departure?"

"Your Majesty's orders!"

The Empress was not long in giving the necessary instruction, and the convoy left. They were altogether at sea and abroad for nine years. His secretary on the expedition, Martin Sauer, who kept an account of the journey, published in London in 1802, obviously did not like Billings, and so his opinion is biassed. Amongst the party was a German naturalist, Dr Carl Merck, assisted by an English medic, John Main, one Robert Hall, and Christian, son of the Danish discoverer Vitus Bering. During his later years, Billings undertook a systematic hydrographic survey of the Black Sea. Of his further life we know very little.

H.I.M. CATHERINE II OF ALL THE RUSSIAS (Reigned 1762-1796)

As I am sure you know, I can trace my ancestry back to the beginnings of Russian history, but I was the first 'foreign' ruler of Russia. It came about because the heirs of Peter the Great, with the possible exception of Elizabeth, were all short-lived, second-rate people, who hardly had time or experience to do anything positive or useful for the Russian nation. I was a German princess, chosen to marry the Russian prince, who eventually became Tsar Peter III. When I married him in 1745, I immediately set about learning all about my adoptive country, and was determined to bring it up to the standard of a European power, such as I had experienced in Germany as a child. To help me in my quest, I corresponded with some great European minds, such as Voltaire and Diderot (whose libraries I purchased after their deaths), and surrounded myself with capable advisers, such as Panin, Sievers, Potemkin and Princess Dashkov. My position enabled me to acquire many beautiful *objets d'art*, including the whole of Sir Robert Walpole's collection from Houghton Hall, Norfolk, which had to be sold to pay off family debts.

Like most arranged marriages, mine did not turn out too well, and my husband had to be disposed of. I russianised my name to Ekaterina (after Peter the Great's wife, as well as my mother) Alexeevna (a good Russian patronymic). I have a very marked inclination towards those who support the throne of Russia, which I consider to be all the stronger for my occupancy of it for 34 years. It needed regeneration after the decades of instability and confusion which had weakened the throne since the death of Peter I in 1725. I admire what he achieved – without him I doubt if I would have been able to rule in the way I have done. When I had the Bronze Horseman by Falconet erected on the embankment of the Neva, it was inscribed in Latin (an international language): PETRO PRIMO; CATHARINA SECUNDA (To Peter I from Catherine II), thereby recording for all time my debt to Peter and his work in opening up Russia to the wider world.

Among my favourite foreigners, the British loomed large: you may have heard of Sir Charles Hanbury Williams, the British Ambassador for part of my reign, Dr Thomas Dimsdale, Charles Cameron, Dr John Rogerson, Sir Samuel Greig, Charles Gascoigne, John Howard, among others. As a woman I naturally appreciate the contribution of my sex to the advancement of learning. Someone very dear to me, who did just that, was Catherine Dashkov (nee Vorontsov), one of the greatest Anglophiles ever. You probably know that all her family were very enlightened characters. She travelled a lot in Europe, especially after her husband's death in 1768. On her return, having seen and learnt so much, she was anxious to elevate Russian to a higher position among the literary languages of Europe. I appointed her Director of the St Petersburg Academy of Arts & Sciences; two years later she was named first President of the Russian Academy of Sciences, which had been founded at her suggestion. None of this would have been feasible without the influence of her mentors in Britain.

My popular title "Catherine the Great" is not entirely deserved, but...I leave it to posterity to judge impartially what I have done.

5 A THRONG OF TRAVELLERS

"...it is certainly a foreigner's fault if he is not well received here. Travellers, unfortunately, forget to leave their notions behind when they come into a strange country; and, unless they will give into the way of the people they are with, it is impossible they should be on a comfortable footing."

Letters from the Continent to a friend residing in England (1790)

John Howard (1726-1815)

I was born in north London, although my father had a small estate at Cardington, Bedfordshire, where I was brought up. He died when I was only 16, and I inherited his considerable wealth and property. As a boy I was interested in astronomy and meteorology, and had some scientific work accepted by the Royal Society, who made me a member in 1756. So I became well known in my county, and was appointed High Sheriff in 1773. In this position I got to visiting the infamous Bedford gaol, where John Bunyan had languished a century earlier. I was disgusted at the condition of the prisoners, and the general lack of organisation in the prison. This led me to tour from county to county, devoting myself to prison reform.

In 1774 I gave evidence before a committee of the House of Commons, prior to travelling all over Europe, spurred on by my Christian zeal, to better the lot of my fellow-men. I not only toured prisons, gaining information on the situation in each country, but visited the prisoners themselves. My first visit to Russia was in 1781, after a long land journey, taking in Denmark and Sweden. On arrival at

St Petersburg, I observed a strict incognito, but Empress Catherine, hearing of my presence in the city, invited me to dine. I have to tell you that I declined the offer, saying that I had come to see prisons, not palaces. It is not recorded what Catherine said to my rebuff. However, it has earned me a reputation for being a snob and a prig! But not to be daunted, I spent the next five years studying the plague in various countries of Europe. One of the worst features of prisons in most areas that I visited was the presence of typhus. Before leaving for what was to be my last tour, I made my will, which included leaving Cardington Manor House to my friend Samuel Whitbread (later to found the well-known brewery!) My 1789 visit to Russia was marred by war against Turkey, but I could not resist helping, if I could, the poor, unfortunate Russian soldiers. On reaching Kherson I myself caught a fever, from which I soon died, attended by my man-servant Thomasson, and Surgeon-Admiral John Priestman, another Briton who had served for four years in the Russian fleet. I am told that he was laid to rest beside me, at Dauphigny, a short way outside Kherson. On my death-bed I asked that a simple sun-dial be put over my grave, as I had no desire to be remembered, but, it appears, Alexander I, who reigned in the early 19th century, had a thirty-foot cenotaph erected not far away from my burial place, and a prison, after one of my own plans: a square courtyard overlooked by the governor's house. Apparently, the cenotaph was inscribed in Russian and Latin, until Mr T.Alcock, M.P., who visited the site in 1828, left funds to place an English inscription. What a fuss! If this was not enough, you can still find my statue in Bedford, as well as a commemoration in St Paul's Cathedral, London. My book 'The State of Prisons in England and Wales' reached three editions in my lifetime. Each new edition had an appendix with updated statistics of my findings. I regret that I did not have time to compile such an account for the prisons in Russia, which were, as you can imagine, every bit as grim as those of Great Britain. I *do* wish I could have done more, but at least I left a legacy, which has been continued ever since my death by the Howard League for Penal Reform.

Samuel Whitbread (1758-1815)

I am the only son of the brewer mentioned previously, and was born at Cardington. My mother died when I was very young, but my father looked after me with great care, sending me to Eton, accompanied by my own private tutor. I was so lucky – after studying at both Oxford *and* Cambridge, I was sent on a tour of Europe, under the guidance of the historian, Rev William Coxe. (He was recommended to my father by no less than Dr Samuel Johnson, and, I discovered, was paid no less than £800 per annum for his services, which were not onerous, as I behaved myself very well all through the tour!) The traditional 'Grand Tour' was rather less desirable, as France was undergoing a 'time of troubles', so it was sensible to avoid that part of the world. We set off first to Denmark, Sweden and then St Petersburg.

In the Russian capital I met, of course, many of the British community. My best friend was J.Browne, who was rather sorry for himself, his business having recently collapsed. I also made friends with Joseph Billings, and Mr Sutherland. My father would probably have been vexed to think that I tended to prefer my own countrymen to the Russians, but I attended one or two court functions, and was introduced to the Empress.

On one occasion, when I was driving past the Winter Palace with my usual six horses, (when more than four was restricted to the Imperial family), I am told that the Police Master was standing at a window with Catherine. "Look at that insolent brewer, how he drives", he is reported to have said. "Never mind him, replied the Empress, if he wishes to drive sixteen, let him do it – it is this kind of people we want here"!

I must say that Mr Coxe was a great scholar: among his published works was 'Travels into Russia', which describes our experiences, and those of his previous tour with young Lord George Herbert, and which ran into six editions between 1784 and 1803. In it he records, among many other things we saw and did, the Vauxhall in Moscow. This was based upon the gardens of the same name in London. It was situated at the furthest extremity of the suburbs, quite a country spot in fact. We entered by a covered way into the splendidly lit gardens, for which the admission price was four shillings. The proprietor was, as you will expect, an Englishman with a half-Russian name: Mikhail Yegorovich Maddocks, also known as The Cardinal, because he always wore a red cape. He was in fact an excellent mechanic, and had made a clock, with a full orchestra and figures, which he offered to Empress Catherine in return for the exclusive patent for presenting plays and public masquerades at his theatre (the Petrovski) in the Vauxhall. I heard it said that he had earned nothing but debts in the twenty-five years he functioned there. But he was fun to meet. I have been sorry to hear that the Vauxhall, like many other buildings in Moscow, was ruined by the fire of 1812, and afterwards built over, no trace of it remaining.

I have to mention someone else who impressed me very much: Rev William Tooke, chaplain to the British community at St Petersburg, who was no mean scholar of languages, and author of several books about Russia, some translated from the French. His two-volume 'History of Russia, from the Foundation of the Monarchy by Rurik, to the Accession of Catherine the Second' is well worth reading. I met his two sons: Thomas, who started his career in a business house at St Petersburg, and William, who came back to England at the age of 15, became a solicitor, and later a Member of Parliament, as I myself did in later life. He was probably more successful than I was: you may not have heard that I got involved in many projects of different kinds, but ended up by suffering from depression and cut my own throat with a razor!

An Account of Russia (1768) by G.Macartney

'Foreigners of almost every nation which we are acquainted with, are to be found in Russia, either as established or temporary residents... All foreigners except Jews and Jesuits are at liberty to settle in this country, and may trade by wholesale, but unless naturalized, they are prohibited by the laws from selling in Russia what they purchase in Russia and are therefore obliged to consume or export it.

'The English are by much the most respectable for their opulence, their integrity and their understanding, but of all foreigners the French are the most beloved, caressed and imitated by the Russians. The English enjoy particular commercial privileges and, in point of honour and justice, are entitled to still greater. For to the early and continued support of the English, Russia principally owes its present existence as a maritime or commercial nation.

'They leave the great advantage of their trade to the stranger; and whilst the products of Russia are transmitted to the most distant parts of the globe, the name of a Russian merchant is utterly unknown.

'Great Britain and Ireland alone export from Russia: iron (24,000 tons per annum to England), clean hemp, clean flax, linens, manufactures, bristles, isinglass, rhubarb, furs, etc....in exchange for imports of cloth, shalloons, woollens and mixed stuffs, flannels, pewter, tin, lead, ale, porter, Carolina indigo, beaver skins, sugar, mahogany ware, mahogany plank, clocks, watches, earthen ware, etc.'

John Parkinson

I am different to most of the others in this book, because I cannot claim to have contributed anything to the development of the Russian Empire, but I certainly became aware of that legacy when I visited in 1792. I was an Oxford don, and was asked to accompany a young gentleman, Edward Wilbraham Bootle, on an extended tour through Stockholm to St Petersburg and right through most of Russia, over a matter of two years. I kept a diary of my experiences.

We were entertained by a Mr Gould (whose first name I have failed to record), an ex-pupil of Lancelot (Capability) Brown, the famous landscape gardener. Gould was responsible for the gardens round the Taurida Palace, which was built for Prince Potemkin in recognition of his part in conquering the Crimea, called in those days Tauris. Gould's home was within the Palace, where our host entertained us with private reminiscences of Prince Potemkin, with whom he had been "very well acquainted". He also told us snippets about Catherine the Great, none of which are worth recording here. I could not help noticing a print of John Wilkes, an English M.P. expelled from Parliament for libel. Gould told us that a visiting Russian priest, who had been in England, warned his host that Russian visitors might offer a prayer before this ikon of his favourite saint, and that this would be "a prostitution of divine honour". It is as well that we British are not so superstitious! Mr Gould, at the age of 73, was entrusted with the laying out of the Admiralty Gardens in the capital – a huge undertaking.

Bootle and I were dined by Mr Yeames, a veteran shipbuilder. We did not sit down until past four, and were obliged to be at the Hermitage at quarter to six, so we did not have much time to enjoy the excellent dinner. Our guide round the Hermitage was none other than Robert Hynam, a clockmaker, who went to Russia in 1776 to make his fortune, and became a member of the Imperial Academy of Sciences! He advised the Russian government on standard measures. In the museum we saw the work of another clock-maker, James Cock, who had a workshop in London, and sold the Horloge du Paon to Potemkin who presented it to Catherine for the Hermitage. It is a curious piece of mechanism, in which a tune is played with balls; a golden peacock unfolds his plumage and a golden *cock* crows!

As you are probably aware, in the Hermitage there are many nations represented in the works of artists and craftsmen, but I must say I was amazed at the amount of British work there was when I went round the exhibition. Take for example brothers William and Charles Brown, master engravers, who are hardly heard of at home: Catherine practically monopolised their work between 1786-96. Previously, she had ordered medallions and casts of engraved gems in 1781 from James Tassie, stipulating that they must be placed in suitable cabinets. These were provided by J.Roach, from designs by James Wyatt, who, incidentally, was offered 'any fee he liked to be court architect' to Catherine. He declined. Then there were several examples of the work of Matthew Boulton, but he will no doubt tell you about them shortly.

Then, what of the Wedgwood porcelain? I was amazed at the so-called Green Frog Service, commissioned in 1773 via the Russian Consul in London. It runs into 944 pieces, and each is decorated with a different picture: castles, abbeys, palaces and parks, as well as ancient ruins and country cottages. Catherine II, who loved most things English, but was woefully ignorant of England itself, requested (nay, ordered) this very original set of illustrations. Part of the service was exhibited in Greek Street, London, prior to shipment to St Petersburg. According to later estimates, this dinner service cost Catherine £3000; Wedgwood made no profit, but much fame.

The Russians still relied on the British for so much: either importing works of art or encouraging Britons to stay and work in Russia. One example is Francis Jacob Gardner, who arrived in Russia in 1746. It is fairly certain he came from Staffordshire, but little is known about him. What we do know is that he opened a small factory in the village of Verbilki, near Moscow, in 1762.

Another Englishman, Charles Milly, helped a Russian, Nicholai Popov, start another porcelain factory in 1805. This was a much smaller concern, and produced small quantities (though finer) of wares for the Russian Court.

Later in our tour, in the far South, my young friend and I were very graciously entertained by a Madame Mordvinov and her brother, Major Cobley. The latter had, in expectation of our arrival, prepared apartments for us in the Palace of the Khan, which had recently been rebuilt by Charles Cameron. He also took us up to the summit of a mountain to see a view of Bakhchisarai. If you have not heard of the Anglophile Mordvinovs and the Russianised Cobleys, you soon will!

John Dundas Cochchrane (1780-1825)

Like John Parkinson, I can only speak about other people's contribution – but also of what they gained from their activity in Russia.

I was the grandson of the Earl of Dundonald, and at the age of ten I joined the Royal Navy, seeing service in the West and East Indies. This gave me the ambition to see more of the world, and on leaving the service in 1820, I decided to tour the world, including Russia, Siberia and North America. I have to say now that the American part never took place: I did not know that I had only five more years to live! But I did get right across Russia, and it was in Kamchatka that I met the girl who was to become my wife. (She was 14 when we married, and we returned to England, where she learnt to speak fluent English, survived me and remarried. Her second husband was the son of a merchant who traded in Russia.) Also in Kamchatka I came across a Cockney, who had been exiled from Moscow for forgery, flogged, knouted etc, but was still welcome in every house.

I also met Peter Dobell, who styled himself Russian Consul-general to the Pacific, with a lifetime of trade in China, a polite, hospitable Irishman. He was later to publish a pamphlet in London, entitled 'Russia as it is, and not as it is made out to be' under a pseudonym 'A Friend to Truth'. He was clearly disillusioned by his twenty years' experience, which was helped by his fluent knowledge of Russian language. Near Moscow I met on one occasion another ex-Royal Navy officer, James Holman, who was travelling extensively through Russia while suffering from total blindness! He told me of some of his experiences of meeting our compatriots: a Scots lady compelled by illness to relinquish her post as governess to the Golitsyn family; a Mr M. an Englishman, who had retired to his estate at Ekaterinburg, given to him by the Russian government in recognition of his services in building steam engines, on condition that he established a cutlery factory on the estate; another Englishman, Mr S. who had returned from extensive inspection of posts in Eastern Siberia; and at Irkutsk a Mrs B., who was born in London, married at 15 to a Russian businessman, remarried at St Petersburg in an Orthodox church, but recently widowed. She expressed a desire to return to England. I am sorry to say that I do not know the end of the story.

Elizabeth Rigby (1809-1893)

I travelled out to Russia, via Denmark, in 1841. After a tiring journey to the capital, I stayed at the English boarding house, kept by Mrs Wilson, where rest and refreshment were promptly given and never more gratefully received. I visited the English Church and the British Factory. The Emperor knew that his sixteen hundred English children would always respect the existing laws, and probably wished that the rest of his family was as peaceable. I was later housed by an army colonel, but managed to catch a fever, for which I was treated by an English physician. The journey to Revel (Estonia) in winter by sledge was notable for two minor things: my sherry froze in its bottle, owing to the intense cold; at a post station where I stopped on the way I noticed a clock, inscribed 'Thomas Hunter, Fenchurch Street'.

I later visited Tsarskoye Selo, where in the simple bedroom, used by the late Alexander I, was a small table, kept intact after his death, on which was his simple English shaving apparatus. In the palace of Nicholas I there was a small print of Admiral Sir E. Codrington. The English red-brick Gothic gatehouse was originally built as an arsenal, in which there was a collection of armour and antique instruments, entrusted for classification and arrangement by – who else but an Englishman?

6 AN INFLUX OF INDUSTRIALISTS

Charles Gascoigne (1738-1806)

I was the son of a London merchant; my mother was the daughter of the Earl of Elphinstone. My first wife, whom I married in 1759, was Mary, daughter of Samuel Garbett, founding partner of the Carron Company. I eventually became a partner of the firm, which first produced iron cannon in 1761. The company was having problems with the quality of its iron, so I introduced many improvements in the technique of production. The Russian admiralty, under Admiral Samuel Greig, ordered 1000 tons of cannon in 1772. We also supplied a Newcomen steam engine for pumping duty at Kronstadt. All of this led to the emigration of skilled workers from Britain to Russia. But you have to have managers! You will not be surprised to hear that the Royal Navy tried to stop me. But I went ahead, looking for a fresh start – fame and fortune! In 1779 I arrived in Russia, having been offered a salary of £4,500 to reform the Ordnance department. I took some key men with me, and the factory was set up at Petrozavodsk, some 150-200 versts from Moscow. Later on I founded the iron works and town of Lugansk in Ukraine, situated strategically to supply arms to the Russian army in their campaign against Turkey. In 1789 I introduced at Kronstadt a foundry using scrap metal, and it was later transferred to St Petersburg to become the basis of the Liteiny Zavod (foundry). Russia was also interested in the British invention of copper sheathing for the hulls of wooden ships, and with Matthew Boulton's co-operation, we installed rolling mills for the steam-powered mint. In 1796 I established a factory at Petrazavodsk to make metal buttons for military uniforms.

I enlisted the architect, William Hastie, to design a new building for the reorganised works at Kolpino, near St Petersburg, and for the first metal bridge erected in the capital. Much of the ornamental ironwork on buildings in St Petersburg was created in my factories. I advised on the reconstruction of the docks at Nicolaev, and played a large part in the introduction of a new Russian statute on weights and measures, which was based on the English inch.

My success must have reached the ears of the Empress, because the cotton factory that had been recently set up at Alexandrovski, on the bank of the Neva, was running at a loss. It was under her special patronage, and she was having to make up the deficit. So she sent for me, and asked me to take over. There was employment for 750 people, which was increased by the introduction of employment for foundling boys and girls, under the supervision of English foremen. So there was an English colony of 70-80 persons. Divine service was performed in the school-room every Sunday evening by the chaplain from St Petersburg.

At the factory cotton was spun, sheets and table-linen woven, and we made playing cards (which were a crown monopoly). I introduced horse-mills to work the machines, which was a great improvement over the former processes, but which still left the establishment so expensive that they could not vie with English manufacturers. I had one third of the profits from the sales, which after several years amounted to a good fortune. I was made a State Counsellor, and known by everybody as Karl Karlovich Gaskoin. My second wife was Anastasia, daughter of Dr Matthew Guthrie, physician to Tsar Paul. When I died in 1806, I was buried in Petrozavodsk; there is a bust of me in Lugansk.

One of the trusted men I had brought to Russia was 'General' Alexander Wilson, as he became known. He was my assistant director, and since my death took over managing the whole enterprise, but without my pay! In the inimitable Russian style, all persons officially employed have a military rank. Wilson was anything but a soldier, and tried as best he could to hide his rank. But in the capital he was obliged to wear uniform, and as there were guardhouses in almost every street, whenever he passed the guard turned out to salute him, which used to annoy him very much. He was always concerned about his future prospects, and had to make do with the Order of St Vladimir. However, as time went on, Wilson introduced steam machines, which reduced the expense of the work, and during the Crimean War, when British imported goods were prohibited, our factory flourished. Visitors to the factory had many good words to say about Wilson: one wrote that he 'possessed a calm, even temper, firm but just, and conciliating, with a competent knowledge of what he undertook to perform, without possessing any considerable amount of invention. He spoke Russian like a native, besides French and German. He therefore most justly possessed a good deal of influence, and was thoroughly liked and respected, from the humblest workman under his orders up to the Emperor, who was very fond of him. Lastly, he was thoroughly honest, a rare thing in Russia.' Nicholas I was reported to have said that there were only three people in Russia whom he could trust not to rob him: himself, Grand Duke Alexander, and General Wilson. Praise indeed! He died comparatively poor. Strange to relate, Wilson employed his own father at Alexandrovski. His younger brother, John, was a partner in the St Petersburg firm of Thompson Bonar.

One of the mechanics at the cotton factory was William Sherwood, who came out to Russia when the establishment started in 1800. His young son grew up at Alexandrovski. He became known to Emperor Alexander I. John, as he was called, seems to have had a good education, learning French, German and Latin, as well as English. On leaving school he was employed as teacher of English in a general's household. Unfortunately, he fell for one of his pupils, eloped with her, but on being caught up with, the young couple were parted, she to a convent, he to the army. Eventually he was promoted to Lieutenant, and served among other places at Kherson, in the deep south, where one day he chanced to overhear some superior officers engaged in deep conversation. It turned out to be a plot to assassinate the Emperor, which eventually culminated in the Decembrists' Revolt of 1825. Sherwood, being anxious to please the Emperor, wrote him a letter, which he entrusted to the Imperial physician, Sir James Wylie. From then on, he was allowed a bodyguard, and asked the Emperor's permission to join the Masonic lodge where several of the conspirators were active. Eventually, the officers were detected and punished. Sherwood was promoted to Captain, and decorated. He and his father were awarded a pension for life, Ivan Vassilievich (John son of William) was given a coat of arms with the Imperial eagle in the centre, and became known as Sherwood-Verni (faithful). Nicholas I thought it might be risky for Sherwood to remain in Russia, and suggested he should retire and settle in England. But the Faithful one preferred to remain where he was, and his bonus was that his wife was restored to him. He died in 1867.

But most of this was after my time. What I do know about is that, even from the mid-eighteenth century, before the Industrial revolution, there were numerous Britons operating in Russia in different fields. We know that, as early as 1753 a Mr John Thompson (under the name of Martin Butler) set up a wall-paper factory in Moscow. I read of his appeal to the Senate to renew his patent on the grounds that he undertook to employ only Russian labour. Thomas Nesbitt attempted to do the same at St Petersburg. William Gomm (a leading merchant since the late 1740's) was also active at Onega, having obtained an exclusive privilege for 25 years, on condition that he paid a certain sum per annum to the Crown, whenever his profits exceeded a given total. His assistance was enlisted in sending Russian boys to train in England. Gomm published a book: 'A view of the Exports from Onega'. He was master of the Perfect Union Lodge of masons (of which Thompson was a member). Charles Brown, a Londoner, came out to manage his brother Lawrence's business in 1804. I am afraid he retired penniless, so took up writing on his return to England, producing 'Narensky, or the Road to Yaroslaf, a new serio-comic opera in 3 acts, as performed at the Theatre Royal, Drury lane, 1814'. It purported to be founded on an event which had occurred in Russia during his residence out here. Not, perhaps, one of the greatest contributors to the Russian Empire!

I will not finish without mentioning John Cavanagh, who died in 1783, and who ran a sugar refinery. His son became a banker in St Petersburg, and did much to assist visitors to the capital. His daughter, Mary, married in 1776 Timothy Raikes, another banker, and member of the Lodge mentioned above.

By 1791 there were at least four shops in St Petersburg with English names: Hoy & Bellis, 74, Malaya Millionnaya; Sam Hawkesford, Nevsky Prospkt; Ben Hudson; Mr Hubbard, in Pervaya Linya on Vassili Ostrov. I hear that by 1830 there were many more commercial houses, including the bankers Hills & Whishaw, and John Thomas & Co. On the English Quay were Carr & Co and Thomas Bonar & Co; Cattley & Co, on the English Back Line (Galernaya), and in Malaya Millionnaya, on the corner of Nevsky Prospekt, was the GRAND MAGASIN ANGLAIS de MM NICHOLLS AND PLINKE, arranged on the principal of a London bazaar, containing articles of every description under heaven. Nearby was Peters the tailors, and Jackson, magasin de modes. In Nevsky itself, the MAGASIN BRITTANIQUE of Mr Andrews. In Gorokhovaya street- Dixon's bookshop.

I am beginning to wish I had lived a little longer!

Samuel Bentham (1757-1831)

I am a son of Jeremiah Bentham, attorney of London, and brother to Jeremy Bentham, the well known writer on jurisprudence and ethics. He went to Oxford, but I, being of a more practical frame of mind, preferred to study the technical skills associated with shipbuilding. After a few years working in various shipyards, I determined to try my hand at something more ambitious. At the age of 22, I undertook a journey, at the instance of Lord Lansdowne, to visit arsenals on the Baltic, but extended it to include large parts of Siberia, studying methods of mining and working metals. As you probably know, Siberia was a largely unknown area to most people, Russian or foreign, and did not become accessible to outsiders until the 19th century.

While I was at St Petersburg, I was appointed a Conseiller de la Cour and given the rank of Lieutenant Colonel. I was put in charge of the Fontanka canal works, and I invented a new pile driving machine. I was amazed and delighted to discover how many English people there were in the capital, but I chose to propose to a young Russian lady, whose mother refused to let her marry me, a foreigner! I was introduced by Joseph Farington, R.A. to Prince Potemkin, who asked me to be manager of his estate on the Don. My commission – to transform a peasant backwater into a self-contained showpiece of advanced experimental agricultural and industrial technology. Although Kritchev, as it was called, was deep inland in the Crimea, Potemkin (a mastermind of improbable stunts) demanded a shipyard as the centre of the community! As there was no industry in the area at all, I was ordered to set up separate factories for every commodity that was needed: lumber mill, glass-blowing factory, tannery, cordage factory, dairy, bakery, school and hospital. This proved to be too tall an order under the circumstances, and I wrote in 1784 to my brother Jeremy, pleading for help. He acted immediately, and arrived in Russia. His preoccupation was with the management of unskilled workers in the factories, whereas I was still involved in inventing ways of installing larger guns on small ships – something that was soon to be needed in the war against Turkey, in which I played a modest part: I was knighted, and promoted to Brigadier-general.

Soon after this, I returned to England to visit my father, and took an appointment in the British Admiralty. Among my commissions was to go to St Petersburg in 1805 to build docks for British vessels, using local timber. By this time I was married, so I took all my family with me; my children picked up some Russian while we were there! Two years later we were recalled, owing to the war, but after Napoleon's final defeat, I visited Russia again, this time including St Petersburg, Moscow, Nijni-Novgorod to see the famous fair, but on return to Moscow, I fell ill. Nevertheless I managed another tour, this time of Southern Russia in 1816, but I eventually died in 1831. I think I made a reasonable contribution to the Russian Empire, which is why I am included in this book!

Col. William Upton

I was a pupil of Thomas Telford, of whom everyone in Britain has heard. I went to Russia to be in charge of all engineering projects in Sevastopol. I designed and constructed, with immense difficulty I may say, a great fitting basin, into which opened five dry docks, three at the end and one on each side of the entrance canal. As there is no tide, these docks were above the level of the sea, and the ships were floated into them by locks, having a rise of ten feet each. To supply the basin and thence the canal, the water was brought eleven miles by an aqueduct of stone, into which the river was turned. At one point this passed through an excavated tunnel 900 feet long, constructed on arches in five or six places. To form a great reservoir, and ensure a constant supply of water, an enormous stone dyke was built across a mountain gorge. Proper sluices were built to prevent too great a pressure in case of unusually heavy rain. But soon after it was all finished, there was a terrific thunderstorm; the valley rapidly filled with water, and a great landslip from the side of the mountain took place, the sluices blocked up, and the flood poured over the top, taking away tier after tier of stones, until there was nothing left of my years of dedicated work but a jumbled mass of ruins.

Another of my projects was to convey drinking water from a great distance to a reservoir above the town. Some Jews, who wanted the contract, conspired against me and sent emissaries in the night to dig up and destroy the pipes. My contribution to Russia was not very conspicuous!

Nor in fact was that of Robert Owen, the pioneer reformer, who managed a cotton mill at New Lanark in Scotland, visited by none other than Grand Duke Nicholas, later Emperor. The Russian visitor talked for two hours, admiring the organisation of the works, as well as the schools for the employees' children. Owen was moved to offer the Grand Duke a silver dessert service; he was, however, restrained by his wife, on the grounds that the gesture was ostentatious, and that the heir to the throne had enough silver plate of his own. Despite this, Nicholas was so excited by what he had seen and heard that he said: 'As your country is overpeopled, I will take you and two million of population with you, all in similar manufacturing communities.' He was, apparently, prepared to provide them with land sufficient to give Mr Owen's ideas a really good chance. Owen declined, as he thought his hands were full enough of work at the time. If he had agreed, this present book would have been a great deal longer! Nor did Owen allow the Grand Duke his other wish: to adopt the Owens' younger sons!

Matthew Boulton (1728-1809)

As a champion of the Industrial Revolution, I started a factory at Soho, near Birmingham, in 1762, making metal objects, such as clocks and jewellery. In 1766, my partner, John Fothergill, a Russian-born Birmingham merchant, undertook a journey to Russia to establish trade links. It was not long before the Russian ambassador visited Soho to acquire works for Empress Catherine, who, as you may know, had a very advanced taste in valuable ornaments. He chose any number of vases, candelabras and wine-coolers, which were later delivered by Lord Cathcart, British Ambassador in St Petersburg. I was told that Catherine said that they were "in all aspects better than the French". Praise indeed!

In May 1796 I was informed that Catherine planned to refurbish her Mint in St Petersburg, and was invited to tender for the job. (I already had experience of coinage production.) The Russian Mint had been started under Peter the Great, who visited the London Mint in 1698; in the 1730's it was established in the Peter-Paul Fortress.

Catherine wanted to improve the currency system, and to have not only coins but medals skilfully produced.

A group of Russian mint technicians visited Soho, including the grandson of one of Peter's original managers. The work of re-establishing the Mint in Russia was, however, delayed by the death of Catherine, and the lack of interest by her son and heir, Paul. But when Alexander I acceded to the throne, things got started again, although the old building was not found suitable for the modern Mint. An Italian architect was engaged to deal with the problem. If you should visit St Petersburg, look out for the elegant building, which still stands.

Our other problem was the rivalry between our team and that of Charles Gascoigne, who, as you probably know, was involved in many industrial activities at that time in Russia. Workmen were affected by the situation, as also by the fact that the Russian 'Table of Ranks', which applied to all classes, classified engineers and mechanics as manual workers, no better than serfs!

Most of our team gradually returned home, but James Duncan stayed as foreman at the Mint. I received a letter from him in 1814 to the effect that he was coining ten million silver pieces a year. So we did achieve something worth recording!

7 TWO VISITORS

Catherine Hamilton

May I be permitted, as a mere woman amongst all these famous men, to add my experience of the Russia I visited late in the 18th century? While touring in Europe, I met Princess Catherine Dashkov (née Vorontsov). The princess and I immediately took a great liking for each other. She let me into her family history, and what a family! Her father, Roman, was Vice-Chancellor to Empress Elizabeth, and Grand Chancellor to Peter III, who stood godfather to the young Catherine. Her sister, Elizabeth, a somewhat coarse woman, became Peter III's mistress, and, it is said, could have become Empress, had Peter succeeded in divorcing his wife. Young Catherine Vorontsov, however, was a refined girl, who at an early age took to reading history, classics and philosophy, Voltaire and Montaigne, and thereby attracted the notice of the future Empress Catherine, herself no mean reader.

Catherine married, at the age of 15, Prince Michael Dashkov, and they had two children: the son, Paul (1759-1807), to whom the great Grand Duchess herself was godmother, and the daughter, accompanied their mother on an extended tour of Western Europe. On arrival in London, Paul was entered at Westminster School, while his mother visited France. Later he studied at Edinburgh University, and during that time Catherine Dashkov took apartments in Holyroodhouse, from where she was able to join in several learned societies, with such notable scholars as Adam Smith. It must have been easy for Catherine to move in high circles, as her brother Alexander was at the time Ambassador in London. But it would have been difficult for a woman in the 18th century to exert an influence in the men's world of universities, diplomacy and politics, had she not had the backing of the Grand Duchess herself. No one will ever be able to measure the influence on the progress and decline of the Russian Empire of such Anglophiles as Princess Dashkov. When she returned from her extended tour, she spent much of her time at either of her country estates: Kirianovo, on the Gulf of Finland, or Troitskoye, near Moscow, reading, writing and fulfilling herself as a member of the Free Economic Society. She was appointed Director of the Academy of Sciences by Catherine II, and first President of the Russian Academy from 1783, until her dismissal by Paul I on his accession. When I was with her in 1784 at Troitskoye, she arranged for me to be presented to the Empress at Tsarskoye Selo, where foreigners were rarely received. Then I was taken to Moscow, where I marvelled at all the curious and interesting sights of that ancient capital, after which my friend took me home to her estate at Troitskoye. I think she was surprised that I, a Briton, so used to beautiful gardens, should have admired her estate, which she told me she had planned entirely herself, and chosen every tree and shrub. She organised a village fete for my benefit. A village had been newly built a few miles away from Troitskoye, and the Princess got all the peasants who were going to live there, dressed in their best clothes. As the weather was very fine that day, they danced on the grass and sang Russian folk songs. Add to that the traditional Russian dishes and drinks, and a really good time was had by all. I was then informed that the new village was to be named Hamilton. I was quite taken aback by the honour, and presented the villagers with the traditional gifts of bread and salt. I kept in touch with them over the years.

My nieces, Catherine and Martha Wilmot were to visit Troitskoye in 1805, and they left their impressions in their 'Russian Journals'. Their real contribution was to induce Princess Dashkov to write her memoirs, a work which sheds so much light on Russian society of that period. Catherine took one copy home with her to Ireland in 1807; a few months later when Martha was taking her copy, she burnt it rather than abandon it to the Customs. Owing to the Tilsit agreement, Anglo-Russian relations were somewhat strained. Princess Dashkov's Memoirs were not published until 1840, well after her brother Semeon Vorontsov's death, for fear he should take offence at her version of events.

George Green

I made 'An Original Journey' to St Petersburg in 1813, and during the course of my stay I had occasion to visit an estate at Falkenhof, in what you would now call Estonia, but at the time was part of Russia. The house was inhabited by a Mr Wilkinson, but it became well known a few years previously as the estate of Elizabeth Chudleigh, Duchess of Kingston (1720-1788), who, after a life crowded with incident, most of it not to her credit, sailed for Russia, and ingratiated herself with Catherine the Great, who gave her a choice of estates. She had one of the best houses in the capital set aside for her use, near the Ismailovsky Bridge, and the country estate at Falkenhof, with the village which took the name of Chudleigh. Although the post-office had the name of the village painted on the door, the place was grossly misspelt on the post map and in the books. It 'abounded with serfs who did not dare to approach the upper petticoats of their mistress, without first kissing the fringe in a posture of genuflexion.' (Incidentally, she freed all these serfs in her will). She paid Baron von Rosen 85,000 silver roubles for the estate, and sent to England for a shipload of animals, birds, plants and seeds and machinery. She had a Mr Clarke and a Mr Maw to farm the land for her, but it proved a worthless scheme. The soil was intractable, and did not respond to tilling. She considered the idea of mining cobalt to bring her in some revenue, but changed her mind to vodka distilling. When this dream failed to materialise, she desperately tried to resell the estate to its former owner, who demurred. When she died, there were two claimants to the property: Baron von Rosen, the previous owner, and a Colonel Garnovski, who failed to carry out her wishes. Her maitre d'hotel, Seymour, who was supposed to receive £10,000, only got £1,000. Many other benefactors were refused payment.

While in Russia, the Duchess recommended her gardener, Mr Mowat, from her estate at Thoresby, Notts, who went out to be a gardener for the Empress. The duchess wanted another gardener for a neighbouring estate, and sent her terms: '£50 per annum, table etc, a good house, and passage home paid after a year.' She sounds generous enough, but I expect the Russian locals despised such ostentatious interlopers, who deserved to be less popular.

8 AN ASSEMBLY OF ARTISTS

Charles Cameron (1743-1812)

I was born in Scotland, both my grandfather and father being in the building profession. At a tender age I was entrusted to the court of the exiled Young Pretender in Italy, since my family were of the Jacobite persuasion. I was able to study Classical antiquities, especially the Roman baths, and on returning to London, published a book on the subject, which was so popular that it ran to a second edition.

Around this time, it came to my notice that a fellow Jacobite, James Wyatt, whose architecture was very much in vogue, was approached by the Russian Ambassador in London with the offer of 'any salary he chose' to settle in Russia as Empress Catherine the Great's own personal architect. Apparently, he was dissuaded from accepting the offer by a certain Mr Wright, who had himself acquired a large fortune in Russia by coach-building. He told Wyatt that Catherine, while keeping her promise about money, would never allow him to leave the country. Several English noblemen combined to pay him to stay in England, and so I took advantage of the position, and offered my services.

Some fifteen miles south of the capital was the Empress's country residence, Tsarskoye Selo (The Royal Village), which had been built in the 1750's for Empress Elizabeth by Bartolomeo Rastrelli, an Italian with French training. He was only one of many Italian and other foreign architects employed during the latter half of the 18th century by Russian rulers to build up and beautify their palaces. But Catherine was not altogether comfortable living in the very ornate, overbearing style of the interior, and she flattered me into redecorating certain rooms of her palace. When I had passed my 'test' she put me to work on designing furniture for these rooms. She was so pleased with the results of my efforts in this and other directions that she entrusted me with the construction of a whole palace, about three miles from Tsarskoye, for her son, Grand Duke Paul, and his wife. This was named Pavlovsk, after the Russian spelling of Paul, and it took me four years to design and build. It was set in a park, through which flowed the small river Slavyanka. On its banks I built The Temple of Friendship, the Colonnade of Apollo, and later, The Pavilion of the Three Graces. In the nearby village, I designed St Sophia's church. Meanwhile the Grand Duke and Duchess travelled around Europe incognito, collecting everything they fancied, such as clocks, Sevres porcelain, tapestries and furniture to fill their new home. Ironically, Paul was never particularly happy with the palace I built: he brought in Vincenzo Brenna to add taller, more elaborate wings to what I suppose was really only a Palladian mansion, and then himself preferred to live at Gatchina, another Imperial residence, south of the capital, where he was eventually murdered!

However, at Tsarskoye itself, I was responsible for the Chinese Village, (a passing fad at that time), the Agate Pavilion, so named from the agate, jasper, malachite and other semi-precious stones covering the interior. When this was completed, Catherine took me by the arm, and walked over the whole building, and said: 'It is indeed very handsome, mais ça coûte!' Not that she spared any expense to build up the prestige of the Russian Empire, especially by this proliferation of impressive buildings. Probably my most important assignment was The Cameron Gallery, which I built in 1783-7. It is a wing of the Palace, set at right angles to the Empress's private apartments, and takes the form of a terrace, or sheltered walk, with slender columns, between which are bronze busts of famous figures from mythology and history, both ancient and modern. Catherine herself insisted that the bust of Charles James Fox, by Nollekens, be placed between those of Demosthenes and Cicero, in acknowledgement of the part Fox played in averting war between Russia and Great Britain. The Empress spent much of her leisure time walking through the Gallery, talking to her guests. At the end, broad steps gently wind down to the lake, which forms part of the English Garden. As Catherine grew older and less agile, the steps proved troublesome, and I built an incline for her use.

During my working life at Tsarskoye, I occupied rooms, which had originally been Catherine's apartments, and was treated with great deference, until the new Emperor, Paul, dismissed me from his service, mainly, it would seem, for being associated with his mother, whom he had grown to hate. After leaving the Imperial employment, I was given the post of Architect to the Admiralty. I designed and superintended the building of the Naval Hospital and Barracks at Kronstadt in 1805.

Before I go, I must tell you about John Bush, who during the 1770's was head of a celebrated nursery garden at Hackney, north of London. He was summoned by Catherine to advise on laying out the gardens and hothouses at Tsarskoye, and a very good job he made of it! What was unusual about John and his wife, Elizabeth, was their kind hospitality to British visitors, the new town being built specially to service the Imperial Palace not yet being equipped with inns. There was one instance of this when Dr Thomas Dimsdale was being entertained by the Empress, his wife was dining at the Bush table, and a footman in green and silver came in and said, if not inconvenient, Sir James Harris, the British Ambassador, and the Imperial Minister were coming to dine! Mrs Bush had the help of her four daughters, so all was in order! (Incidentally, I married one of the daughters, Catherine.) When John Bush returned to England to see to his affairs, his son Joseph remained as one of the Imperial gardeners at St Petersburg.

Another of my contemporaries was Thomas Banks, who started life as a sculptor, and was employed in London by William Kent the architect, who himself had enjoyed a spell of favour at the court of Empress Anna in the 1730's creating landscape gardens. Banks produced his masterpiece in 1780: a marble statue of Cupid over 4 feet in height, but was disappointed at the little interest shown in it when it was exhibited. So, being unemployed, he embarked with his work for St Petersburg in search of a patron. He arrived in the Russian capital in August, 1781, where the Cupid was brought to the notice of Catherine, who immediately bought it for 4,000 roubles, and had it placed in the Grotto in the garden at Tsarskoye. The Empress was so pleased with the statue that she asked him to make another, to be called 'Armed Neutrality', but either the climate disagreed with him, or he was discontent at his prospects, and he returned to London in 1782, not before he had made a model for a statue of Catherine herself, which he left with Prince Potemkin.

Mr Gould (1732-   ), a pupil of Lancelot (Capability) Brown, was responsible for the gardens around the Taurida Palace, St Petersburg. These gardens, 'created out of a mephitic bog', in the shade of which Potemkin, Catherine the Great and two succeeding emperors sought tranquillity and repose from the oppressive weight of public duty, excited the admiration of all who were privileged to walk through them. Gould went on to lay out Admiralty Walks in the capital, described as 'a new and beautiful promenade consisting of long alleys, planted on each side with rows of trees with flowers and shrubs at intervals.' It was much frequented by people of distinction. There were benches, placed at intervals, and coffee, tea and confectionary were sold.

By about 1779 I was getting fairly dissatisfied with my assistants, so in the Empress's name, I placed an advertisement in the Edinburgh Evening News, inviting applicants, such as stonemasons, bricklayers and a smith. Perhaps we would get ten applicants. Despite discouragement from the British Ambassador, 73 craftsmen arrived – some with families! We housed all these Britons in sixteen wooden houses in a tightly-knit community, largely isolated from Russian life, called the English street – with their own Masonic lodge. Among these was the distinguished Adam Menelaus (1756-1831), no mean architect, who soon realised that he was surplus to my requirements, and after a year worked for Nicolai Lvov on the quest for Russian coal, along with another Scot, William Hastie. Their aim – to save importing coal from Great Britain. Menelaus worked for the Razumovskis during the 1800's, and later for the Stroganovs, and - Alexander I. During that reign he was responsible for building The Cottage, a modest Gothic style palace in a wooded parkland on the Gulf of Finland, opposite Kronstadt; nearby was The Farm. Unfortunately, Alexander did not live to enjoy these country retreats, but I am sure they served succeeding emperors as refuges from the stress of public life.

John Field (1782-1837)

Born in Dublin of a very musical family, I was fortunate to learn the keyboard at a very early age. My father was a professional player in the orchestra at the Theatre Royal, my grandfather was organist at a Dublin church. Both lived in the same house, teaching music. I made my debut in Dublin at the age of ten, and my father, realising that I had promise, took me to Bath, which was at the time a great cultural centre, and on to London. I became apprenticed to Muzio Clementi, the foremost pianist and piano-maker of the day. It is well known that the piano had not long been invented to take the place of the harpsichord, and many fashionable people wanted their children to learn to play. My job was to demonstrate pianos in Clementi's showroom in London, and when the head of the firm undertook a tour of Europe, he took me with him.

In 1802 we arrived in St Petersburg, and opened a branch of the business; I was hard put to it, speaking only English. But the following year, the master left Russia, and I was made branch manager, and lived as the guest of General Merklovski, Governor of Narva. The shop did not last long, but long enough for me to pick up a large aristocratic clientele, and while teaching and performing for my rich patrons, I acquired a mastery of French, German and Russian, as well as a considerable income! Among my pupils were Charles Neate, the English pianist and composer, Sergei Rachmaninov's grandfather, and Leo Tolstoy's mother. I met most of my contemporary composers, and many acknowledged their debt to me. One wrote: 'The silvery cadences of his music were to float out across the snows, lingering in the birchwoods and lilac thickets.' Michael Glinka, at one time my pupil, wrote of me: 'Field's playing was at once sweet and strong and characterised by admirable precision. His fingers fell upon the keys as large drops of rain that spread themselves like irridescent pearls.' I invented a new musical form – the Nocturne, which was later adopted by Chopin. Liszt edited the Nocturnes, and added a fulsome appreciation. My Concertos were played and praised by Schumann.

I married in 1808 one of my Moscow pupils, Mademoiselle Adelaide Percheron: unfortunately we had no children. I made friends with Dr James Quinlan, a fellow Irishman, who held the post of Head Physician at the Imperial Hospital in Moscow for 35 years until 1827. In 1832 I visited London on a concert tour, which coincided with Clementi's death, and I was one of the chief mourners at the maestro's funeral in Westminster Abbey, where I met Mendelssohn. From London I went on to Paris, where I was announced as 'Chapel Master to the Emperor of Russia'! In Italy I fell ill, and was taken back by the Rachmanov family to Russia, where I died in 1837. On my deathbed I was asked if I would require the ministrations of a priest. 'Are you a Catholic?' they asked. 'No'. 'A Protestant, then?' 'No'. 'A Calvinist?' 'No, I'm a pianist!'

My grateful friends and pupils erected a monument to me in Moscow, but I would prefer to be remembered by my contribution to music, and I dare to think that I am.

George Dawe (1796-1829)

I have been asked to speak for British painters who worked in Russia or provided pictures for Russia.

I cannot help mentioning Nicholas Dixon, who worked between 1667 and 1708: he painted a miniature portrait of Tsar Alexei Michailovich, but as far as I can ascertain, never visited Russia. On the other hand Alexander Cosens, a water colour painter, was commonly held to be the illegitimate child of a Mrs (or Miss) Cosens, a woman from Deptford that Peter the Great picked up and brought back. Alexander had the ?dubious honour of Prince Menshikov as his godfather. (He had a brother, Peter, whose godfather was the Emperor himself!) Alexander went back to England in 1746, taught drawing at Eton and Christ's Hospital, and died in London in 1786.

Another English painter, who needs no introduction, was Sir Joshua Reynolds (1723-1792), commissioned to paint a picture for the Hermitage. He was given a choice of subject, and no limit to the fee. He chose a subject which pleased the Empress: the infant Hercules strangling serpents, figurative of Russia surmounting her problems. She paid him 150 guineas, and a gold snuff-box with her portrait on the lid, encircled with diamonds. The picture was removed by Emperor Paul (who hated his mother) into a private apartment below the gallery, with the explanation that 'Russians have a superstitious horror of death…and the subject was unpopular'.

So the first real British-born painter to work in Russia was Richard Brompton (1734-1782). He studied in London, where he was well known for his extravagant habits, which led him into the King's Bench prison for debt. He was let out only upon his appointment as portrait painter to Catherine the Great. He died in St Petersburg.

I will mention in passing the contribution made by James Tassie (1735-1799), who trained in Scotland, but worked in Ireland. He was responsible for providing the majority of the cameos and intaglios for Wedgwood's first Catalogue in 1773. Tassie's catalogue of 1775 contained 3106 examples, and Catherine the Great ordered a complete collection of Pastes in imitation of Gems and cameos, which were arranged by a German, to be exhibited at Tsarskoye Selo. After Tassie's death, his nephew William completed the Imperial Collection.

John Augustus Atkinson was born in London in 1775, and was taken at an early age to St Petersburg by an uncle to study in the Imperial galleries. He soon gained the patronage of Catherine, and, strangely, retained it under Paul. I always wondered if the young

Alexander was his pupil. In 1799 Atkinson had two pictures hung in the St Michael's Palace: 'The Victory of the Don Cossacks over the Tartars' and 'The baptism of Count Vladimir'. He travelled within Russia sufficiently to be able to make drawings of peasants, their manners and customs, which he incorporated in a Russian version of Hudibras, published in Konigsberg in 1798. Atkinson returned to England in 1801, and was made a member of the Royal Academy in the following year. His 'Picturesque Representations of the Russian People', written in 1803-4, did not appear until 1812. But in collaboration with Walker, an engraver, he brought out 'Panorama of St Petersburg' and a portrait of Marshal Suvorov in 1805. The same team produced 'Foreign Field Sports' in 1814, which contains two pictures of Russian hunting.

Sir William Allan was born in Edinburgh in 1782, studied in his native city, and then continued at the Royal Academy in London. In 1805 he left for Russia, but after being shipwrecked at Memel' in the Baltic, was forced to travel overland to St Petersburg, where he had influential friends, including Sir Alexander Crichton, physician to the Emperor. Having learnt enough Russian to survive, he travelled into the interior of Russia, Ukraine, and eventually Turkey, studying the customs of the Cossacks, Tartars and others, and collecting arms and armour, His picture 'Russian Peasants keeping their Holiday', painted in 1809, was exhibited at the Royal Academy when he returned to England in 1814, having been previously prevented from doing so by the French invasion of Russia. Allan 'commuted' between London and the Russian capital more than any man I know. On a visit in 1844, I understand he executed for Nicholas I 'Peter the Great teaching his subjects the Art of Shipbuilding', which I believe is still in The Hermitage. He died in 1850.

Another northerner who made a name in London at the same time as Allan was Robert Ker Porter (1780-1842). He was appointed historical painter to Alexander I in 1804, and his contribution was immense: vast canvases, depicting historical scenes, were hung in the Hall of the Admiralty in St Petersburg. Porter courted a Russian princess, Maria Scherbatova, but, his matrimonial hopes not coming immediately to fruition, he left the Russian capital and toured in Finland and Sweden, where he was knighted by King Gustavus IV in 1806. In 1809 he published 'Travelling Sketches in Russia and Sweden, 1805-8', which are delightful as well as useful in understanding the life of provincial people in the Empire at the period. On his return in 1811 he married his princess, who bore him one daughter. Meanwhile he had written 'Narrative of the campaign in Russia during 1812', and had been knighted by the Prince Regent. The Princess, now Lady Ker Porter, died of typhoid fever in St Petersburg in 1826, and, I understand, Sir Robert returned to England in 1841, but not for good: on a visit to his daughter, now married to a Russian officer, he chanced to favour the Emperor with a call, and on the journey back from the Palace in a droshky, died of apoplexy. Or so I am told. He was buried in St Petersburg, but there is a memorial to him in Bristol Cathedral.

I have been called 'the most celebrated painter ever resident in Russia'; I am not sure I deserve that title, but I certainly made a very good living out of my work, and created a large repertoire of pictures, mostly portraits of famous people of my time. I was a Londoner, born in 1796; my father was an engraver, who sent me to study at the Royal Academy. I was present at Brussels after the Battle of Waterloo, and was invited to Russia to paint a series of portraits of the heroes of the Napoleonic wars. In less than nine years I executed between three and four hundred such pictures, and amassed, as far as I remember, about one million roubles. One long room in the Raphael gallery of the Hermitage was dedicated to the exhibition of these works. Naturally, other commissions followed, which included full-length portraits of Wellington, Kutuzov and Barclay de Tolly. But of all my work, the masterpiece is a study, 23 feet high, of Alexander I mounted on a grey horse, which was hung in the St Petersburg Arsenal. I can say, with my hand on my heart, that I never solicited favours or honours, but the Emperor conferred on me the title of First Portrait-Painter to His Imperial Majesty.

All this work told on my health, and I was advised to leave St Petersburg. I did so, finally returning to London in the spring of 1829, where I died the following October. I must, however, mention my younger brother, Henry, who copied some of my pictures of Russian officers.

H.I.M. ALEXANDER I OF ALL THE RUSSIAS (Reigned 1801-1825)

I do not expect you are surprised at my appearance in this collection of portraits of Britons who helped Russia become a European, even a world, power. I pride myself on being one of the biggest influences in enlightening my nation, with the help of many of your countrymen.

As in the case of Peter the Great, I was given a different or unconventional name – as were my two brothers, Constantine and Nicholas. It was as though a new era was starting with a new century, and I was determined to achieve greatness – not tyranny or reaction – but enlightened power to lead my people to greatness, especially after we had relieved Europe of Napoleon.

As you must realise by now, I was born in 1777, and brought up largely by my grandmother, Catherine II, who regarded my father as weak and incapable. She appointed all the staff in the palaces, including nurses, tutors and governesses, and had a very marked preference for Britons. My first influence was Pauline Primrose, who arrived at Court with her sister, Sarah. They were probably the first English nurses at any overseas royal Court. (They had an aristocratic ancestry, although I understand their father John had fallen on bad times). Pauline (whom we called Polly) married my valet Johann Gessler. They were both held in very high esteem by everyone in and around Court. I quote from Grandmother's words, that Mrs Gessler was 'a woman of rare merits. She is tidy, clean, simple and sensible. I feel sure that if Monsieur Alexandre had a son of his own, brought up by the same Englishwoman, the throne would stand secure for more than a century to come!' (Unfortunately, as you know, I did not have a son, but was succeeded by my brother, and the throne did stand secure for more than a century!) When Dr Thomas Dimsdale came on his second visit in 1781 (I was four at the time), his wife Elizabeth was intrigued by the way my brother Constantine and I were handled, dressed and played with. Among other childhood playmates was G., with whom I always talked in English. I played the flute with another English boy, who had to leave Russia when things got difficult under my father's regime. The last time we performed together, I remember holding the flute in my hand, and addressing it: Adieu, sweet instrument! You have charmed away many an hour of care, often and deeply shall I regret the absence of your enchanting sounds; but you are going to breathe them in the best and happiest country in the world.' I had not then visited England, but when I did much later, I realised how true my words were!

When we were in our teens, our brother Nicholas was born, and Grandmother (who was by then very old), chose for him Jane Lyon. (Later in life he called her his lioness). She was the daughter of a sculptor who worked under Charles Cameron. She was only 17 when she was appointed, but was a young woman of moral determination, standing up for her rights and those of her young charge. You must know what a strong character Nicholas was, and how he confronted the problems that I left behind! Ironically, he ended up fighting the British in the Crimean war. Some of his qualities were surely instilled by his beloved Jane. When he had children of his own, he employed Englishwomen, such as Miss Brown and Miss Higginbotham. This tradition continued down the century: Kitty Strutton (born 1811), daughter of a bricklayer from Hackney, was nurse to Alexander II's children from 1845…

I could go on and on, but my brief was to inform you of the 'English' influence that surrounded me in my life and reign. (Many of the so-called English were in fact Scots, such as Sir James Wylie). In addition, several of my close Russian advisers were what we could call Anglophiles. Take, for example, Count Matvei Ivanovich Platov (1751-1818), hetman of the Don Cossacks. He had fought in 1770 against the Turks, and took a leading part in the Napoleonic campaign as a general. Appropriately, he accompanied me on my triumphant tour of the capitals of Europe, including London, where the Prince Regent gave him a watch, the City of London a sword, set in gold, with his monogram, which is, I am told, still on display in the museum at Novocherkassk. He was made an honorary Doctor at Oxford. This visit to England stands out in my memory – the first of its kind by a Russian ruler since that of Peter the Great over a century earlier. After the official part was over, I met so many interesting *ordinary* people.

But back to Platov: I always knew him to have a soft spot for the English. This is borne out by a book I read in 1818 by Lieutenant Colonel John Johnson: 'A Journey from India to England', in which he describes stopping off at Platov's seat for two nights. On hearing that a party of Englishmen had arrived in town, the Count sent his secretary to welcome them, and asked to be allowed to send them food etc. The next day they were invited to dinner, and were introduced to the Count's ménage: three English ladies, one of them a protégée of Platov's, and her two friends. They had accompanied the Count back from England. While in Russia they were chaperoned by Mr Wood, keeper of the Count's stud.

I must mention the Vorontsov family, all of whom distinguished themselves in service to the Russian Empire, and all of whom were distinctly Anglophile. I am sure you have already heard of Catherine, who became Princess Dashkov. My namesake, Alexander, a lifelong bachelor, spent a period as Ambassador to Britain during the reigns of Peter III and Catherine II, but he was not too popular with the Empress, who compelled him to retire from public life in 1791. When I acceded to the throne, I summoned him back to office and appointed him Imperial Chancellor. I relied on his experience and his wide grasp of history. He was an implacable opponent of Napoleon, and with Alexander's support, I got myself out of the ridiculous alliance that my father had made with the French.

Their brother, Semeon, was Ambassador in London from 1785 until 1800, when my father recalled him, because he did not approve of the liaison with Napoleon, and all his estates in Russia were confiscated. I, of course, reinstated him, but ill-health and family affairs induced him to resign in 1806, and he lived out his days in London, dying in 1832. His son, Michael, was born in 1782 in St Petersburg, but spent his childhood and youth in London, where he received a brilliant education. He became known as a Regency buck, earning himself a reputation as a dandy. Pushkin called him 'Polu-milord' (a half-lord). He came back to Russia, married Elizabeth Branizky (who was generally supposed to be an illegitimate daughter of Potemkin), but I can overlook some of his indiscretions, since he played such a big part in our campaign against Napoleon. Semeon's daughter Ekaterina was a linguist, who at the age of twelve translated a French tragedy into Russian, as well as a musician, who is seen at the organ in a painting by George Heyter. In 1808 she married as his second wife George Augustus Herbert, 11th Earl of Pembroke, and their eldest son, later 1st Lord Herbert of Lea, was a friend and inspiration to Florence Nightingale.

In 1823 I appointed Michael Vorontsov Governor General of New Russia and Bessarabia. Michael spent a lot of his time rearing English cattle. His castle, at Aloupka in the Crimea, was designed by Edward Blore, architect of Sir Walter Scott's house at Abbotsford. It was said that when the Vorontsovs eventually moved from Aloupka, 50,000 roubles were offered for one of the six marble lions at the entrance to the estate! Of course, like all the Russian nobility (and royalty!) of the time, Vorontsov had a succession of English doctors. One of these was Dr Hutchinson, who wrote a thousand pages to disprove the existence of God, and five years later became ordained priest in London! Another doctor, John Prout, this time at the other estate at Marsanda, was buried under a walnut tree in the churchyard, with a plain but neat monument. Michael Vorontsov has been credited with the development of Odessa as a major port and city. I believe he was the first to start steam-boats on the Black Sea, and made energetic efforts to prevent the plague penetrating into Russia from Turkey. Two other facts I would rather forget: when Alexander Pushkin visited Odessa, he formed a liaison with Vorontsov's wife. However, I am told, this relationship resulted in some of his finest poems.

You will undoubtedly be wanting me to disclose to you how I ended my reign. I am not going to give you the satisfaction of a straight answer. One thing I will say – *if* I disappeared from Russia, as many believe, to live the life of a hermit, dying in obscurity later in the century, I enlisted the help of – a British Officer. As I have often been heard to say, (and mean it!), is that the man within whose reach heaven has placed the greatest materials for making life happy is – an English country gentleman.

9 A MASS OF MEDICS

Dr Thomas Dimsdale (1712-1800)

I came from an old Quaker family – one or two of my ancestors were involved with William Penn, founder of Pennsylvania, a century before my time. I studied medicine at Aberdeen University, but most of my family lived and practised in Hertfordshire. The scourge of the 18th century was undoubtedly smallpox, and I made a speciality of devising a method of inoculation against it: inject a healthy patient with matter from someone who already had the disease. The patient would then suffer an attack of smallpox, but with adequate preparations was able to recover quickly and become immune to further infection. (Later, Edward Jenner inoculated with the cow-pox virus to build immunity against smallpox, which has substantially remained in use ever since, I believe.)

I published a paper on the subject in 1767, and the following year was invited to visit Russia to inoculate the Empress Catherine the Great. What an honour! I took my son, Nathaniel, with me. The Empress had arranged a team of post horses ready to whisk us away, should the inoculation go wrong, and the Russians want to seek vengeance on us. But fortunately, all went well. Not only Catherine herself, but her son, the future Tsar Paul, underwent the treatment, and soon others of the Court followed. The Empress was so grateful that she created me a Baron of the Russian Empire; £12,000 a year, and an annuity of £500; miniatures of herself and her son, set in diamonds; a rose-cut diamond ring mounted in gold; she added a Russian Imperial black eagle to my coat of arms. My son was rewarded with a magnificent four-colour gold snuffbox. The Russian boy who gave blood for the operation was raised to the nobility, and called Ospenny (which, I am told, is Russian for someone with smallpox!)

In 1780 we came home to England, and I resumed my practice at Hertford, and represented my town in Parliament. But in 1784 I was recalled to Russia to inoculate the Empress's two grandsons: Alexander (later Tsar Alexander I) and Constantine. This time I was presented with the Empress's own muff, made of fur from a black fox, normally only allowed to royalty. The idea of inoculation, originally entirely abhorrent to the superstitious Russians, gradually caught on, and we set up hospitals expressly to isolate and treat cases of smallpox. I enlisted a fellow-Scot, Matthew Halliday, who was twenty years my junior; he supervised the hospitals, administered free inoculation to the poor, and later on went to Moscow to help treat and cure victims of the plague. He eventually established a merchant firm and bought an island in the Neva. His eldest son, William, who was born at St Petersburg, trained in Edinburgh and London, before returning to the Russian service in 1785. I do not think there is any doubt we Britons did the Russian Empire a lot of favours! But some of us did very well out of it. Before I died, I requested to be interred in the Friends' burial ground at Bishop's Stortford, where other members of my family were. My third wife, Elizabeth, who died twelve years later, was laid alongside me.

Dr John Rogerson (1741-1823)

Having graduated at Edinburgh, I arrived in Russia at the age of 25. Immediately I was called to examine the son of a Russian noble-lady, Princess Dashkov. The boy was suffering from croup, but I was able to save his life. His mother being a very well-placed and influential person, I was very soon appointed Physician to the Court, a position I held for nearly fifty years. My duties included examining each of the Empress's prospective lovers, since she had a dread of venereal diseases. It brought me very close to Her Imperial Majesty, who, I admit, preferred me as a companion rather than as a doctor. On one occasion she was heard to say: "To put oneself in Rogerson's hands is to be a dead man"! I even heard it said that I applied my science not only to bleed the Empress, but to inspire her choice of favourites!

For services rendered, I regularly received a snuffbox, and just as regularly took it straight to a jeweller's to sell it. The jeweller would sell it to the first nobleman who wanted it as a physician's fee. So I obtained my snuffbox more than once. All doors to Russian society were open to me; I think I caused some merriment among the card-playing fraternity. I was very fond of whist, but by all accounts played it badly. On one occasion Count Bezborodko annoyed me by ordering cannons to be fired whenever I revoked in the course of a game! Another thing that angered me was the fabulous cures claimed by Count di Cagliostro, who was on a tour of Russia in 1779: I challenged him to a duel; he responded by offering a duel of arsenic pills. You will not be surprised to hear that I declined! I suppose my most traumatic moment was when I was summoned to the Empress's apartment in November, 1796. I found Catherine the Great stretched on the floor, with her feet against the door. She was speechless. I supposed it to be an attack of apoplexy, and ordered her to be bled twice. She appeared to be somewhat relieved, but was unable to articulate. She died the next day.

I was given an estate in Belorussia, with 1600 serfs, and was made a Privy Counsellor by Emperor Paul. But when I retired in 1816, I returned to Dumfriesshire, where I was able to buy some land and have a fine mansion built on the proceeds of my career in Russia. I died in 1823. I hope that my epitaph is not what was recorded in 1800 by Rev W.Tooke in his 'History of Russia': "In general, the physician finds a very ample subsistence in Russia; but his richest veins of gold are Petersburg and Mosco. In London alone, perhaps, is the mine of diseases so productive as here."

Another Scots physician who lived and worked in and for Russia for over forty years was Matthew Guthrie, who, among other distinctions, became physician to the 1st and 2nd Imperial Corps of Noble cadets in St Petersburg, and Council of State to the Emperor. His wife, Maria, who had formerly been acting directress of the Imperial Convent for the Education of the Female Nobility of Russia (!), made a tour of the Crimea in 1795-6, and died there, not before sending a series of letters to her husband in St Petersburg, describing her adventures and impressions of the South. Matthew published these in 1802, and, dedicating the book to Alexander I, received a valuable diamond ring. He also contributed topics on Russian affairs to the Edinburgh journal 'The Bee' during 1792-4. His elder daughter married in 1797 Gascoigne, director of the Olenetz iron works, from whom you have undoubtedly heard, as he made a considerable contribution to the Russian Empire, like the rest of us.

Before I go, I will just mention my kinsman, James Mouncey (1710-73) who attended Empress Elizabeth, became the first corresponding member of the Society of Arts in Russia, but whose main claim to fame seems to have been that he managed to smuggle a rhubarb root to Britain, when he returned in 1762.

Sir James Wylie (1768-1854)

I was born at Kincardine on Forth, Scotland, of a modest working-class family. As a youth I attempted to run away to sea, but my mother literally dragged me back from the docks: looking back, I am glad she did, because the ship I would have boarded sank within a day during a violent storm. On completion of my apprenticeship, I started attending the University of Edinburgh, where I took classes in anatomy, surgery and medical theory and practice from such great scholars as Alexander Monro, Joseph Black and William Cullen. I did not graduate when I left university, and in 1790 left for St Petersburg, where I was to spend the rest of my life and career.

Shortly after my arrival in Russia, I joined the Eletsky Regiment, and as Regimental Surgeon I was present with my men at the Siege of Warsaw in 1794 and of Cracow the following year. The immediate fortune I had been led to expect was not forthcoming, and I was about to return home in disappointment, when I was invited to enter the service of Prince Alexander Golitsin, a very highly favoured nobleman. My appointment as Surgeon to the Imperial Court came about in this way: Count Kutaisov, a favourite courtier of Emperor Paul, was in danger of suffocation from an abcess in his neck. His doctors jealously guarded their position, and refused to enlist my help. Eventually, when they could do no more, I was asked to intervene, and immediately performed a tracheotomy, and the man lived. Immediate fame! Later I boasted that I owed my promotion to cutting Count Kutaisov's throat!

In 1801 the Emperor was strangled by a group of officers. I and two colleagues performed the post mortem and issued the death certificate declaring apoplexy, and I personally superintended the embalming of his body. Well, I wanted to keep my job and my relationship with Prince Alexander, to whom I was physician, and who now became Emperor – and my great friend. Much has been written about Alexander I, who had a great preference for the British, and was a much loved and benevolent monarch. I knew him personally all his life, and I had great respect and affection for him. When I was Inspector General of the Army Board of Health, I travelled with the Emperor when he went to war. An incident occurred in Moravia in 1805, when Alexander was taken ill and had to sleep on straw in a peasant's hut, with no medical help but mine. At 3 a.m. he was so ill that I feared for his life, so I rode to the nearest town and asked an officer at the Austrian headquarters for some red wine to warm the Emperor's stomach. When the officer refused, I bribed a servant. On my return, I found Alexander's condition was much improved. Just an example of my devotion to duty – and to my friend.

My biggest ordeal was undoubtedly at the battle of Borodino (7 September, 1812). I performed over 200 operations on the field of battle, many of them amputations. As you probably know, amputation in my day was performed without anaesthetic, and the only instruments were those available at the time, usually a saw! In one case, a Cossack had ridden 20 miles after having been struck by a cannon shot. He never spoke during the operation, which took me four minutes. The fellow talked afterwards quite composedly. The year after that at Dresden General Moreau, commander of the anti-Napoleon coalition, had one of his legs shattered by a cannon. I amputated the limb while the General was talking to the Tsar. The gallant patient died shortly afterwards. I must add that on one battlefield I myself lost a finger while dressing a soldier's wound.

In recognition of my services to my adoptive country and Emperor, I had the honour of accompanying Alexander I on his triumphant tour of the western European capitals after Napoleon's downfall. While we were in England, I was knighted by the Prince Regent on Ascot Heath, using Hetman Platov's sword. By request of the Tsar the knighthood was converted into a baronetcy!

I was with the Emperor on so many great, and not so great, occasions. On one tour of Finland, the Imperial party was obliged to walk, there being no transport on the island. Alexander outwalked us all. We arrived at a lonely hamlet, where the only living creature was a cow, which, on seeing us, began to caper at a fearful rate. I could not help pointing out that even the cow knew it was the Emperor, and she was dancing with joy at the unexpected visit. Another time while out travelling in the northern winter, the Emperor and I were forced by the weather to stop at a post-house. Alexander had frost-bite on one of his cheeks. Not being able to procure anything else to cover the Imperial face with, I sacrificed a pair of my pantaloons, and between us it took two hours to effect the conversion.

In October, 1825, I went on a tour of the Crimea with the Emperor. It was, of course, the duty of the Provincial Governor, Count

Vorontsov, to attend upon His Majesty. The Count was a great Anglophile, and you will not be surprised to learn that he had an English physician, Dr Robert Lee. At Nicolaev, one day over dinner, one of the oysters served to Alexander had a small worm adhering to its shell. I told him it was common and harmless, and a conversation ensued about tainted food and similar medical topics. So the discussion turned inevitably to homoeopathy, which was in vogue at the time; I tended to favour it, whilst Lee did not. Suffice it to say that Lee made an impression on the Emperor for his opinion and outspoken manner. On one occasion I saw the two men walking round a garden talking.

Within a month, while we were at Taganrog, the Emperor was taken gravely ill, and the Count hastened there, with Dr Lee, but they arrived three days late. I satisfied Lee with the cause of death, but I did not allow him to see the dead Emperor's face when he visited the corpse lying in state. I was not going to allow him to spread rumours about the final illness, because, as you may know, there has been ever since this episode a suspicion that the Emperor did not die, but fled his responsibilities and went abroad. If you are unfamiliar with the story, the brief outline is as follows: Major General Earl Cathcart, British Ambassador in Russia for many years from 1813, actually accompanied Alexander on his campaigns against Napoleon, and not unnaturally became a close friend and confidant. It is suspected that Cathcart was involved in a plot to smuggle the sovereign from Taganrog on his yacht to the Holy Land, where he could study to be a hermit. It is certainly curious that all accounts of the yacht's movements during November and December, 1825, are conveniently missing from its log. I am told that early in the 20th century, when scholars were anxious to get to the bottom of the mystery, Alexander's body was missing from its coffin! But I signed his death certificate, giving the reason for his demise, so all speculation can cease forthwith.

At the state funeral held in St Petersburg, George IV was represented by the Duke of Wellington, attended by Sir George Cathcart, son of the yachting Earl, and who, ironically, was killed in the Crimea in 1854, fighting against the Russians.

My contribution to the advancement of medicine in the Russian Empire did not stop at my ministrations towards Alexander, and his brother, Nicholas I. Indeed, you have already read of my involvement in the military sphere. I drew up plans for hospitals, which had to submit annual mortality and morbidity statistics to me. I established case records for all patients for the first time. I wrote several important medical texts, ranging from field surgery to pharmacopoeia and water purification. I promoted the training of Russians as doctors rather than importing foreigners, to study at the Medico-Chirurgical Academy that I set up, and of which I was President for 30 years. I founded the journal of the Academy, improved the legal and financial position of doctors, establishing examinations and certificates for doctors, to avoid bogus practice. Quite a record!

But, despite my accomplishments, there were those who criticised me: for example, a certain Dr Lefevre, whom I met at St Petersburg, later was quoted as having been uncertain as to what my native language was. 'It most resembled Scotch, but in his ordinary conversation he made use of such a Babylonish dialect that it was difficult to ascertain the root from whence all sprung. In the society of savants he was fond of talking Latin; it was the language which he wrote the best and which I believe he understood thoroughly.' At least I did something right! Another comment on my speech was from Captain G.Colville Frankland, who visited Russia in 1830: he said that I spoke 'English with considerable hesitancy and difficulty.'

I never married, so I bequeathed my considerable fortune to Emperor Nicholas I, for the foundation of a hospital to house the pupils of the Medico-Chirurgical Academy. Within five years of my death, two statues were erected in the capital. My funeral at the English Church in St Petersburg on 15 February, 1854, was attended by Emperor Nicholas I, and three Grand Dukes. During my lifetime I had been honoured by successive Emperors with the orders of St Vladimir, St Alexander Nevski and St Anne. My crest bore a picture of a Cossack, a people for whom I had a great respect and affection.

Edward Morton M.B.

A member of Trinity College, Dublin, and of the Royal College of Physicians, I was asked in 1827 to replace Dr Lee as travelling physician to Count and Countess Vorontsov. As I was not free at once, Dr Granville (note the name) deputised for me. By the time I left, I had had time to read up the latest accounts of life in Russia, such as Bishop J.T.James's 'Journal of a Tour to Russia during 1813-14', and Dr MacMichael's 'Journey from Moscow to Constantinople'. During my stay in Russia, I managed to meet several of our compatriots, some of whom you are already acquainted with: George Dawe, Alexander

Cobley, and the redoubtable Mrs Cochrane, widow of the eccentric Captain.

Some of the Russian nobles were very fond of having English medical attendants. In one family there were four physicians in seven years, all of whom left to seek preferment, often in the Imperial service. You have already met Dr Robert Lee, whom I replaced. I would also mention Dr John Prout, physician to Admiral Greig. Other British medics were employed at the various hospitals: Dr Steen, at the Artillery hospital; at the Marine hospital were Dr Leighton and Dr Gibbs. I was told about a delicate operation for aneurism successfully performed by Gibbs and a German doctor, under Leighton's supervision. This operation had been attempted only three times before: twice in Paris, once in London. Around the table were assembled the whole staff of naval surgeons, booted, spurred, some with stars! The operation was long and painful: for two hours the patient was forcibly held in position by his superior officers, and dared not complain! When the operation was finished and the poor fellow regained his composure, he kissed Dr Leighton's hand! Leighton is elsewhere reported to have plunged the poet Alexander Pushkin into a bath of ice to cure him of gangrene fever. But he did have his kinder side: he arranged with those responsible for some ships, which were to be brought from Archangel, to be launched earlier in the year, so that the seamen did not have to endure such bad conditions from ill-laden vessels in winter weather.

Two Scots doctors, members of the same family, were Sir Alexander Crichton (1763-1856) and his nephew Sir Archibald Crichton (1791-1865). The senior of these was born in Edinburgh, practised in London, among his patients being the Duke of Cambridge, brother of George IV. He brought out a treatise on mental health in 1798, and would appear to have been a successful and popular figure in England at the turn of the century, but something (or someone) induced him to go in 1804 to St Petersburg, where he immediately became physician in ordinary to the Emperor, and just as popular as he had been in London. He was soon made Head of the Civil Medical department, and was knighted by Alexander I in 1809, the year in which he helped allay a serious epidemic in some of the eastern provinces of Russia. He spent much of his time on the study and treatment of consumption, and his findings on the uses of the vapour of boiling tar in the cure of pulmonary consumption were published in 1817. He was knighted by Frederick William of Prussia in 1820, and by George IV the following year.

His nephew, Sir Archibald, was educated at Edinburgh, the son of a captain, but went to Russia in the 1820's, already knighted, and honoured by Oxford University. He became physician to Nicholas I, a member of the Russian Medical Council, and a Counsellor of State. His various orders included those of St Anne (1834) and St Vladimir (1836).

I earlier mentioned Dr Granville: his temporary stay in the Count's employ produced a book on St Petersburg, but more interesting is his Autobiography, published in 1877, which tells us about his tour in the summer of 1849, in attendance on Princess Chernichev, wife of the Russian Minister for War. The doctor had sailed from Hull in May, but even at that time of year the ship struck an iceberg, which broke both paddle-wheels, 150 miles off Kronstadt. Eventually Granville reached the Russian capital, safe and sound, but only to find a distinctly cooler attitude towards foreigners than had hitherto been the case. Nicholas I had been on the throne for 25 years, and he was certainly not the Anglophile his brother had been. Here is a typical entry in Granville's diary:

'St Petersburg, May 30. There are two (? only two) English physicians settled here: not one of them is known by name in the circles I frequent. In former times none but English were employed, and preferred; now the contrary is the case. The Emperor Nicholas has been striving to make the higher classes really Russian, and nothing but Russians or Russian Germans hold the sway. This extends even to the nurses. They say the English are too extravagant, and that they can procure as good nurses from Germany for half the money.'

I cannot help but wonder who the two English doctors referred to could be. However, in 1849, before leaving Russia, Dr Granville presented a copy of the Waterloo medal by Pistrucci to the Emperor (who happened to be absent in Hungary). As this valuable work of art was never acknowledged, he assumed the Emperor never received it. This he calls 'an example of ministerial morality in Russia, A.D.?1849'. Do you share with me the feeling that Granville was a little unlucky in all his dealings with Russia? Or do we sense the gradual approach of an anti-British attitude as the Crimean War got nearer?

There is also a distinctly sour note in the writings of Sir George Lefevre, whose 'Life of a Travelling Physician' was published in 1843. Russia was not the El Dorado he and many more had been led to believe. As an example he describes a concert in Odessa, given by an English musician, at which the Empress was present. It went off 'with great éclat. The emoluments amounted but to a modicum, and in this respect he was disappointed; for, like myself, he had been led to believe that professional men could not fail to make their fortunes rapidly in Russia; but if such things have happened, the times had passed before the musician and myself had tried the experiment. The pagoda tree had been plucked of its fruit – nay, the branches even well shaken.'

Lefevre helped to stave off poverty by holding the position of physician to the British Hunt. He was entertained in St Petersburg by 'the first accoucheur, who had maintained an unblemished reputation in the obstetric art during 40 years' residence in the country. He had presided at the birth of all the Imperial children, and encouraged the Empress by his presence in the most trying moments and an unparalleled success had crowned his endeavours.' Who could he have been referring to? Incidentally, I think that Dr Lefevre is going to contribute to this collection later: perhaps I had better let him speak for himself!

10 A MINISTRY OF MISSIONARIES

Rev Arthur Young (1769-1827)

I was born in 1769 and educated at Eton and Trinity College, Cambridge, after which I was ordained. My father, also called Arthur, was an eminent agriculturist: he imparted an enthusiasm for, and knowledge of, farming methods, taking me on a tour of Essex and Kent when I was only 15. But by the age of 28 I was contributing articles to my father's periodical 'Annals of Agriculture'. I really got enthused about the idea of revolutionising farming, and, I am ashamed to say, I neglected my duties as a clergyman. My living was in Ireland, and I was absent as much as possible! In 1804 I was invited to make surveys of the agriculture in at least some of the provinces of Russia, with all expenses paid, plus £1200 per annum. So I took my wife Jane as my (French) interpreter, and, despite quite a lot of prejudice, misunderstanding and unpopularity, managed to travel in several parts of Russia. From St Petersburg, I wrote home to my father my first impressions: "the Russians detest all foreigners, especially our countrymen, who live in a most respectable manner and spend a deal of money, caring for the Russian no more than the Russian cares for him, and besides, the Character of a merchant they affect to despise...French, Germans, Swedes, Foreigners of all descriptions incorporate themselves with the natives, but never thc Englishman... Stockings, cannon, ships are manufactured here by Englishmen, gardens laid out, deserts converted into cultivation by Englishmen. There are English architects, physicians and surgeons. Their coin is stamped by Englishmen, their leather and cotton goods made by

Englishmen, yet we are detested. In forty other branches have Englishmen been employed, but they kick them out whenever they have sucked them and set Russians in their place." I was not too popular with some influential Russians, such as Princess Dashkov, who was insensed at the nature of my employment, which she thought 'tended to overturn the Government and execute discontent in the people'. This did not stop me doing what I came to do.

While in the Crimea, I bought a considerable estate at Karagoss, where I was visited at least once by Alexander I. I died in 1827, and my son followed me a year later, without an heir. A Greek steward was left resident on the estate, and the agent was a German merchant at Theodosia. He did not remit a single rouble from the produce of the estate to my family in England. I feel sure there was some tricky business going on. In fact, I have been told that, with the connivance of the agent, somebody impersonated the heir to the estate and ordered the chopping down of trees. A few days later wagon loads of valuable pear, apple, plum and other fruit trees were for sale as firewood in the market at Theodosia.

Incidentally, I may have failed in my attempt to reform the Russian agricultural system, but at Voronova, near Moscow, where Count Rostopchin had set up an English farm, there is (or was) a statue of me, and a building dedicated to my memory!

John Paterson (1776-1855)

I arrived in St Petersburg in 1812, with the intention of printing scriptures in Finnish, and to do something for the circulation of the Bible throughout the Russian Empire. You must understand that for many, many centuries the Russian Orthodox church had reigned supreme in the country, but it was not exactly forthcoming in expounding the Gospel of Christ, even to those who could read (which, admittedly, were few.) I represented the British and Foreign Bible Society, which was set up expressly for the purpose of spreading the Word across the globe. In the Russian capital there was not a single type-foundry worth a name. There was no lead available: what little there had been was all used for making musket balls. This was, I admit, a momentous year for the Russian army. Even paper in large quantities was not to be obtained from one factory, so it had to be got from several, even if not all the same size and quality.

So I and my party set out for Moscow, hoping to see a bit more of the country. The conditions for travelling were atrocious: inns were uncomfortable, the post-boys tried to take advantage of us. But, eventually, we arrived at Moscow – at precisely the same time as Napoleon! Not the best time for getting co-operation from the authorities! On returning to St Petersburg, the road was crowded with refugees from the Napoleonic advance. Vehicles of all descriptions, with foot passengers, cows, sheep and other domestic animals, all fleeing from the French army to Jaroslavl. Among the carriages was the coach of the Bishop of Smolensk, closely shut, in which was the Bishop and the famous Mother of God of Smolensk (an icon). She was by repute a miracle-worker, but at the time I am talking about, she could neither save herself nor her votaries.

I decided to draw up an address, stating the objects and efforts of the Bible Society, pointing out the advantages such a society might produce in Russia, with the positive support and encouragement of the British Society. I managed to get a public translator to turn it into German, imagining it would be more acceptable than in English. The translation was so bad I could not use it. For instance, where I expressed a hope that friends of Revelation would take part in the plan, he wrote 'the friends of revolution'! I do not think I would have been too popular in the Russia of 1812, or of any other time!

However, I managed to enlist several influential members of society and government, and I had heard it said that Emperor Alexander himself was not averse to such a movement.

I was right: on December 25, 1812, Alexander gave approval to the founding of the Society, to which he was asked to be patron, but he declined in his typically modest fashion, saying that it was an honour to which he had no claim, but requested to be enrolled as a member, with a donation of 25,000 roubles, and an annual subscription of 10,000 roubles. Other members of the Imperial family followed suit. The President of the Society was Prince Alexander Golitsin; among the vice-presidents were three Metropolitans, four Archbishops, two bishops, the Minister of the Interior (Count Kotschubey,) eight Privy Counsellors, as well as (surprise) the Roman Catholic, Greek, Armenian and Lutheran archbishops, and Count Lieven.

For all that, I still found myself doing all the work: making type, printing, selling and buying. Occasional help appeared in different ways. I also managed to get permission for a place of public worship in English for missionaries passing through St Petersburg. This was in addition to the so-called English Church, of which you have probably heard, which served the needs of the British Colony in the capital. By 1815, my work was somewhat eased by the supply of printers and other staff from Britain: Mr Thomas Rutt, with two young men, came to manage the stereotype press. Three years later, Mr Rennie, with his wife and adopted daughter, and four young unmarried men, arrived with all their book-binding equipment.

The sixth anniversary of the Society was celebrated in the rotunda of the Taurida Palace on 27 September, 1819. It was a really impressive assembly, composed of all sorts of people, from peasants to rulers, Christians of all denominations, military and naval officers, representing the 173 branches of the Bible Society in the Russian Empire. In the six years of its existence up till then, 371,600 copies of the Scriptures had been printed, translations were made into many tongues. No doubt changes were observable in the peoples of the Empire, many of whom were hearing the Word of God for the first time in intelligible language. Alexander I ordered the Scriptures to be introduced into the seminaries, and into such schools as there were.

In 1821 I accompanied Dr Ebenezer Henderson and Mr Serov, assistant secretary of the Society, on an eleven-month tour of the Empire, to advance the interests of the Society. We started out from St Petersburg, and travelled via Novgorod, Moscow, Tula, Orel to Kiev, then by the Dniepr to the Black Sea, Crimea and back through Novocherkassk, up the Volga, stopping at Vladimir, Moscow and on to St Petersburg. At Bakhtsisarai we were given a very warm welcome by Rev Mr Carruthers, at whose home we had the pleasure of meeting Rev

Messrs Glen and Ross, who had recently arrived from Astrakhan to tour the Crimea, and investigate the possibility of establishing an Institute for instructing the Tartar youth. In the neighbourhood of Nikita, we visited the Imperial Garden, run by Mr Christian Steven, an eminent botanist, who had made a collection of insects, valued at the time at £500, which he had presented to Moscow University, on condition of being able to nominate annually two students to be educated at the expense of the University. He was a real scholar, who was doing good work for the benefit of the Russians: he wrote a Catalogue des Plantes Rares, and a Manual on Silk Production, of which he was the Chief Inspector, and a Councillor of State. In his Garden there were all kinds of tea plant. Not far from there we inspected another British institution, Mr Young's farm, of which you have probably heard. I was very impressed by his profound knowledge of agricultural science, as well as his religious outlook.

At Astrakhan we reached the headquarters of the Scottish Missionary Society, an undertaking that I had been involved in at its foundation, but which was finding life difficult for various reasons: supply of materials was a problem, the climate in winter made the printing presses stiff and the ink hard. They were continually invaded by Circassians, and they found it hard to keep workmen. In addition, there was nobody there who spoke or understood Arabic!

You must be aware by now how attracted Alexander I was to all things British. No doubt much of this attitude came from his upbringing by his grandmother, Catherine the Great, of whom you have read. Well, the Emperor, on his triumphal tour in England in 1816, gave an audience to a delegation of Quakers, and went to the Friends' Meeting House which Peter the Great had attended over a century previously. On his return journey from London to Dover, Alexander called at a farm run by a Quaker, and was so impressed by this man's husbandry that he resolved to have a Quaker farmer from England come to Russia to drain and cultivate the waste lands near St Petersburg and form a model farm. He asked me to procure such a man. Somehow the matter became known, and a presumed Quaker arrived in St Petersburg from Hamburg, and told me he had come to offer his services. I took up a whole packet of references, which proved to be forgeries. It appeared that the man in question was not a Quaker at all, had left his wife behind, and taken up with another woman, and supported himself selling tea. However, such was the spirit in Russia at the time, he was employed by a Russian nobleman on his estate. Then I found a genuine Quaker, Daniel Wheeler, who was received most graciously by Alexander. Wheeler went back for his wife and family, who joined him without hesitation, and they settled at Okhta, a village not far from the capital. I had been allotted ten thousand roubles to set up a house to be ready furnished for their arrival. One room was fitted up for Friends' worship. In 1823 Mrs Wheeler and her daughters returned to England unwell. It was while they were away, and Wheeler and his son remained to carry on the good work, that one day Emperor Alexander, while passing by in his carriage, alighted and sprang over a ditch towards where Wheeler was working. He gave him his hand and immediately entered into conversation with his usual freedom. He enquired about the Wheeler family, and when told that the wife was away ill, the Emperor asked why. When told it was the coldness of the house, he immediately gave orders for an architect to ascertain what needed to be done, and within days the house was invaded by builder's men, and quickly made more habitable.

On another occasion Alexander spent three hours at Wheeler's home, talking confidentially with the Quaker. During the course of the interview he gave Wheeler his hand and attempted to describe his own feelings of disappointment and despair, which, looking back, must have been a premonition of his untimely death. He even read scripture with Daniel Wheeler, who was clearly captivated by Alexander's personality and piety. Wheeler returned to England more than once during his stay in Russia, but in 1833 he finally got the call to go elsewhere to serve his Lord. Prince Golitsin, who, you may remember, was President of the Bible Society, asked Daniel Wheeler to write to him from wherever he may live, and ordered a certificate to be prepared in English for the satisfaction of Wheeler's friends, which he signed on behalf of the Emperor. Mrs Wheeler stayed on in St Petersburg until her husband had made all his arrangements, then they left without delay for Rio de Janeiro, and on to New Zealand to do missionary work. Daniel Wheeler eventually died in 1840, and his Memoirs were published two years later.

The land that had been put under his care near the Russian capital was what had been previously regarded as impracticable, either barren or marshy. When Wheeler left, there were 3000 acres in full cultivation, fifteen farms established, and 2700 more acres drained in preparation for farming. He introduced various implements and methods, previously unknown in Russia. I think I can say for certain that Russia had reason to be grateful to him – and perhaps to me for introducing him!

Another Quaker who made an impression about this time was William Allen – but perhaps I will let him speak for himself.

William Allen

When Alexander I was in London I was favoured with a private interview, in which the Emperor invited me to come to Russia to spread the news of God's word among his peoples. I was by profession a chemist, and a Fellow of the Royal Society. With my colleague, Etienne Grellet (1773-1855), I set off for Russia in 1818. At St Petersburg we engaged apartments at the home of an Englishman (whose name I have forgotten), met Dr Paterson and Walter Venning, both members of the Bible Society, and were interviewed by Prince Golitsin and his secretary, Popov. We were introduced to Metropolitan Michael at the Alexander Nevsky monastery, taken on visits to the Foundling Hospital, the Wilson cotton factory, and finally interviewed by the Emperor in 1819. I called on Sir James Wylie and Alexis Olenin, President of the Society of Arts, who showed me a supposed fragment of a manuscript of the Epistle to the Galatians dating from the 3rd century. All this entertainment did not prevent us from achieving the object of our visit, which was to send twenty sledges loaded with Bibles in Greek, Armenian, Persian, etc, to the Bible Society in Tiflis. We travelled the length and breadth of Russia, visiting such sects as the Memnonites, Molokani, Dukhobors and Sabbatarians. In Odessa we encountered Jesuitical activity – burning of Bibles and other distasteful things.

So concerned was I about the degrading condition of the poor in many parts of Russia that I secured an interview with the Empress Elizabeth, mother of Alexander I, at which I convinced her that the answer to the nation's ills was to invite Sarah Kilham, a member of the Society of Friends, who ran a school in Sheffield for poor girls, and who was willing to come over and set up a similar school. She would train teachers throughout the Empire, to go out and teach poor children. The Emperor gave his go-ahead and the Empress Mother was its patroness. The school, which was situated near the river Neva, was flooded during the exceptional tide of November, 1824. The furniture floated down the river, and Sarah Kilham was obliged to house her students elsewhere. A temporary setback! She also assisted Walter

Venning in a school for 120 poor little foreign boys rescued from begging in the streets.

I returned to England, taking with me the twenty-year-old son of General D'Junkovski, to receive instruction in English, mathematics and agriculture.

I will leave you with this unsolved question: who was the Quaker given permission by the Emperor to enter the Kremlin gates with his hat on?

George Borrow (1803-1881)

I was born in Norfolk, and from an early age was passionate about travelling and languages. When I was thirty, as a member of the Bible Society, I travelled to St Petersburg with letters of introduction from John Venning, a Norwich merchant. John had gone to Russia himself in 1793, set up a business, and returned home at the turn of the century. His younger brother, Walter, you have already met, however briefly; he joined the family firm in St Petersburg, and was responsible for founding the Prison Society. It was his son, James, that introduced me to Prince Golitsin.

I found the Russian capital entrancing: no other city in the world compared with it. The meeting and harmonious mixing of East and West attracted me. In addition, it was with great kindness that I was received by both the English Colony and the native Russians. It helped that I had a working knowledge of the language.

I got permission to print Scriptures in Mongolian, and with the assistance of Mr Swan and Mr Stalleybrass, we created a Mongolian-Russian-English Lexicon. Among other works of mine were translations of several Pushkin poems, which we printed and published in St Petersburg. I like to think they went some way to making known to the English-speaking world the work of Russia's greatest poet.

I visited Moscow and Nizhni-Novgorod, but was not allowed to go further, owing to an edict of Nicholas I forbidding passports for foreigners to Asiatic Russia, so I returned to England. You may have heard of me as a writer of romantic travel books, such as 'The Bible in Spain', 'Wild Wales' and 'The Romany Rye', and may even have read some of them!

Rev. Lewis Way (1772-1840)

I am Lewis Way, a barrister of small fortune; one day a Mr John Way, a gentleman totally unconnected with me, passed my chambers, and saw my name written on the door. He made my acquaintance, and soon afterwards died, leaving me £300,000, with the condition that I should employ it for the glory of God. I immediately took Holy Orders in the Church of England, and made a vow to devote the rest of my life to the conversion of the Jewish nation, and the promotion of their welfare, temporal and spiritual. I had several endeavours at converting Jews in Britain; but unbeknown to me, at the same time, Emperor Alexander I was employing a converted Russian Jew, J.C.Moritz, who did much good work baptising Jews into the Orthodox Church.

The Emperor also sent a letter of introduction to a certain B.N.Solomon, of the London Jews' Society, assuring him of assistance in spreading the Gospel among his Jewish subjects. So Solomon and I set off on a missionary tour to Russia, and gained an interview with Alexander, during which we read together the 44th chapter of Isaiah. When we came to the passage in the 28th verse, that says of Cyrus: "He is my shepherd, and shall perform all my pleasure, even saying to Jerusalem, thou shalt be built, and to the Temple, thy foundation shall be laid", I looked at Alexander, and Alexander looked at me, both thinking perhaps that the Emperor might be the instrument, as Cyrus was, for bringing back the Jews to their own land.

Solomon and I went to the Crimea, taking another recent proselyte, Sultan Kategerry-Krimgherry. I returned two years later, leaving missionaries in the field. A year later, Solomon came back to me, pretending he had a doubt about the Trinity. I sent him to a learned theologian, and he seemed to be more settled, and offered himself for ordination. All seemed to going well, when suddenly Solomon ran away with £300 of the Society's funds, and was never seen again!

I do not know if you are interested in reading about someone else who tried the same thing as I did, but he was not British. Joseph Wolff was born in 1795 the son of a rabbi in Germany, and spent his early life travelling in Europe, meeting Christians of all persuasions. Being a talented linguist, he always managed to get in touch with the learned and influential wherever he went. In Switzerland, wandering about penniless, he was offered asylum in England by Rev Thomas Jones. Wolff soon learnt to understand English, and attended every denomination of church service, finally settling down in the Church of England. When I met him in London, I suggested he should sit at the feet of Rev Charles Simeon and Charles Lee, Professor of Oriental languages, both of the University of Cambridge. In two years he learnt everything there was to learn, except how to shave himself! In 1821 he set off via Gibraltar, Malta, Egypt, Palestine, Armenia and Georgia, everywhere preaching to the Jews. In Tiflis he preached in German and English, as well as Yiddish. At Vladikavkaz Wolff caught typhus fever and became too ill to go on, and lay down in the street to die. A good Samaritan, Col. James Russel, a (!) British officer, picked him up in his carriage and delivered him to a Jesuit monastery. There he was pestered to convert to Catholicism while he was in a delirium, so he actually crept out, only to be rescued again by Col. Russel, who this time took him to a German doctor. When he was feeling better, he went to Karass, where he was well received by the missionaries. At Nicolaev he was well treated by Admiral Greig, who gave him letters for Count Vorontsov, the Governor-general of Odessa. At Taganrog, Alexander I sent a message that the Emperor would receive him the next week. But it was too late: in the meantime, Alexander had died. At Sympheropol, Wolff lodged with my old colleague, Sultan Krimgherry and his British wife. At Odessa he was allowed to preach, not only in the synagogues, but in the open street.

In 1826 he returned to England, and married Lady Georgiana Walpole, was naturalised as an Englishman, and set off on more travels and adventures, though not again to Russia. When he had enough of travelling abroad, he continued his missionary work the length and breadth of the British Isles on behalf of the Missionary Society, finally settling down as vicar of Ile Brewers, Somerset, where he died and was buried. (I have been told that his grave is at the back of the church, on the way to the rubbish dump!) His last act was to send his friend, Rev George Williams, Senior Fellow of King's College, Cambridge to St Petersburg, to fulfil a promise made many years previously to the Armenian and Russian Patriarchs to help establish hostels in Oxford and Cambridge.

So, I suppose we must admit that some good came out of all this activity, and a small contribution was made to the development of the Russian Empire.

Mrs Mary Holderness

May I be permitted to add my experience, and give my opinion, of the part played by the British in Russia in the early 19th century. Their influence was everywhere! I made a journey from Riga to the Crimea, so saw a cross-section which many others never experienced, as it was rather off the beaten track.

I crossed the Western Dvina to visit Count and Countess Creptovich, who, I was amazed to discover, spoke English with the greatest correctness, and had accustomed their children to speak it. They were well supplied with English books from St Petersburg, which helped the Countess when she gave English lessons. They had a servant brought up in an English family at St Petersburg. When I stayed there, I noticed several rooms with English grates. There was a magnificent riding house in the English style. Unfortunately, the pack of English fox-hounds were lost at the time of Napoleon's occupation, and dispersed over the country. At nearby Gomel I was entertained by the Count's steward, Colonel Hince, who made me very welcome and showed me over the incomplete mansion being built in the town by an Englishman called Clarke. Not far from there, I was told, there were glass factories, but did not visit them; there was also a candle factory, run by a Scotsman, Mr Stephens. All the British people here were glad to see me at so great a distance from home.

You have probably heard of Joseph Lancaster, a Quaker, who opened a school in London very early in the century for poor boys. During his visit to London, Alexander I visited the school, and was so impressed that he arranged for four students from the St Petersburg Pedagogical Institute to study at the Lancasterian School, and in exchange teach Russian to their teacher. On the completion of their course, a Mr James Heard went back with them, and was invited to establish a school on the estate at Gomel. The plan was for two hundred peasant boys, and with assistance Heard would teach them reading, writing, arithmetic and handicrafts. When the hopeful young teacher arrived at the estate, there were no quarters available for him, so Mr Clarke the architect gave him a room in his house. Eventually he was given a wooden cottage, with chinks in the floor which were very draughty. He received £15 for his first four months, during which, he told me, he made a ceaseless study of Russian, as he had nothing else to do: the school was not yet built! When this eventually happened, it was difficult finding candidates for tuition! Heard moved into a wing of the Count's house, and gave Russian lessons to the son of Mr Harbottle, who had come out to look after one of the farms. There were two more British farmers on the estate: Mr Stewart, a Scot, and Mr Scott, from Norfolk.

After a while James Heard received a letter in English from Prince Radziwill, asking him to go to Kursk to open a school, on very attractive terms. But he had promised to return to England to his ageing mother, but not before he was given a small tie pin as a souvenir, and a letter to William Allen, who offered him a post as inspector of the Society's schools in Surrey and Sussex for four years. He wrote a 'Practical Grammar of the Russian Language', which I hope helped aspiring visitors and settlers in the Empire, and also translated Oliver Goldsmith's 'The Vicar of Wakefield' into Russian.

At Uman was the seat of Countess Potocki, who employed as steward a Mr Henley. Over several years his conscientious discharge of his duties earned him the civil rank of Major, and he became a naturalised Russian. We stopped at Tulchin, another village on the Uman estate, which was under the management of a Mr Davison. Behind the house there was a pretty garden laid out in the English style.

When we eventually arrived at Odessa, my children and I were shown much kindness by Mr James Yeames, the Consul-General. Somebody I met described him as 'a most amiable man, who possesses the esteem and respect of all who have the happiness of knowing him'. Other British settlers there included Mr Simond, Mr Hearn, Mr Lauder, 'a very respectable English merchant, and partner in business with the Consul, to whose sister he is married'. At Odessa there were enough Englishmen to organise horse races, which attracted all nationalities, both as spectators and jockeys. There was a move afoot to have the races annually.

Taganrog, a city considerably to the east of Odessa, had an equally lively British community: Mr Hare, 'one of the most respectable merchants'; Mr Gray, who had been the Emperor's gardener at St Petersburg for over thirty years; Mr Caruthers, the Consul; and Mr Yeames' brother, the vice-consul.

My modest book about my travels, which was published in 1823, was originally intended for the amusement of a friend in England. When it got into print, it was hailed by none other than the New Edinburgh Review, which acknowledged that, as I had resided in Russia for upwards of four years, I was in an advantageous position to acquire information superior to that of a passing traveller. With apologies to any 'passing travellers' you may hear from, I frankly think the Review was right!

We also visited General Cobley, a man with a remarkable story: somebody told me that he had been esteemed 'the handsomest man in the Two Sicilies', and had an impressive career in the British army. His children were all born in England, but brought up in Italy. One daughter, Henrietta (1764-1843), met and married at Leghorn a young Russian Anglophile, Nicholai Mordvinov (1754-1845), who took her back to Russia, where they had four children. They considered moving back to England, but that did not materialise. After all, the rest of Henrietta's family lived at Nicolaev, and Nicholai's two sisters, Elizabeth and Anne and their families, shared the house with them. It must have been quite a ménage – and a large house, if we are to believe that Henrietta's brother, Major Thomas (Mayor of Odessa), lived there too, and that their daily visitors included Vice Admiral George Hamilton of the Russian navy and another officer, called Heyden. (Incidentally, I learnt that Mordvinov's father, Semeon, had been adjutant-interpreter to Vice-Admiral Gordon, who, though high up in the Russian Navy, knew 'not one word of Russian'!) The young Nicholai went to sea, I was told, at the age of twelve, and by seventeen was appointed adjutant to Admiral Knowles, who arranged for him to travel with him to England, in 1774. He stayed for three years, intent on improving his English. Not only that but he met among others Jeremy Bentham, and witnessed the publication of Adam Smith's 'Inquiry into the Nature and Causes of the Wealth of Nations'. I have not heard that it did him any harm during his career in the Russian Empire.

But, to get back to General Cobley: as British Consul, he had an estate outside Odessa at Troitskoye, a village of some 300 serfs (the property of the landowner), he was a rich sheep-farmer, and had, in addition, a troop of Cossacks at his command. However, modesty forbids me to describe the General, so I will hand that task over to Sir George Lefevre, who is much better at describing colourful characters like General Cobley.

Sir George Lefevre (1797-1879)

On the map of Russia there was, near Odessa, the town of Coblevoy: country house of the British Consul, a post house, five cottages, a pond and fields of sheep. In the course of my travels in southern Russia, I was taken to visit the old general, who, though a landsman, could challenge any son of the seas at swearing. In the presence of kings and princes, maids of honour or ladies of high rank, Cobley prefaced, intermingled and concluded every sentence with oaths – and all in English! When I arrived, he was engaged in lashing a peasant with an English hunting whip on an indescribable part, saying: Sir, you'll get drunk on a Sunday again, and give the sheep nothing to drink!'

It was clear to me that he thought more of his sheep than of his employees. His hobby was to improve the quality of Russian wool, and he proposed to do this by first improving the quality of Russian mutton. He boasted of the best sheep in the area, and could abuse all other mutton, putting an excellent leg on his own table, as I can testify.

It is singular how tolerant all foreigners are towards the English; how much they will bear from them, without being excited to anger; and how seldom even the most despotic governments take notice of their outrageous conduct.

We also visited Nicolaev, where we found an Englishman with a numerous family, occupying one of the best houses in the town: Mr Upton, (of whom you may have heard) a civil engineer anxious to show his skill in carrying the water of the river Bug to Odessa. His tea and cold mutton, which must surely have had a cross of Cobley's sheep, were not unwelcome.

At Climovski, the estate of a Russian Count was under the superintendence of an English steward, who was not one of those barbarians to be met with on most estates, who squeeze the last farthing out of the poor peasant to enrich themselves. He was a well-educated man, who left England fairly late in life, and so was more aware of how to treat people than the average Russian in a responsible position. I was surprised and pleased to find a Lancasterian school on the estate.

11 EAGER ENGINEERS

Sir John Rennie (1794-1874)

You must have heard of my father, also John Rennie, who hailed from Scotland, studied at Edinburgh University, then worked under James Watt. Father was asked to design Waterloo Bridge and London Bridge, as well as various canals and harbours. My brother George and I were chosen to carry out our father's design for London Bridge between 1824 and 1831. We were also involved in the construction of George Stephenson's Liverpool & Manchester Railway in 1830. We were well into the Industrial Revolution, and, Britain being to the fore in this matter, it was no surprise when my firm, Rennie brothers, was asked by Nicholas I to build a yacht for reviewing his fleets in the Gulf of Finland, as well as for pleasure excursions. The yacht, equipped with two steam engines, and weighing about 260 tons, was completed in 1850. Being a small vessel, she carried a large amount of coal, which lowered her flotation level. A severe storm in the Baltic threw her out of course, and the captain, who was not a very sharp fellow, ran aground and could not be got free. There we were, stuck hard and fast on the island of Dago, off Estonia, realising that the Emperor would brook no more delay (the completion date was already late). My son and I set off with difficulty to St Petersburg, only to be laughed at by Nicholas (who was a different man to Alexander):

'Now, if this had occurred under the command of Russian officers and sailors, what would the English have said? Why, that no wonder an accident has occurred, when the vessel was confided to those stupid fellows, the Russians. Now, you see, it has happened with the English;

and they, with all their pretended knowledge, don't know the Baltic yet, and are more stupid than the Russians.'

We were all fully insured, and all that was lost was time: we were asked for a repeat order, the original yacht was repaired and sold by the underwriters. We then built four iron steamboats, with their engines, for the Caspian Sea, the first ever afloat there. The vessels were built in England, then taken to pieces and sent with a number of workmen to Odessa, thence by land to the Caspian, where they were put together again. We made a pair of iron gates for the docks at Sebastopol, as well as several warships for the Black Sea fleet.

The municipality of Odessa asked me to cost the whole process of paving their streets and laying a system of sewers. I went out in 1860, and my first impression was of a magnificent city, with its numerous palaces and winter residences. I got a warm reception from all the important people, was lodged in handsome, spacious, well-furnished rooms at the Hotel de Londres. But on closer inspection of the state of the streets, I was appalled: bullocks and horses were used to pull loaded wagons and carriages through thick mud, many getting fixed there and joining the other carcases lying around. During the wet season it cost as much to get the corn from the granaries to the harbour as to take it from Odessa to London! You can imagine that the country roads were no better. About 28 miles out of Odessa there was a kind of depot for the vast quantities of corn brought down from the interior. When I visited, there were immense heaps of corn lying there to rot, because it was so difficult and costly to move it. In the city the sewers were mere gullies at the side of the street, into which all the filth was thrown, so that in the dry season it created the most offensive smell; in wet weather it would not run off, on account of the gullies being blocked up with mud. As to paving the streets, I asked where suitable stone was to be had, and was told it was about 150 miles away, and could be got with great ease and at a comparatively trifling cost. So I made my report, and returned to England. I heard nothing more of the project.

So this is one of the less impressive chapters in our history. But, before I finish, I am tempted to tell you about a British firm of engineers that was hugely more successful in Russia, but I see Capt Jones waiting in the wings, and I will leave him to fill in the details.

Capt. G. M. Jones, R.N.

When I toured Norway, Sweden, Finland, Russia and Turkey, in the 1820's, I kept a diary of everywhere I went, and later published it. In Russia, my first stop was, of course, St Petersburg, where I observed that the British trading houses, which had flourished under Catherine, showed a definite decline during the short reign of Paul, who had a decidedly anti-British policy. I visited some notable institutions, such as the Hermitage, the Alexandrovski cotton and linen manufactory, the Kolpena iron works, and also sailed to Kronstadt in one of Baird's steam boats.

In case you do not know about the Bairds, I will put you 'in the picture': Charles Baird was born in Scotland in 1766, went to Russia during the last quarter of the 18th century, inherited a small business from his father-in-law, and set up in 1792 an iron and copper foundry on one of the islands in the Neva that form St Petersburg. Among products of the foundry was the steamship *Vesta.* It operated for many years between the capital and Kronstadt, under a monopoly from the Empress, and made an enormous amount of money. I was told that in one week alone Baird had amassed 70,000 roubles by conveying passengers to Peterhof at the time of a fete. He certainly had a large work-force, which included many of the British settlers in the capital. The firm, which carried on after Charles's death (1843) under his son, Francis (1802-64), a naturalised Russian, continued and expanded: there were saw-mills and a sugar factory, iron bridges, machines for boring cannons. Along with his cousin, William Handyside, he was responsible for building the Alexandrian Column in the Winter Palace, for erecting the cross on the dome of St Isaac's cathedral, and for spanning the Neva with the first permanent bridge, St Nicholas Bridge. Francis married in 1828 Dorothea Halliday, who gave him ten children, one of whom, George, joined the company.

The head of the firm was in constant communication with England: as soon as a patent was taken out there for any new invention, if it was applicable to Russia he at once imported it and patented it, thus obtaining a monopoly. He cultivated all the officials, and anyone else with influence, especially the police and customs. Even Sir John Rennie, who could have been a rival to Baird, did not begrudge the fortune they made, and also the service performed to the native work-force, without which Russia would have been the poorer. In 1860 the Baird works were flourishing with between 1200 and 1500 employees, and were producing half a million roubles' worth of goods per year.

I have heard that later in the century, when the grandson, George Baird, took over the company, he came across, among the confidential papers of the firm, a very large contract that had been made with the Imperial government for the supply of iron bars and wedges to prop up the walls of St Isaac's cathedral, the huge foundations of which periodically showed signs of subsidence. One of the conditions was that it was to be kept secret, as the government was so sensitive to anything becoming known at all disparaging to the site chosen by Peter for his capital!

To get back to my tour: I had the pleasure of being shown around the hospitals of the capital by none other than Sir James Wylie. I had an audience with Alexander I, who first addressed me in French, and then said in English: 'I speak a little English, but I am afraid.' It then transpired that, although the Emperor knew English well, he had been put off by a lady who corrected him on one occasion two or three years previously. He referred to "Naple", to which she exclaimed "Oh, I suppose you mean Naples, don't you?" It was a shame, because I found Alexander very amenable for a ruler. He was particularly partial to the English character, and sometimes drank tea with one or two of the English merchants, and never failed to stop and converse with Mr Anderson, the oldest resident, when he met him in the street.

At Revel I met Mr Whittock, the agent for Lloyds, who assured me that the northern climate had worked a complete cure for his rheumatism. He also added that the cost of living was much better than in England, citing the example of chicken that cost 4d each. At Moscow I saw a theatre being built by a Mr Davis. At Sheremetiev Hospital, Dr Kieran, one of the directors, showed me an interesting ceremony: distribution by lottery of various sums to thirty-eight poor but respectable girls who were ready to marry. One of these was the daughter of a gentleman from Birmingham who held a situation at the arms factory at Tula.

This factory was one of the most well-known and successful industrial endeavours in Russia. As with so many other enterprises, it owed its foundation to Peter the Great, who first entrusted the management of it to an Englishman, called Trewheller. I understand that the railings and gates of the Summer Palace gardens in St Petersburg were made by metalworkers from Tula, and that Catherine II got artisans from England to teach the Tula workers how to make spectacles. When they could not sell all they had made, she bought them up herself! When I was there, the superintendent was my namesake, John Jones, who, unfortunately did not speak Russian, which was not an advantage when dealing with the Russian workers. But he was an expert craftsman, who invented machines for gun-making. Under his orders a hundred workers worked the smithy, the furnaces, the bellows, the anvils, the hammers. Apparently, Mr Jones's contract had been for five years, at 12,000 roubles per annum, with house, coals, candles and servants. When this term expired, the government hesitated to renew, hoping to save money, which struck me as a very poor investment. One of the negative features of an otherwise successful firm was an immense steam engine, supplied by Baird, and erected in a large building near the smithy, but for some reason they could not work it and it stood derelict.

See if you can see the significance of the following tale, which was later enshrined in a story by Nicholai Leskov (1831-95): Alexander I on his visit to England in 1816 was presented with a steel, wind-up flea. The Emperor flattered the makers of it thus: "You are the best craftsmen in the world, and against you in competition my people can do nothing". (He was a master of tactlessness, as well as flattery.) On his deathbed he handed the toy to his confessor, asking him to pass it to the Empress. She was not interested in such triviality at such a time, and it eventually passed to his brother Nicholas I, who had a copy made at Tula to prove the skill of native workers. The man assigned to the task was left-handed and cross-eyed, but he made an exact replica, with one addition – on its feet were tiny horseshoes. Nicholas wanted to show it to the English, so the smith was sent to London, where he stayed in a hotel, was treated like a V.I.P., but could not face the overland journey home, took an English ship, was sea-sick, got drunk, and returned a broken man. He died without an opportunity of passing on to the Emperor some important information he had learnt in England. The writer concluded that this was the reason Russia did so badly in the Crimean War!

In Moscow again, an Agricultural School had been established under a Mr Rogers, who in winter taught the theory, and in summer the practice of husbandry. Gentlemen sent their lads from all parts of the Empire. I was told that potatoes had been introduced into Russia in the 1780's by a Mr Rowand. The Empress Catherine was so pleased that she wanted to bestow an order on him. He refused, fearing he would be called 'the potato knight'. Another very successful venture was the stud, run by Mr Jackson, who had brought five beautiful stallions from England at great risk and expense. He demanded 500 roubles for their services, and employed two English grooms.

On my way through the south towards Turkey, I met a curious gentleman in the grandson of the last Khan of the Tartars, who had been conquered by Catherine and granted a pension and asylum in St Petersburg. The Khan's son retired to the Caucasus, where his own son, at the age of thirteen, met 'the Scotch Missionaries' (about whom you may have read). They persuaded him to be baptised. His family were enraged at this, so the boy sought protection from the Mission, then joined the Russian army. He was later discharged to allow him to go to Edinburgh to be educated at Alexander I's expense. In Scotland he got to know a Mr Neilson and his family. When he became intimate with the daughter, he was sent packing back to Russia. Next he was persuaded to go to Ireland, but there was regarded as an impostor, so he sailed to Scotland, where he (?) accidentally met again Miss Neilson, married her and took her back to Russia. Their son had Alexander I as his godfather. Eventually the family went to the Crimea to work for the propagation of the Gospel. Alexander I enjoined him to start schools for the local children, to be reimbursed either by the Russian government or the Society for Promoting Christian Knowledge, but he never received any such money. He claimed to have converted two Tartars for Christ, and generally cultivated good relations with the Moslem priests.

At Kherson, I saw a Lancasterian school under the direction of an Irishman, Captain Hamilton, of whom somebody told me that 'the Captain is too honest to be rich'. At Baktcheserai I met Mr Carruthers, one of the Scotch Missionaries, whose wife was 'in the habit of visiting the harem of the only man in town to keep two wives'! I think we had better leave it there

12 HOTELS & CLUBS FOR ALL

Captain G. Colville Frankland (1797-1876)

Although I did not exactly produce anything to be remembered by, I kept a record of my visit to the Russian capital in 1830-1, which I published later in two volumes. One of the most interesting things I observed was the provision of Clubs for gentlemen, based on the model of the London Clubs. The so-called Commercial Club occupied the former residence of Earl Cathcart while he was Ambassador, and was situated conveniently and appropriately on the so-called English Line. There was a very magnificent suite of rooms for the accommodation of merchants (who, of course, were not normally welcome in the houses of the great). The entrance was extremely stately, and there were rooms with billiards and dice tables. There was a library, and newspapers in English, French, German and Russian. Elegant dinners were served up to such as chose to partake, at the extraordinary low sum of two roubles, or 1s 8d a head. Strangers (excuse me, non-British) were introduced gradually, thanks to the falling off of the British population in St Petersburg itself, as more and more of them spread country-wide, until eventually there were more Russian gentlemen, citizens and officers than Britons among its members. But – it was we who taught them this civilising facility. When I visited, there was a great deal of champagne drunk. I had to make one or two speeches in return for compliments paid to the Royal Navy. (And why not?) I had the pleasure of making the acquaintance of Sir James Wylie, and was introduced to several of the merchants, among whom was Mr Cayley, the British Consul. After dinner, an old fellow with a long beard, apparently a Russian merchant, insisted on kissing me, 'as a mark of affection for my principles', he said. I allowed him to kiss my forehead!

One evening I went after dinner to another establishment, the English Club. This had been founded in 1770 by Francis Gardner (of whom you have no doubt heard) a man who made and sold pottery, and the Club was from the start, the choice of political men: affairs of state were discussed between and over games of chess. Its modest quarters in the Galernaya soon proved inadequate, and in the 1790's it moved to the Moika, where, I am told, it was to stay for the rest of the 19th century. It was very select, consisting of Russian and Polish noblemen, foreigners of respectablity, and English merchants (not necessarily in that order). Its membership was limited to 350, (it was originally 300) and it took three years to effect an admission, as it was so popular. The Committee consisted of three Russians, two Germans and two Englishmen. The subscription of 4-6 guineas per annum was supplemented by revenue from wines, cards, billiards etc. Dinner was obtainable three days a week. Each member could introduce a friend, but strangers to St Petersburg were admitted for six months, 'their names being put in a book'. At table gentlemen of each nation tended to sit together. There were a number of boarding houses and private hotels, run by Britons among others, but as I had no experience of staying in any of them, I will leave it to someone else to deal with.

A Conversation overheard in St Petersburg (1836) between Mr Leith Ritchie (1800-65) and Rev R.B.Paul (1798-1877)

Leith Ritchie: Excuse me, sir, but are you staying in the capital for any length of time?

Rev R.B.Paul: Just on my way to Moscow. What do you think of St Petersburg?

L.R.: My first impression is that the love of foreigners, so prevalent here, is very advantageous to the traveller. If decently introduced, one may spend every evening in very agreeable society; and the oftener one frequents a particular soirée the more welcome one finds onself.

R.B.P.: Yes, that is my impression. I am staying at Mr Ray's, a most comfortable boarding-house, it costs me 8 roubles a day for board and lodging. Mr Ray's daughter, Mrs Cotesworth, runs a similar house nearby, where, I am told, the cost is the same. It seems to be the normal charge. But, I was reading the visitors' book last night, and was surprised to read an entry by a certain Captain Cochrane, who described the Ray house as 'an ill-attended, dirty and extravagant hotel'.

L.R.: Oh dear! I met Captain Cochrane, who moved on to Mr Page's, which, he told me, was the best, most respectable and cheapest in St Petersburg. I have certainly heard good things about Mrs Cotesworth's. A Mr Bremner states that those who like English comfort and English cleanliness cannot do better anywhere than at Mrs Cotesworth's.

R.B.P.: I also met a Captain: R.Mignan, of the Bombay Army, on his way through Russia to Kurdistan. He stayed at Mrs Howard's, which had been a private residence of Emperor Paul, but, according to the Captain, the kitchen had never been altered from the time it belonged to royalty, but stood as a memorial to the rudeness of the age in which it was built. I visited someone there, and found it clean and comfortable, but by no means cheap: 10 roubles a day for breakfast and tea, 5 roubles for dinner, excluding wine, of course.

L.R.: It is possible that things have altered over the years: in 1809, the first American Ambassador, John Quincey Adams, had to find accommodation temporarily, and the man who undertook to hire lodgings for him at the Hotel de Londres, got into hot water because he had engaged an apartment of five indifferent chambers, said to be the best in the city. But I read a book by a certain John Barrow, who made his 'Excursions in the North of Europe' in 1830, and who quickly after arrival 'experienced the bad accommodation which the Russian Empire notoriously affords to travellers'. He and his companion had no luck at Damuths, which, he wrote, has the reputation of being the best; they tried the 'London', and were 'shown up into a dirty, miserable-looking attic, not unlike a hay loft over a coach house, and equally void of every appearance of comfort'. They next tried one of the private lodging-houses kept by the English in the Back Line. Which one?

G. Poulett Cameron (1805-1882)

I wonder if you have heard of the Marquis de Custine, a Frenchman, who did much harm to Anglo-Russian understanding by writing a travel book, widely read at the time. An acquaintance of mine, Major Shadwell Clarke, a veteran of the Peninsula War, and who had himself served with the Russian Imperial forces, decided together with me to check the torrent of ill-feeling against the policy and government of the Russian Empire.

During my excursions around the Empire, I met up more than once with Russian officers who spoke very good English. One such, a cuirassier of the Imperial Guard, serving in Kislovodsk, Georgia, struck me so much with his fluent English, free from the slightest foreign accent, but partaking somewhat of a broad Yorkshire dialect! When challenged, the officer laughed, explained that he was a member of a noble Russian family, who had a nurse from the north of England, and he picked up her accent as a tiny child. I became friends with this Anglo-Russian to the extent that when I eventually reached Moscow on my journey home, I was invited to the cuirassier's family seat, where the style and furniture spoke of English taste and comfort. I met, among others, a former governess, who, though retired, had found honourable asylum in the home of her erstwhile employers. The officer's younger sister, seating herself at the harp, gave a very convincing rendition of 'My heart's in the Highlands'. The Count himself spoke excellent English, having learnt it from an English tutor; for many years he had English horses and grooms in the family, and kept Southdown sheep, providing produce from his farm to a hotel in the capital.

At Moscow, I stayed at Mrs Howard's boarding-house, where the charges are moderate, and was very glad of truly English comfort after a long and uncomfortable journey. At St Petersburg I put up at Wilson's, remarkable for its cleanliness and comfort. I also received hospitality and invariable kindness from Messrs Cayley, Barnes, Plinkey, Anderson, etc, members of the British merchant body in the capital.

W.R.Wilson (1772-1849)

I was one of many Britons who travelled in the early 19th century around Europe, including Russia, and saw for myself the influence our compatriots wielded in that country. I am sure you have heard a lot about St Petersburg and its British contingent; I will tell about my impressions of Moscow, the original capital, which had fallen into comparative obscurity since the foundation of Peter's city. When I was in Moscow in 1828, the number of horse-dealers and grooms was very great. They were in high favour among the nobles; English saddles and bridles were selling at very advanced prices. The Governor of the city was particularly skilful in choosing horses. It was usual to hear the nobles recounting the pedigree of their favourites, as if on an English race-course; I have a feeling their grooms had taught them such jargon.

There was an 'English Club', with a limited membership of 600. Strangely, most of the members were Russians. It was housed in a more splendid building than the Club in the capital. It was open every day until midnight for billiards, cards and conversation; the dining facilities were not too impressive, but most visitors to Moscow were invited to call in: Captain Frankland, in his 'Narrative of a Visit', complained that he 'never sat so short a time at dinner anywhere', and that no English newspapers were taken at the Club. But, think of the compensation, when 'at noon, Pouschkin (the Russian Byron) called, and sat with me about an hour. His conversation is entertaining and instructive. He seems to be thoroughly versed in the political, civil and literary history of his country, and is also fully aware of the faults and vices of the Russian administration…' Praise indeed!

A member of the Club, whom most visitors met, was Mr Rowan, who had great delight in showing various official records, left behind by Napoleon's troops, who were billeted on him in Moscow in 1812. Mr Rowan was the oldest British resident, and a member of the committee of management for all matters connected with prison discipline. It was his peculiar province to visit from time to time the establishment on Sparrow Hills, whence prisoners left for Siberia. Another small contribution to the Russian Empire!

It might seem strange that there should be British businesses at this time in this semi-Oriental city; but let us not forget that this is where it all started – long before St Petersburg was founded. There was Mr Gillibrand's counting house, and Piggott, a tailor, from London. What about Israel Barnett, who ran a tavern? As for hotels, there was (and is) Howards' with its excellent board and lodging for 12 roubles a day, Pickersgills'. Mme Billet was English by birth, not to be confused with Mr Billot, at both of which houses men of commerce stay, especially in winter. The dinners have always been good, substantial, and *à la Russe,* with a few homely English variations. The beds are soft and clean (a welcome exception in this country!)

Last, but by no means least, there was an Anglican church in Moscow, just as there had always been in St Petersburg, with one difference. During the conflagration of Moscow in 1812, the church, which was situated in the suburbs, was destroyed, along with the house and contents of the chaplain, and the communion plate, the total amounting to 40,000 roubles. After a few years, it was realised that meeting for services was desirable, nay, essential, and Earl Cathcart, who was Ambassador in 1817-18 was influential in providing a permanent English Church. It was opened in November, 1825, when 100 persons attended divine service, that is, about a quarter of the English residents. The Minister at St Petersburg, Mr Law, whom you may have met, was very helpful in the setting up of this place of worship, and the congregation from his church in the capital presented communion plate to the amount of £100. The church itself was in Tchernichev Pereulok, which was half street and half country lane; the building itself was a brick cottage of one storey above a basement, with a door on one side, and the modest residence of the chaplain on the other.

George Augustus Sala (1828-1895)

I was born in London, my father being the son of an Italian theatre producer, and my mother an actress and teacher of singing. So no surprise that after leaving school I worked on scene-painting and book illustration. I tried my hand at writing, and attracted the attention of none other than Charles Dickens himself, who published some of my articles in 'Household Words' and later in 'All the Year Round'. He sent me to Russia in the fateful year of 1856 as a special correspondent.

At St Petersburg I stayed at Heyde's Hotel, on Vassili Island. It was clean and comfortable, dear and noisy and out of the way, managed by the Barnaby brothers, but run almost exclusively on Germanic lines. I wish I had heard before I arrived about the Misses Bensons' boarding-house, where ordinary and sensible travellers usually turn up on their first arrival in Petropolis. A few years after my visit, I came across 'A Handbook for Travellers in Russia, Poland and Finland' by T.Michell. In this he treats of the Misses Bensons' boarding-house 'No 78 on the English Quay… The apartments are quite English in their neatness and cleanliness. The table d'hôte is well loaded with substantial English fare, varied with dishes taken from the "Dîner à la Russe". The charges vary from rs.3.50 to rs.4.50 per diem for bed and board. The waiters understand English, and the worthy and obliging proprietresses are ever ready to assist the helpless traveller with their knowledge of the country, and particularly with information respecting the sights of the capital. A commissioner in attendance. The Queen's messengers put up at this house.

'Vehicles: Miss Benson will send a carriage if telegraphed to, but there is no difficulty in making a Russian coachman drive to the address given above.'

I never had the pleasure of visiting Russia again, taken over as I was by my journalist's career. Nevertheless, I thought you would be interested to hear about the arrangements available to British visitors and residents in the Russian capital. But there is someone else who can supplement my experience.

Henry Morley

I was Professor of English Literature at University College, London, when I paid a visit to St Petersburg in 1866. While I was staying in the city, I was told of a 'great birthday' that was going to be celebrated in a certain well-frequented English lodging house and private hotel in the Galernaya street (The English Back Line). That street, though narrow and gloomy when compared with other of the city thoroughfares, was one of the best known in St Petersburg, particularly to foreigners. I had, before I went to Russia, read a book by one R.B.Paul, who observed a numerous array of signs, 'bearing such classical inscriptions as John Smith, tailor and habit-maker, Thomas Williams, upholsterer, and James Jenkins, watchmaker'. Paul had enlisted the help of a Mr Russell, 'an emigrant blacksmith, who practised his art in the English Back Line, and who took his visitor to a rag-fair to buy a carriage and harness, but owing to an impediment in his speech, 'was not very clever when dealing with Russian dealers'. So, not to be put off by what I had read, I visited the house appointed for the gatherings, although used principally by the humbler classes of English residents and visitors. The street contained many lodgings and counting houses of foreign merchants. One end, flanked by the Senate House, faced St Isaac's cathedral and the Admiralty buildings, where

Peter the Great rode (and, I believe, still rides,) on his warhorse. At the other end, flanked by the building yard of the new Admiralty, stood the lodging house in question, for 90 years the home of a certain class of Englishmen and Americans. It stood (and probably yet stands) in a court, and had the least possible claim to elegance. Crossing the dirty court, under the low wooden porch, and an old horse shoe nailed over the threshold, we passed through a narrow passage, and at once entered the large dining room of the establishment. There was a long table, and round it on paralytic chairs sat some thirty or forty Englishmen, smoking and drinking. Seeking a more retired spot, we passed through to a room adjoining, but here the noise was worse; and as the tobacco smoke rolled by in clouds, we could discern on the walls Bendigo, Tom Spring, The Flying Dutchman and Voltigeur, in company with the Queen, Prince Albert and Lord Palmerston. They looked down upon a company of eager men, smoking cigars, spinning cotton (verbally), making machines of all kinds, weaving calico, building ships, bridges and engines. During the short time we could endure the smoke, the words that most assailed the ear were such as 'Valves, eccentrics, parallel motion, vacuum', and, as ten arguments were going on at once, the cry was of 'turbine, water wheel, self-actors, gearing, power-loom, sewing machines, shuttles, spindles, wheels, shafts, pulleys'. My friend whispered to me that more had been made, more engines built, more calico woven, out of tobacco smoke, in that small room during the last thirty years than in all Russia and England together!

Cards were in use at two tables, the players being grooms and horseboys – managers of the studs of Russian counts and princes. In respect of horse flesh, English skill has always been paid for in Russia at high salaries. Considerable numbers of grooms from St James' and trainers from Newmarket were employed both at St Petersburg and in the provinces. One such man, who was to become well known in another direction, was John Southee (1772-1852), a substantial Kentish yeoman from near Canterbury, who, after the death of his wife, undertook a tour in Europe, and, at the suggestion of Count Shuvalov, visited St Petersburg, staying at a hotel in Little Morskaya street, along with four of his twenty children. While there, he was offered employment as stud manager to Prince Kurakin at Krasnoe Selo near the capital, and the use of an eleven-roomed flat in Galernaya Street. Of his children, Caroline married Nicholai Popov, of whom you may have heard, the owner of a porcelain factory; another daughter, Ellen-Sarah, married Sergei de Poltoratsky, becoming mistress of a huge estate at Avchourino on the Oka, employing English stewards and governesses.

Englishmen were responsible for introducing horse-racing, and began to have the satisfaction of seeing Russians beginning to imitate them. There were also a few packs of fox-hounds, but it seemed that the Russian nobles were not prepared to risk their necks with our countrymen in the field as much as they did their money in the club house.

But to get back to the dining table: that old veteran with the iron-grey hair and the massive forehead is a Scotsman, known locally as Old Wallace; his namesake, Young Wallace, sits next to him, a highly skilled engineer from Napier's on the Clyde. I was told that he was engaged only a few weeks before the Crimean war, fitting up to 600-horsepower engines in Russian ships. As soon as he heard of the possibility that his handiwork would be put to active service against Britain, he withdrew his labour. Beside him sat Hargreaves, lately engineer of the Emperor's yacht, Donaldson, Young, Thomas and Wilson, engineers of boats belonging to the Baltic Fleet. There were also managers of the various departments of Bairds, perhaps the most famous engineering establishment in the capital, responsible for much more than ships. Among this company was an assortment of clowns, singers, clerks and salesmen, captains of ships, paper-makers, tailors, furriers, coal agents, all of them English, Scottish, Irish or American.

Something else which the English introduced in the early 1850's was a boat race: one team from the British legation, the other made up of merchants. The course went from the English Quay to a bridge opposite the Suvorov monument and back.

Many respectable English families lived on the Vassilii Island and in other quarters of the capital, but the more fashionable part seemed to prefer what was known as the English Quay, where the establishment known as the English Factory stood, and still stands. This is a very handsome building in the Grecian style, near the Custom-house. The principal time for business was from 4 to 5.30, when the Russian merchants go home to supper. A typical English Factory party comprised 20-30 guests. The table service was generally of English ware: some sported silver forks – napkins always on great occasions. The host and hostess sat at the extreme ends of the table, as in England.

Someone I wish I had met was Captain Davison, whose Russian 'career' started as secretary to Count Novosil'tsev, an influential statesman under Alexander I. On his retirement from this position,

Davison ran a model market garden outside St Petersburg, from which he supplied the principal houses of the capital with meat, vegetables and butter stamped with the Imperial eagle. He was said to be one of the few Britons who acquired a perfect knowledge of the Russian language. Someone told me that he was sent to England to stock up with implements, seeds, workmen, dairy maids, etc, so that his farm should be an 'imitation of that of His Majesty the King of England'.

Finally, I would like to mention one house in particular which enjoyed a very respectable rank in the commercial world of St Petersburg: Anderson & Moberley. John Anderson sent his son to the High Commercial School, where he gained a silver medal, carrying with it the freedom of St Petersburg. He went on to King's College, London, and later became manager and then partner of an ironworks. Edward Moberley married Sarah, daughter of John Cayley, English consul in St Petersburg and had eleven children. Sarah was a friend of Lady Pembroke, daughter of Count Vorontsov (of whom you have no doubt heard). Of their children, George was to become Headmaster of Winchester, later Bishop of Salisbury; the eldest daughter, Fanny, married Charles Cattley, vice-consul at Kertch on the Black Sea. A notable family, indeed, and typical of the involvement of Britons in the commercial, industrial and social life of the Russian capital. I only wish I could say I had done as much in that direction!

13 A CLUSTER OF CLERGY

Rev William Tooke (1744-1820)

I thought you might be interested to hear about the arrangements that are made for the spiritual health of our British residents and visitors to the Russian capital.

The provision of a place of worship has always been co-terminous with the so-called British Factory, which was at first, of course, in Archangel. The register of that church dates from 1706, but there was no permanent appointment to the chaplaincy, any suitable clergyman who happened to be in the locality was asked to oblige. Notable among these was Thomas Consett, who died in 1730. He appears to have been something of a scholar: there is extant his translation into English of the Archbishop of Pskov's oration at the funeral of Peter the Great, printed in St Petersburg, and his Latin version of an oration by the Bishop of Riazan and Murom.

In 1723, when the British Factory moved to St Petersburg, it was resolved to do something more strenuous to secure the services of a regular minister, by making his salary 600 roubles per annum, as well as a free house and travelling expenses from England and return; this was not, however, enough to attract anyone, until 1731. Much of the time even then the post was held by chaplains to Ambassadors. This did not prevent the British Factory from building a church in 1753.

From 1763 to 1774 the chaplain was John Glen King, a Cambridge man, who, although he held a living in England, came on a visit to Russia, and was appointed Medallist to Empress Catherine, as well as filling his spare time studying the history and liturgy of the Orthodox church. His works include 'The Rites and Ceremonies of the Greek Church in Russia' (1772), illustrated by copper plate engravings; 'Letter to the Bishop of Durham about the Climate of Russia' (1778), a work of 23 pages, almost entirely devoted to a description of the cold weather. One wonders whether the Bishop had asked for this essay, or whether he was really interested in the appended 'View of the Flying Mountains at Zarsko Sello near St Petersbourg' (1786). The author was a Fellow of the Society of Antiquaries, and a Fellow of the Royal Society.

I was born in 1744, and after my ordination was offered a living in Essex, which I declined on being appointed chaplain to the British in Kronstadt. I held this post until 1775, when Glen King resigned the St Petersburg post. Throughout my ministry here I made it my business to become acquainted with Russians from the upper strata: literary men, scientists, bishops and land-owners. I met some of these at the annual *diner de tolerance* given by Catherine II to clergy of all denominations in the Empire.

As a linguist, I had translated such writers as Diderot from the French. I was made a Fellow of the Royal Society in 1783, the same year as I became a member of the Imperial Academy of Sciences and of the free Economical Society at St Petersburg. In 1792 I inherited a huge fortune from an uncle, so I returned to England to publish: Life of Catherine II, translated from French, but with much added by myself (1798); the next year saw my 'View of the Russian Empire during the reign of Catherine II and to the close of the present century', closely followed by the two-volume 'History of Russia, from the Foundation of the Monarchy by Rurik, to the Accession of Catherine the Second', with an appendix of over 100 pages, and a 'Sketch of Mosco'. Both volumes have 'Plates of the Sovereigns of Russia, drawn and engraved by J.Chapman from a series of medals' in my possession.

As I say in my last book, 'all foreigners…go to Russia in the design of making a fortune, and then quietly to enjoy the fruits of their labours in their native country. But, owing to the liberty enjoyed by foreigners in Russia, very few of them have any aspirations to return home.' I do hope you do not think I am among their number!

During my lifetime, I received a bouquet from a fellow-writer, Rev William Anderson in his 'Sketches of the History and Present State of the Russian Empire' (1815). He admits that the material for his first three chapters was principally drawn from my 'View of the Russian Empire', adding: 'Mr Tooke is a laborious and accurate writer; and, though partial to the Russians, usually adduces such facts as may enable his reader to form his own judgment without danger of mistake.' I can only hope I did something to help the British understanding of Russia, and so encourage them in their work of developing the country materially, politically and spiritually.

Although I went back to England, I kept in touch with events at the St Petersburg chaplaincy. Mr Percival, who took over when I resigned, was forced to seek another climate owing to ill-health. Mr Loudon King Pitt, who died in office in 1813, was appointed a Director of the Bible Society, and was proposed as teacher of classics and English to the Empress and her children. His widow was invited to live in the Palace, and continued to do so for years.

The Chapel was rebuilt in 1815, described by one visitor as 'a neat and substantial edifice, situated about the centre of the English Quay, where it presents a notable front to the river, being decorated by a colonnade and ornamented at the top by three figures, Faith, Hope and Charity. The interior is neat and simple, and has the great advantage of being well warmed and comfortably fitted up. The State pew for the British Ambassador is on the right as you enter, opposite the pulpit. It is surmounted by the Royal Arms of England. The altar piece is a deposition from the cross, a very creditable painting (in fact it was a copy of Rubens' Descent from the Cross, presented in 1815 by Sir James Riddell, Bt.); on each side of the altar are two handsome Corinthian pillars of marble (casts of the apostles Peter and Paul)'

There always were two entrances: one from the Quay, the other a large gateway from the Back Line. No bell is permitted to be rung; the burial ground is on the other side of the river. The Russian police are expressly prohibited from entering the church or the clergyman's residence. Within the large court behind the church is a library of some 7,000 volumes, as well as a large collection of maps, for the sole use of the British (of whom there were in my time some 3,000). The church itself seats 600, and is well supported by the generosity of the British residents, as well as a small tax levied on all British vessels trading to St Petersburg.

From 1820 for many years the incumbent was Rev Edward Law, who filled the post with great distinction. During his incumbency the greatest event was the Memorial Service to Alexander I in December, 1825, at which Mr Law, of course, preached an extremely worthy sermon, extolling the virtues of the late Emperor. This was only just, seeing as how Alexander had favoured our people throughout his life, from cradle to grave, as you must by now be aware.

Rev. R.W. Blackmore

I thought you might be interested to know a little about Kronstadt, the island fortress and naval base, where I have been chaplain for several years. It is situated about 20 miles from the Russian capital, and serves partly as a defensive outpost, and partly as a shipyard. As you might expect, it owes its status to Peter the Great, who, in 1703, erected the Kronschlot Fort on the island. The name Kronstadt was given in 1723. The town, which was well drained by Commodore Greig, is roughly half a mile in length, leading down to the Mole, or mercantile harbour, where some days you seem to meet none but Englishmen. There are shops, with English inscriptions over the door, like 'Grogs and Porter sold here'. There are inns, with signboards in English. You can never feel lonely!

Naturally, there is an English church here, for which the records of chaplains go back to about 1762. I think you have already met William Tooke, who served here in the 1770's. I myself have been 'in charge' since 1819, a matter of some twenty-two years. My background is from Oxford, where I was a contemporary of John Keble at Merton College. I actually married (in 1824) Miss Harriet Hembry a member of a British family from St Petersburg. The service was conducted by Rev. Edward Law, whom you know, in the presence of three members of the Booker family. John Booker has been the father figure at Kronstadt for over fifty years. He is known as the British Resident, and an exceptionally conscientious and popular man. He has, curious to relate, an English garden, which abounds in the hardiest of our fruits and shrubs, as well as flowers and table vegetables. Many a British visitor to Kronstadt has been entertained by the Bookers. Of their children, Thomas was born in 1807, one of his godfathers being Admiral Robert Crown; he was later to marry the widow of the famous and eccentric Captain Cochrane. Catherine Booker married Charles Vertue of London in 1817.

The original church building was made of wood, and was replaced in 1824 by a plain but elegant building, nearly 100 feet in length, with eighteen windows on each side. At the official opening ceremony, in the presence of the British Ambassador, the British Consul, Mr Booker, Rev Edward Law, Admiral Crown, as well as clergy of the Orthodox church, the procession route was lined by 150 British seamen, a select body of whom formed the choir to sing at the service. As a structure, the church is an ornament to the town, as well as a monument to those who were active in founding it, securing an important advantage to the

British population and visiting seamen. The building cost £15,000, part of which sum was defrayed by the liberality of the English-Russian Company, and part by a duty imposed on English vessels using the port. (I have an income of 7000 roubles, with a house provided).

Kronstadt is the first place at which ships bound for St Petersburg arrive. Here the traveller is conducted to the harbour-master's vessel, and his passport is examined. He is then allowed to go up to the town, attended by an interpreter, and at the offices of the port admiral and the military commandant the passport is registered. He is then free to go where he pleases. (The services of the interpreter are not charged for, but I hear that most people give him a rouble.)

At the request of Nicholas I, Rennie brothers designed a complete naval establishment, utilising as much as they could of the old construction dating from Peter's foundation. There are docks and basins for repairing men-of-war, but not the slips for building them. They are therefore built at St Petersburg and then floated down the Neva and out to sea on large caissons, called 'camels'. There is a generally held opinion of the Russian naval establishment, that they are not as reliable or honest as their British counterparts. I met a Mr John Moore, who stopped here on a journey from London to Odessa in 1833. He himself met a sea-captain engaged in the St Petersburg trade, who assured him that officers of the Russian navy were in the habit of going on board his ship on her arrival at Kronstadt, offering him for sale anchors, cables, cordage, and all sorts of naval stores, stamped with the Imperial mark, quite new out of the arsenal. It seems that the storekeeper had an understanding with the officers, and issued fresh articles, declaring that the stolen goods had been worn out in the service. The honest British captain, of course, never bought so much as a rope-yarn from these 'honourable men'.

I, of course, cannot vouch for the accuracy of this story, as I keep always to my own calling, that of the spiritual welfare of the British community here; but one cannot help occasionally hearing things that go on under one's very nose, as it were...

I have added a little to the development of British understanding of the Russians: my works include: The Doctrine of the Russian Church (1845); a translation of A.N.Mouraviev's History of the Church in Russia (1842); and Lives of the Russian Prelates (1854). I also had a visit from William Palmer of Oxford, who wrote 'Notes of a visit to the Russian Church', in which he speaks highly of my relationship with the Russian clergy, but mentions that I have not even heard of my old colleague, John Keble's, 'The Christian Year'. I have been isolated here in Russia so long, and newspapers, periodicals and books all cost so much, not to mention the postal charges!

William Palmer (1811-1879)

Forgive me, but I do not think I shall contribute much to the understanding of the Russian Empire, for I spent most of my time finding out for myself all about the Russian Orthodox Church, which included a year-long visit there in 1840. After graduating from Oxford, I became a lecturer at the newly-founded University of Durham, later returning to my old college as a tutor. While occupying this post, and having come under the influence of the Oxford Movement, I went to investigate the Russian church, as one part of the non-Roman Catholic Church.

When I arrived in St Petersburg, I stayed at a lodging-house kept by two ladies with English names, in Galernaya. While in St Petersburg, I made copious notes, and these were much later published by Cardinal Newman. I met Mr Blackmore from Kronstadt, and Mr Law the chaplain at St Petersburg. I am supposed to have scandalised some of his flock by making the sign of the cross. Such a thing was apparently unheard of in this remote, benighted section of the Church. After a while in the capital, I wrote in Latin to Count Protassov, Procurator of the Holy Synod (sort of Minister for Religious Affairs), asking for the right to learn the Russian language, and study the doctrines, discipline and ritual of the Church. If this request was granted, I hoped to translate Russian books into English, and to do something towards promoting in England, and especially at Oxford, a fuller and more accurate knowledge of the Apostolic Churches of the Easterns. I had heard that there was someone in the Spiritual Academy who read English, and as I had brought with me a selection of books, donated by living authors, I offered them to the library of the Academy.

When I asked a certain Archpriest for admission to Holy Communion in an Orthodox church, I was told: "You have your own chaplain here; you need not come to us." I tried, in vain, to explain to him that there cannot be two confessions, or two bishops, in one place. That I was no member of the Church of England in Russia, but of the Church of Russia. Nothing would convince him: the Russian church was not ready to broaden its outlook towards other Christian communions in the 1840's – but, for that matter, nor was the Church of England!

I had better luck at the Troitsa-Sergeevsky Monastery, near Moscow. There the Archimandrite said that he intended to learn English for the good of the church, and actually asked me for a list of good English books, which I do not have to tell you I readily provided. I met one of the more forward-looking theologians of the day, Alexei Khomyakov, who showed warm affection for me, and I kept up a correspondence with him after I returned to England in 1841. He professed to be deeply hurt when the Russian authorities displayed complete indifference to my desire to become an Orthodox. I took Mr Blackmore's translation of Mouraviev's 'History of the Russian Church' to revise and publish in England. Like my model, John Henry Newman, I joined the Roman Church in 1855, and actually died in Rome.

14 A GAGGLE OF GOVERNESSES

Dear Reader: please do not be put off by Mrs Gaskell's opinion in 'Wives and Daughters'(1866): 'To be a governess in Russia was the equivalent of taking the veil, or a lady-like form of suicide.'

Mrs Elizabeth Stephens

Would you think that a woman would go out to Russia in the 18th century to be governess to a noble family? You may be surprised to learn that there were many such, even as early as the reign of Peter the Great. As you must be aware, the young Peter was brought up in the house of Mary Hamilton, and was probably influenced by how many more Scots?

If we go back to the 1730's, we read in Mrs Elizabeth Justice's 'Voyage to Russia' how she was found a post as governess to the three daughters of a Mr Evans, a British merchant in St Petersburg. She had to leave England through marital and financial problems. If you should get hold of her book, you will be astounded by the list of subscribers. I must say it deserved to be well-read, since it is a reliable source of information about that period, and it is a distinctly feminine book, consequently rare and precious. But this was not the only account of those times.

Miss Goodwin was born in 1700, daughter of a clergyman of large fortune, who married Thomas Ward at the age of 28, and then accompanied him on his appointment as His Majesty's Consul General to Russia. Peter the Great was not long dead, and Mrs Ward was to meet people who had actually spoken to, and in some cases slept with, the Great One. She mentions Mr Lapuchin, who had an English wife forced upon him by Peter: the girl was a niece of an officer called Munce, whose own daughter was one of the Emperor's mistresses. At the time the British Resident in St Petersburg was Mr Rondeau, and on the occasion of the King's Birthday every year he invited the British living in the capital to a splendid entertainment and ball, which of course the Wards attended. Nothing is said further about Mrs Rondeau or Mr Ward, but in November, 1731, Mrs Ward married Mr Rondeau! When her book "Letters from a lady who resided some years in Russia" came out in 1777, she calls herself Mrs Vigor! I will leave the matter there.

Having been appointed governess to a noble family in St Petersburg, I took up residence with my two daughters, little realising that within a relatively short time, one of them, Elizabeth (who knew no Russian) would marry a civil servant, son of a country priest, Michail Michailovitch Speranski; he was later to become one of Russia's great though ill-used statesmen. (Incidentally, he knew no English!) They met at Fr. Samborski's house in St Petersburg. (Andrei Afanasievich Samborski had been chaplain at the Russian Embassy in London, was married to a Miss Fielding, and was well acquainted with the British way of life, as well as Western religious thinking. He was to become tutor in religion to the Grand Dukes Alexander and Constantine, and undoubtedly contributed to their unusually liberal thinking where religious matters were concerned.)

My poor young daughter died in the first year of her marriage giving birth to their only child, a girl, and so I was called in to take her place. It was not a happy situation: in these early days there was a lack of funds; in 1812 Speranski was exiled to Nizhni-Novgorod, later to Perm, on account of his somewhat too liberal views on the reform of the laws. I naturally followed him wherever he went. When he was restored to favour in 1816, and appointed Governor of Penza, my grand-daughter was sent to St Petersburg to be educated, but unfortunately I died at this point, and cannot tell you any more...

However, I was aware of the influential part played by British nurses and governesses at the Russian Court. You should understand that Catherine the Great was convinced that her son, Paul, was incapable of organising anything, so took over responsibility for his children. The young prince, Alexander, was assigned to Pauline Primrose, one of two sisters, both nurses, who arrived when their father was forced to seek service overseas, having lost property during the 1745 Jacobite rebellion. Pauline, who married Johann Gessler, a footman/valet at

Catherine's court, was described by Alexander's (Swiss) tutor, Cesar La Harpe as 'a woman of rare quality who … inspired in Alexander the first of those good habits that set him apart.' The Empress herself is quoted as saying that Mrs Hessler was 'a woman of rare merits. She is tidy, clean, simple and sensible. I feel sure that if Monsieur Alexandre had a son of his own, brought up by the same Englishwoman, the throne would stand secure for more than a century to come.'

Alexander did not have a son, but his brother and successor as Emperor, Nicholas, had a Scots nurse, Jane Lyon, who was appointed at the age of 17 for seven years. She was daughter of a sculptor who worked under Charles Cameron. Jane taught the young Nicholas his letters, rudiments of English history and literature, and had an altogether benign influence over the future ruler. Would you believe that even the princesses had an Englishwoman, Miss Ramsbottom, who taught them English and Italian, and later left to marry a clergyman? Suffice it to say that Nicholas himself employed Englishwomen among his governesses. I feel sure that as the 19th century progresses, you will meet more of these devoted women, as well as some notable gentlemen tutors to Russian princes.

Miss Kitty Strutton (1811-1891)

My father was a bricklayer in Hackney, near London. I was always interested in children and nursing, and as my elder brother worked as a coachman in a grand part of London, I was lucky enough to be introduced to some influential people, who eventually got me my job as nurse to Grand Duke Alexander, born in 1845. His elder brother, Grand Duke Nicholai, had an English nurse, Jane Isherwood, as did their sister, Grand Duchess Alexandra, (Margaret Hughes). Of course, this was nothing new, as you have probably heard, there had been English nurses and governesses in the Russian Court since the time of Catherine the Great.

Life as a relatively humble employee of the Imperial family could be very interesting, not to say exciting, at times. We were treated very kindly and generously – so long as we did our job properly! We had access to the private moments in the lives of these very famous and important people, who were, after all, human and fallible like the rest of us. But the most important feature of our careers was that we were able to influence the young princes and princesses from their very formative years. If the British had any part to play in the progress of the Russian Empire, we nurses and governesses certainly contributed what we could, although at the time we were probably not aware of what was going on all around us in the wider society.

I was able to recommend my great-niece, Millicent Crofts (1852-1941), as nurse to Grand Duke Vladimir from 1876. It was through Milly that the children in that family spoke English first: she used to sing nursery rhymes to the little ones, and later introduced them to the works of English literature, first of which were 'Barnaby Rudge' and 'Oliver Twist'.

When I retired, the Imperial family provided me with an apartment in the Winter Palace, as well as a little house near their palace at Tsarskoye Selo. I was therefore able to keep in touch with successive generations of 'my' children. When I died, the Tsar, Alexander III, led the mourners, to my resting-place, the Smolenska Cemetery. No one could ask for a greater honour than that!

Miss Hannah Tardsey (1847-)

My father was a gardener at Windsor castle, where I was born. My sister was already governess to the Lvov princes, and she arranged for me to accept the post of nurse at Yasnaya Polyana, the country estate of Count Tolstoy, the famous Russian novelist. He wanted his children to be able to read English literature in the original, so later I was to be governess to his two eldest sons, Sergei (born 1863) and baby Ilya. I am sure they both loved me and I became like one of the family. Ilya has since written:

'She was part governess, part nursemaid, kind, serene and always cheerful. Hannah remains a bright memory in my life. She was well loved and we obeyed her...I have no recollection of learning English, but it seems to me that I began speaking it at the same time as Russian. 'Wash your hands, breakfast is ready' and other nursery phrases came quite naturally to me, without my ever having to learn them... At Christmastime we had a tree and she always made a plum pudding for us. Rum was poured over it and it was brought flaming to the table. When we walked in the garden with her, we always behaved properly and did not soil our clothes on the grass.'

That is surely as it should be. But I think it took the children some time to get used to me, a foreigner, as the family were accustomed to a

Russian nurse. I enjoyed the life, and was not put out at doing menial tasks, such as scrubbing the nursery floor with brushes I had brought from England; I introduced daily baths for the children in a tub I arranged to have delivered from back home (and which is still in the Yasnaya Museum!). But it was not all work: I imported some English ice-skates; we played lapta (a Russian ball game); we went for country walks. Count Tolstoy knew some English people in Tula, where I would visit from time to time, and when we held a fancy-dress party for the Tolstoy children, I was able to introduce little Kitty to them. I took to the life of governess very quickly. I am so glad that I did not heed Mrs Gaskell's opinion in her book 'Wives and Daughters', which was published the year I started my career. I like to think that I contributed a little to the development of Russian society, even for a short term.

Unfortunately, in the autumn of 1872 I caught consumption and was sent to a warmer climate, and, very conveniently, the Kusminski family needed a governess. But my life changed two years later, when I married the Georgian Prince Matchudatze.

After I left Yasnaya, they employed Dora, who, I have heard, was sweet, but completely lacking in authority; when she left came Emily Tabor, who was recommended by the clergyman who had introduced me to the Tolstoys. She was, apparently, 'plain, taciturn, round-shouldered, walked very slowly and rarely smiled.'

On which of us did Tolstoy model his Miss Hull? She appears briefly in the early pages of 'Anna Karenina' as the governess to the Oblonski family.

Mrs Elizabeth Franklin (1834-1913)

I took up my post as nurse to Grand Duchess Olga, daughter of Alexander III in 1882. In this capacity I was given full scope for bringing up royal children just as if they had been English royalty – or even English commoners. I introduced bread and butter and jam and English biscuits for tea; for lunch we had mutton cutlets, peas, baked potatoes; porridge for breakfast; and, of course, Christmas pudding on the appropriate occasion. I never allowed eating between meals. When the Empress became jealous of my influence over the children, and put Olga into the care of a lady-in-waiting, the Princess went to her mother, and made a scene:

'Alicky (her elder sister) had her Mrs Orchard brought to Russia. What shall I do without Nana? If you send her away, I will run away myself. I will elope with a palace sweep. I will go and peel potatoes in someone's kitchen, or offer myself as a kennelmaid to one of the society ladies in St Petersburg. And I am sure that Nicky (her brother) will be on my side.' (You may judge, from that quotation, the girl's command of English, for which I, of course, take credit.) The Mrs (Mary Anne) Orchard mentioned was an Irishwoman, who had been nurse before me, having served the Empress in Germany before her marriage. I am afraid she has gone down in history as a most dictatorial nanny, who finally left the palace in a huff after a particularly bitter altercation with the equally dictatorial Empress. She was replaced by a Miss Eager, an eccentric, who insisted on talking about the Dreyfus case, even to the exclusion of her duties. On one occasion she left the baby Grand Duchess in the bath. The child scrambled out and, naked and dripping, ran up and down the palace corridor. This little episode did *not* appear in her 1906 book of recollections!

Near the end of my life I read a book called simply 'Moscow' by Henry M.Grove, in the course of which he recounts his delight at being spoken to in perfect English by an aide-de-camp of one of the Grand Dukes. When asked how long he had been in England, the gentleman replied that he had never been there, but had had an English governess. Till he was ten he had never spoken any language but English, and only started speaking Russian when he went to school! I think this little example could serve as a motto for our present collection of witnesses: *WHAT WE DID FOR THE RUSSIANS*. Grove also had an amusing interview with an izvozchik (cab driver), who asked his passenger what nationality he was; on being told he was English, the driver addressed him in very fair English. He had apparently been a cabbie in Kronstadt, following in a family tradition. He had left his native town as 'the good old times had passed' when all, or nearly all the izvozchiks spoke some English. (Is this an example of *WHAT THE RUSSIANS DID FOR US?)* He added that 'now all sorts of foreign (sic) ships come and the people on them will not speak English'.

I died in 1913 at Olga's house, and was buried in the park at Gatchina, under a favourite tree, where I used to sit and watch the children at play; I was happy that I had at least fulfilled my ambition to serve this notable family to the best of my ability.

Annette M.B.Meakin (1867-1959)

I went to Russia in the very early 1900's , and met many of the governesses in the course of my "Travels and Studies", which I published in 1906.

At Moscow, there was an aged Englishwoman who had lived in Russia for the last thirty-eight years, and was now a teacher of English to the younger pupils of Madame Fisher's Classical School for Girls, established in 1872, and the first of its kind in Russia. The pupils were drawn from the best families in the country, the fee being 600 roubles per annum. The senior classes were taught by professors from the Moscow university, the juniors by resident lady teachers. Among the dramatic performances put on by the school were Greek tragedies, and on such occasions they were patronised by the Imperial family. The lady I mentioned told me that English books were in great demand among the pupils, and that they eagerly read such authors as Charlotte Yonge, Mrs Henry Wood and Jane Austen. But, she said, English novels are not now what they once were!

She told me she had no desire to go back to England, as she had made her home in Russia, had joined the Orthodox Church, and wished to die in it. I did not meet many others who had gone so far to identify themselves with the Russian way of life, but most of the governesses I talked to tended to stay with their pupils and their pupils' children till the end of their lives. Not only that, but they taught them English so thoroughly that it became a by-word for good breeding towards the end of the Empire to be able to speak English. It was indeed the hall-mark of a Russian aristocrat, just as to know German was that of a Russian businessman. On the other hand, one governess I met told me of one of her pupils, the son of a nobleman, who had difficulty getting into the diplomatic service despite the fact that he was fluent in French, German and English, but had great difficulty expressing himself in his own language!

I remember reading in 1940 an autobiography by Nathalie Majolier who, born in 1903, lived most of her life in exile. From childhood in pre-Revolutionary Russia she recalled mainly her governesses. The first was Miss Lena, who taught her English, including all the nursery rhymes. Apparently, she was Irish, and left the child with a marked accent. When she left, the new governess was Miss Rata, an Englishwoman from London, with whom the pupil had a much better relationship, except for the habit of slapping the child fairly often, if something was not quite right. But on the whole Nathalie called Miss

Rata 'a dear, and we got on like house on fire'. How about that for idiomatic English! At the outbreak of war in 1914, the governess married the riding master, Mr Bennett, while in England with the family, but accompanied them back to Russia without her husband.

1914 was a difficult year for many of the governesses and tutors in Russian families: not only were some of them dismissed from their posts, but also had difficulty leaving Russia. Rev. W. Mansell Merry, who was in Petrograd as relief chaplain to the British community, left some recollections of meeting people in that predicament. He remarked how brave he thought most of these 'plucky, enterprising, independent-spirited girls were, a good many of whom have taken the long journey from home purely 'on spec', trusting to their luck to find the work, which, as a rule, sooner or later offers itself, though never at a very exalted rate of pay.' As he pointed out, there were various agencies in the Russian capital that took a sympathetic interest in their well-being: the Girls' Friendly Society sent a representative, when and where possible, to meet the steamer on its arrival; the Princess Alice Home, under the auspices of the English Church, provided comfortable lodgings at quite reasonable charges until they were suited with a place; and, he added, 'all and every are welcome to the flourishing Girls' Club actually on the Church premises'.

If the War meant hardship for some of those employed privately, how much more difficult was the Revolution, with the expulsion of so many Russians, let alone foreigners! We could like to know more about Prudence Brown, from Tipperary, who was governess to the Bobrinsky family from 1910. Of course, some stayed on through thick and thin. Take, for example, Mary Fellows (1868-1941), who went to Russia as a governess in 1911, and whom Fitzroy Maclean met in Tiflis in 1937!

When *H.M.S.Marlborough* picked up Empress Maria Feodorovna and other members of the Imperial family and nobility who had escaped the Revolution, they were accompanied by their staffs, which included four governesses: Miss Coster, Miss Turk, Miss King and Miss Henton. In 1956 I read the book 'Close of a Dynasty', written by Sir Francis Pridham, Lieutenant Commander on the ship. In this book the author relates conversation with Miss Coster: she spoke in an affectionate way about the Imperial family, particularly of the Empress Maria, and the latter's goodness to all dependent on her. It was from Miss Coster that the author heard that the Empress Maria would not believe the rumours that the Emperor and his family had been put to death by the Bolsheviks.

Finally, I must relate what I know about Miss Florence Farmborough (1887-1978), who went to Russia in 1908, and after two years in Kiev, she moved to Moscow, where she stayed with the family of Dr Pavel Sergeyevich Usov, a famous heart surgeon, teaching English to his two daughters, Asya, 19, and Nadya, 16. In 1914, after a holiday in England, she spent what she described as 'a carefree summer in their dacha near Moscow.' Miss Farmborough lugged around with her a heavy plate camera, taking pictures of people and places, which, I understand, were published after her death in her 'Russian Album'. She trained as a V.A.D.-qualified surgical hospital nurse, but eventually escaped in 1918 on the last goods train to Vladivostok, where she boarded *H.M.S. Suffolk* to Japan, and home.

Tatiana Metternich (1915-2006)

Allow me, as a Russian child brought up at the end of the Empire to give my point of view on the subject of English nannies. In our family we had two nurses, Miss Thompson and Miss Menzies (as well as my sister Irina's governess, Miss Scott). What I recall most of my childhood is the familiar routine of regular hours, insipid English Benger's baby food, all mashed and slushy, relieved by copious teas, Beatrix Potter stories, nursery rhymes and long walks. When Miss Menzies returned to her family in Scotland, my mother wrote her a recommendation as for a subaltern returning from the front line of battle: 'Cool-headed and resourceful when in danger, tireless under stress, indomitable courage.'

We children missed her fearfully at first, but then got distracted by the advent of baby Georgie and Nannie Hillyard. Later in emigration in Paris, the family still had English nurses, French governesses, a Swiss tutor, and German maids. They were all engaged to ensure that all three languages could be spoken, but in priority order: nursery English, literary French and rather rocky German!

Rothay Reynolds: 'My Slav Friends' (1916): "Lawks!" interjected the daughter of a Russian Cabinet Minister in the course of a conversation with a Scotchwoman. "My dear!" said the horrified Scotchwoman, "where did you learn that dreadful expression?" "My English governess always uses it", replied the girl.

Kyril Shishmarev

I am another Russian with a tale to tell, this time with an English governess, Miss Matthews. We lived, when I was a boy, at Tsarskoye Selo, not far from the Imperial Palace, and indeed I was on familiar terms with the young Tsarevich, three years my senior. On one occasion His Imperial Highness was on the parade ground, uniformed as a member of the Cossack Guard. An aide-de-camp came up to me and told me that the prince wished me to join him on the reviewing line. Of course, I was surprised but delighted, and I left Miss Matthews spellbound!

Miss Matthews had taken over where the Russian nurse left off, i.e. when I had grown out of being pushed in a pram. And what prams we had! Large, complicated things with big wheels and brakes and movable covers. I think they came from Harrods of London. They were definitely not Russian. The nurses' uniforms had big white cuffs and collars – all linen. Our clothes and sailor suits came from London too. We must have looked like a British fifth column in the nest of the czars. When I matriculated from nurse to governess, my doom was sealed. Miss Matthews not only looked English. She was English. She was a pretty brunette, and her diction was perfect Oxonian. Mother had chosen her with care. Having started out as the English Baby, I remained the English Baby, no matter how much I grew, as long as Miss Matthews in her prim English dress was hovering around. That was just about all the time. It got to be a joke. I got damn' tired of it. Even Alexei and the Emperor were in on it a few times. Someone would say "Oh, there's the English Baby!" Then up would come the answer: "Oh no – he's not English. He's Russian-English. Only his nurse and clothes are English!" But the nickname stuck.

However, I must admit that my grounding in English stood me in good stead when I emigrated, and later in life, when I became a scenarist in Hollywood.

15 THE RUSH FOR RAILWAYS

George Washington Whistler (1800-49)

As you might gather from my name, I am an American, and so do not exactly qualify for inclusion in this collection of British contributors to the Russian Empire. But – my father, an Irishman, emigrated to the States in 1775, so the connection is better than it might be! I was born in Fort Wayne, Indiana, graduated from the U.S.Military Academy at West Point, New York at the age of 19, and landed a job with the Baltimore and Ohio Railroad, which sent me to England to learn more about railroad technology. My expertise and reputation got to the ears of the Russian government, who employed me from 1842 as a Consultant on the building of their first major line, Moscow-St Petersburg.

I have to admit that mine was not *the* first railroad in Russia. That one was built about five years earlier, naturally and properly, between the capital and Tsarskoye Selo, the Windsor of the Imperial family. One Franz Gerstner, possibly a Czech, seems to have been instructed to build it, at 6-foot gauge, with materials obtained from – where else? – England, home of the Industrial Revolution and the railroad industry. The lines were laid and everything was ready, except for one requirement: the locomotives (from England, of course) were not delivered on time for the official opening. So the first trains were horse-drawn. The line consisted of a single track, with a half-way station, called Srednyaya Rogatka (Central Turnpike), where the trains, which left the termini at identical times, met and turned off at an elbow for the purpose of passing. The engines, which eventually appeared, were supplied by none other than Stephenson, Hackworth and Tayleur. The company received glowing tributes from the local papers. Only one accident was reported in the first four years of operation: one of the engine drivers, Robert Maxwell, having taken too much to drink, failed to stop at the centre station, and the two trains suffered a headlong collision. Maxwell had the prudence to jump clear of his locomotive before impact, was arrested, found guilty of breach of duty and imprisoned for nine months.

The line proved to be commercially less than satisfactory, so it was extended to Pavlovsk, where, as I suspect you are aware, there was a Vauxhall (the latest craze, copied from London). The Vauxhall and the station were adjoining and therefore closely associated; the word 'vokzal' went into the Russian language as the standard word for every railroad station thereafter, or so they would have you believe. (One small example of the British contribution!) However, I have another version: a delegation of Russians went to London to investigate the feasibility of having railroads in Russia, and, reading the name 'Vauxhall' on the station of that name, thought that it was a common noun, and forthwith called all their stations 'vokzal'. Take your pick! Later in the century, I understand, the Pavlovsk line got into full swing, and a second, parallel track was laid, reserved for the Imperial train.

But to revert to my role in the affair: the line from St Petersburg to Moscow was called, of course, the Nicholas Railway, after the Emperor who ordered its construction. There has been an anecdote flying around for many years about the arbitrary attitude of the autocrat: at least two alternative plans were submitted by competing contractors, but Nicholas settled the problem irrationally (or rationally) by placing a ruler across the map and drawing a straight line (the only bend was where his thumb held the ruler!) The resulting cost in tunnelling and bridge-building, not to mention the distance between many stations and the towns they served was, apparently, of little importance to Nicholas I, who only wanted the quickest way of getting troops moved. The Nicholas Line was completed in 1851. I was responsible for selecting the 5-foot gauge, which became standard for all Russian railways, with later implications for international travel! (I have heard that, very late in the 20th century, the last remaining minor bend in the line, where it crosses a river, has been straightened out to allow for high-speed electric trains.) When I first went to Russia in 1842, I left my (second) wife and family in America, but once I had established myself in Russia, they came to join me. On the occasion of a visit from some of my wife's English relatives, the family was introduced to Sir William

Allan, the Scots painter, who later made a habit of calling on Mrs Whistler for what he called 'excellent home-made bread and fresh butter, but above all the refreshment of a good cup of tea.' My eldest son, ten-year-old James, was impressed by Allan's picture of Peter the Great teaching the Russian peasants to build ships. Allan for his part remarked to my wife that her 'little boy had uncommon genius', and the child was accordingly enrolled in the Imperial Academy of Fine Arts. You may know the outcome: James McNeill Whistler (1843-1903) American artist of great acclaim, and the apple of his father's eye!

We had a home on the English Quay in St Petersburg, but owing to the incidence of cholera in the capital, my family went back to England. Two years later I died from the disease: Nicholas I offered his private barge to transport my body from the English Quay to Kronstadt, where it was put on an American steamer. He also offered to educate my two sons, but their mother declined. Otherwise, James, the 'Victorian Outsider' as he has been called, might have become a Russian painter, or engineer...or even civil servant...

The Nicholas Railway was finished about two years after my death. It was found that there would not be full work for it as a military road, so as a great favour to the inhabitants of the two capitals, they were allowed to travel up and down it. The speed in those days was limited to 20 miles per hour, so the journey took two days to complete. At each of the principal stations the train stopped for half an hour, and the tradition of restaurants on the station came in to stay. It was also necessary to provide pillows, until sleeping cars were introduced. I am in no doubt that you will be hearing more about the British involvement in Russian railway-building in due course, but, before I leave you, I must remark on a coincidence: I mentioned Robert Maxwell, the locomotive engineer, above. Well, in a novel, called 'Beloved Prisoner', by Catherine Dillon, there is a James Maxwell, who takes a locomotive on an American ship from Chatham to the Black Sea. He turns up later in the book, surveying land with a view to laying a railway, 'long overdue' between St Petersburg and Moscow, in 1856, five years too late. I beat him to it. But what sort of coincidence is that?

James Nasmyth (1808-90)

I was born in Edinburgh, but was present at the opening of the Liverpool and Manchester Railway in 1830. I think this was what gave me the enthusiasm for mechanical invention, including railway engines. During my early career I was involved in the construction of the famous steamship, the *Great Britain,* for which I patented my well-known steam hammer.

With my partner, Mr Gaskell, I made a journey to Germany to get a close-up view of the work we were contracted to do, which led us on to make a visit to St Petersburg, with the object of obtaining an order for locomotives for the newly constructed line between the capital and Moscow. At a dinner I was introduced to Major Whistler, who informed me of the situation concerning locomotives. The Emperor, Nicholas I, apparently wanted to train Russian mechanics to supply engines, and also to keep them in repair. He did not wish to depend entirely on foreign artisans. So he had given over the entire premises of the Imperial China Manufactory to the building of locomotives.

Major Whistler appointed Messrs Eastwick, Harrison and Wynants to supply the entire mechanical plant of the railway. So I quickly realised that my idea of building engines for the railway was unrealistic, but, when I met Joseph Harrison, the chief mechanic of the firm, I was offered a large order for boilers, and for detail parts, which helped him in the completion of the locomotives. I also supplied many of our special machine tools, without which engines could not then be very satisfactorily made or kept in repair. I was highly remunerated for my journey to St Petersburg!

In addition to this, the Emperor sent me a magnificent diamond ring in gratitude for the manner in which my steam hammer had driven the piles for his new forts at Kronstadt, which he had seen in full action. The steam-hammer pile-driver had also been used in building the great bridge at Kiev. I received an order for one of my largest steam-hammers for the Imperial Arsenal, and it was followed by many more.

Sir Samuel Morton Peto (1809-1889)

I was born in Woking, Surrey, and was apprenticed as a bricklayer to my uncle, who ran a building firm in London. When he died in 1830, I went into partnership with my cousin, Thomas Grissell. Together we were responsible for many well-known London buildings, including the Reform Club, the Lyceum, Nelson's column and the London brick sewer.

But in 1834, when I realised the potential of the newly developing railways, I left the building firm and went into partnership with Edward Ladd Betts (1815-1872), who married my sister. Together we carried out many large railway contracts both at home and abroad, including the South Eastern Railway, the London, Chatham and Dover, and in partnership with Thomas Brassey the London, Tilbury and Southend.

In 1854 during the Crimean War, we constructed the so-called Grand Crimean Central Railway between Balaclava and Sevastopol, to transport supplies to the British troops at the front line. I was made a Baronet for my services, but you may well be asking what contribution we made to the development of the Russian Empire!

However, someone the Russians had to be grateful to was Robert Weatherburn from Northumberland, a member of one of the oldest railway engineering families. His father (also Robert) was a partner of George Stephenson, taking part in the famous Rainhill trials. In fact, one of his uncles married a niece of George Stephenson's. He served his time as an engineer at the famous locomotive works of Kitson & Co. of Leeds, for whom he carried out many projects in Britain. He was sent to Russia and did business for the firm in Riga, St Petersburg, Moscow and, famously, Odessa.

AN IMAGINARY CONVERSATION (CIRCA 1835) BETWEEN TWO RUSSIAN WRITERS:

ALEKSANDR SERGEYEVICH PUSHKIN (1799-1837) and

NIKOLAY VASIL'YEVICH GOGOL' (1809-1852)

ASP: Have you noticed what a lot of foreigners there are about nowadays? There have always been quite a number, especially the English in St Petersburg, but they are on the increase.

NVG: Yes, it makes me sick. They are everywhere – English Johnsons and French coques, walking arm in arm with the young gentlemen entrusted to their parental care; and the typical governess, a tall, thin Englishwoman with a reticule and a book in her hand...I once wrote home to my sisters that 'an Englishman is a rather tall man, who always sits down jauntily on a chair, crossing his legs, and turning his back on his lady.' That was soon after I arrived in the capital; I still think the same. To drink like an Englishman is to bolt the door immediately after dinner and get dead drunk in solitude...

ASP (sarcastically): And when you go to a ball, there is a lot of snobbery – using English and French words.

NVG: English culture is one thing; English people is another.

ASP: Yes, I have read a lot of English literature – Byron, especially, and Shakespeare, of course.

NVG: I have noticed a pronounced Western influence in your writing. I prefer to stick to good old Russian subjects – inefficiency and corruption in administration, landowners, the deep Orthodox faith....But I am hoping to travel abroad sometime.

ASP: I haven't travelled much. In any case, I was banished to the country for several years for my involvement in what was called dangerous revolutionary pronouncements connected with the Decembrists.

NVG: Oh, of course. But what I cannot face is crossing water. I have been as far as Ostend once, on my way to Paris and Rome, and even once to Malta, which I thought was an English colony, but, to my horror, it lacks all the comforts one associates with the English: the locks on the doors are defective, the furniture is of Homeric simplicity, and the language is quite incomprehensible. One hears almost no English.

ASP: I would have thought you would have welcomed that! I occasionally call in at the English Club and meet visitors. I find it useful to hear their opinions of the way this country is progressing, seeing that they have had so much influence. I am thinking of people like Charles Cameron, John Field, the late George Dawe…

NVG: My interest would be to live in England, and study not only the class of the proletarians, which has become so fashionable an occupation nowadays, but all the classes of the population without distinction. You must admit, most of your contacts are upper-class people…

ASP: Well, I cannot stop any longer. I have an appointment to meet an English gentleman who is writing a Guide to Moscow, and needs some help with putting the Russian point of view.

NVG: Who could do that better than yourself?

ASP: You are very kind.

16 INDUSTRY AGAIN!

George Hume

Born in London, I was apprenticed at an early age to a firm of engineers in East Anglia. But my work eventually took me back to London, and thence on a commission to deliver a new ship, the *Mithridates*, for the Russian government. We sailed for Odessa with a scratch crew. The Russian Steam Navigation Company was formed immediately after the Crimean war, with the object of training and employing officers and sailors that had previously formed the crews of Russian warships sunk at the defence of Sevastopol. I was some time in Odessa, refitting the vessel, and attended the English church, where I got to know a very remarkable Scot, Mr Melville. He was tall and gaunt in appearance, but truly British in thought and feeling. We soon formed a firm friendship. He was the Agent for the British and Foreign Bible Society, and had remained in Odessa throughout the Crimean war, devoting himself entirely to the work of distributing the Scriptures among the Russian soldiers. He offered to teach me Russian, after I related to him my amusing experience: trying to buy woollen underwear in a Russian shop by gestures and sheep noises to the young lady assistant. (The story got into the local papers, and I got the reputation of being a mad Englishman.) I accepted Mr Melville's offer. Through him I became acquainted with most members of the British Colony, especially Mr Wagner, a wealthy and generous man, who owned much property in Odessa. Between them they gave me the idea of visiting the interior of Southern Russia.

While I was on a short visit to Constantinople, I met, by sheer coincidence, and old fellow-apprentice from Ipswich, by the name of Graham, who happened to be looking for an occupation. After some deliberation we agreed to form a partnership to introduce reaping and threshing machines into Russia, and persuaded Mr Wagner to underwrite the scheme. While waiting for the machines to be delivered, I left for Berdiansk, where I was kindly received by the British Consul, Mr Cumberbatch. That gentleman took me on shooting excursions. The German Consul, Mr Jansen, introduced me to the Mennonites, who lived a sort of Quaker-like life, objecting to the bearing of arms. They had been exempted from military service by Catherine II, and settled in colonies of farmsteads in this far southern part of the Empire. I also met Mr Dick, who was a preacher, much respected throughout the colonies, but who had seen something of the world beyond the village, having been to Moscow and St Petersburg, and had inspected mechanical contrivances used by manufacturers, which astounded him. He allowed me to try out a reaping machine on his field, to the astonishment of the Russian peasants, who thought the contraption was an invention of the devil! Something else I discovered, which surprised me, was the custom for Russian parents of an only son to adopt temporarily an English lad of the same age to be his companion and fellow-student, mainly with a view to perfecting the boy in the English language. One such boy, now grown up, was Mr Popoff, who not only spoke English perfectly, but was well versed in English literature. I stayed with him, and we made very good friends, having much in common.

When news of the steam thresher's introduction into Russia spread among the manufacturers of agricultural machinery in England, a Mr Lister, of Marshall & Co, from Gainsborough, Lincs, came out to Russia with a view to establishing an agency for their machines. I was invited to join him in partnership, and we worked together for over twenty years. When I got married, I had a town house in Kharkov, where, in recognition of my contribution to the life and economy of the region, the municipality named a street after me. (The only other British family in Kharkov were a Mr & Mrs Cameron, her mother, and their four children.)

I took part in an extensive tour of Southern Russia, and another took me through the entire Caucasus area. Being invited to join 'some engineers from England to the rich coal-bearing estates in the Government of Ekaterinslav', I was surprised and delighted to meet William Gooch (nephew of the manager of the Great Western railway in England), who had finance and ambitions to try his luck in some industry in Russia. We made plans together for the building and operation of a steam flour mill, involving a capital expenditure of £21,000. Mr Gooch and his new wife settled in the house adjoining the mill, which he was managing under my supervision. One night the mill burnt down, as well as large stocks of flour, but owing to insufficient insurance cover, the project had to be abandoned. The building was taken over by my company, Hume & Lister; we set up in it a factory for making pearl barley and for cleaning rice. Another project of which I have been long proud was the search for coal and iron deposits. For this I was fortunate in meeting a man who has gone down in Russian industrial history as a pioneer. I speak of John Hughes, son of a blacksmith from Merthyr Tydvil. He was at one time a director of the Millwall Ironworks on the Thames, and was responsible for building the Plymouth Breakwater Fort. His company won worldwide acclaim for its iron cladding of wooden warships for the British Admiralty. In 1864 he came to Russia and built the Constantine fort at Kronstadt. This brought him to the attention of the Imperial government, and so in 1870 he and his family sailed to the Ukraine with eight shiploads of equipment and around a hundred specialist ironworkers and miners, mostly from south Wales. Together, armed with the geological works of Murchison, we set up workmen's huts in a spot where at the time flocks of sheep grazed the open steppe, and in a few years the New Russia Metallurgical Company was started, and the town was called Hughesovka. The foundry was the first in Russia to use mineral fuel for smelting, and turned out, among other things, rails for the ever increasing mileage of railways that were being built. By the end of the century the New Russia Company owned 60,000 acres at Hughesovka and 2,500 acres of iron ore at Krivoi Rog nearby, employed 12,000 men and paid out £50,000 a month in wages. In addition, there was a hospital with 100 beds, staffed by six doctors, and ran a school with places for 800 children not to mention bath houses, tea rooms, a fire brigade and an Anglican church – St George and St David. In short, it was one of the most successful and long-lasting ventures by a Briton in Russia, and, I have heard that Hughes' legacy was one of the features of Russia that was not destroyed at the Revolution! But trust the Communists to rename the city Stalino, and thus remove the credit due to this British pioneer. As to Mr Hughes himself, it was said that he was able to trace the passage of the first workers in metal over Russia from the Caucasus right through to Spain, and into Wales and Cornwall. A romantic Celt, perhaps, but also a very successful businessman!

Thomas Witlam Atkinson (1799-1861)

I was born in Yorkshire, and trained as an architect. My curiosity led me, as so many others, to St Petersburg in 1846, where, among other things, I met Miss Lucy Beavington, who had been there for eight years, superintending the education of General Muraviev's only daughter. We married, and decided to travel together through the Empire, our sole object being to sketch the scenery of far-flung areas, such as Siberia, scarcely at all known to Europeans. Not everyone from Britain clung to the well-beaten tracks, but braved the elements, the language and the hostility of the authorities, without much help from the natives. In six years we covered forty thousand miles and in so doing we met several British pioneers, who qualify for inclusion in this study.

In the Urals we met a good practical English mechanic, who was superintendent of the machinery at the Mint at Ekaterinburg, which coined large amount of copper money for the Russian government. He had under his care English tools and machines, such as Nasmyth's steam hammer. At Ekaterinburg also had been a young mechanic, named Major, who had been appointed under Emperor Paul, to supervise a small mechanical establishment. He was allocated Russian peasants as workmen, with whom he managed to communicate, despite his lack of Russian language, by novel means. For example, he invariably wore three pairs of stockings, with a pair of wide Russian boots over them. On his daily tour of inspection of the installations, at the first sign of dirt, he would take off a stocking, personally wipe the dirt off with the stocking, repeating it, if and as necessary, at each stop. Sometimes he went home bare-footed if necessary, and the offending peasant had to take the soiled stocking to be washed, or the birch would be sure to refresh his memory the next morning. When Alexander I visited the Urals, he was said to be pleased with Major's work, and gave him a plot of land, in which there were known to be minerals. He set about building himself a house, and excavating gold from his land. As he used local labour, the workmen and consequently the whole neighbourhood knew how much gold he had in his possession. Not surprisingly, he was killed by a burglar who took a box of gold. This was the price to pay for pioneering in Russia.

Another young engineer, Mr Patrick, of Manchester, was for several years highly respected at the iron works. After work on one occasion he went out hunting with several others of his colleagues. Patrick went alone up a mountain side and was never seen again. It was generally concluded that he was killed by a bear. However, three years later a peasant went into a shop in Ekaterinburg with a watch to sell; the jeweller, on opening the watch, found it to be English, with Mr Patrick's name inside. The peasant was arrested and whipped.

S.S.Hill

In 1847 I travelled into Siberia, and left a very full account of my journey. I was accompanied by a Mr Marshall, with whom I had seen part of the two Russian capitals, and left Moscow by diligence for Nijni Novgorod to see the famous Fair. On the way I happened to meet Admiral Ricord, who was Italian by birth, but spoke perfect English, owing to his having served as a midshipman in the Royal Navy under Nelson. He assured me that 'there is no Englishman of my rank in the Russian service', which statement surprised me. At Nijni I had dinner at Government House: my noble host had two fine children, led in by an English nurse, from whom I learned that Russian parents are not less apt to spoil their children than the fondest among ourselves. At Ekaterinburg I met Mr Tate, owner of an extensive iron manufactory, also Mr Jackson, who had just arrived, sent by the Russian government to aid and extend operations. Tate had a yacht on the lake. Pleasure trips for parties of official gentlemen took place in summer, with music.

'Nearly 300 years have elapsed since England greeted Muscovy. So great have been the benefits to trade, the arts and industry in general arising from the friendly relations between England and Russia.'

-- Dr J.Hamel: England and Russia (1854)

17 THE SOCIETY OF SCIENTISTS

James Marr (1779-1874)

I started out in business, but was unsuccessful, and became a gardener on a prince's estate at Guria in the Caucasus. I was offered serfs of my own, but I refused on principle. I married a young native girl and lived in Russia until my death. I did a great deal of research on tropical plants, tea, cotton and other Caucasian specialities. I founded and directed an agricultural school at Kutaiss, the huge garden of which still existed down to 1949, when the life of my grandson, Nicholai Yakovlevich Marr came to be written.

A fellow Scot, McLothlin, was manager of Count Kuchelev's estate at Ligovo, and carried off a large gold medal at the 1850 St Petersburg Exhibition, following that up with two medals at the Great Exhibition in London in 1851.

You will undoubtedly have heard of Sir Rodney Impey Murchison, who was born in 1792, and in his forties was doing geological work in Britain and Europe. In 1839, along with de Verneuil, and 'greatly assisted by officials and savants of Russia, he planned a visit to Russia, where the comparatively undisturbed palaeozoic rocks presented fewer difficulties than in Britain.' The party crossed to the shores of the White Sea, up the Dvina to Nijni Novgorod, and back via Moscow to St Petersburg. In 1840 Murchison returned to Moscow to examine the carboniferous rocks there, and thence to the Urals, the Azov sea and back to Moscow. His third visit, in 1844, was to St Petersburg, via Scandinavia. The book 'The geology of Russia and the Ural Mountains' (1845) by Murchison, von Keyserling and de Verneuil earned the Order of SS. Anne and Stanislaus, as well as valuable presents from Nicholas I.

It was Murchison who encouraged Richard Cobden, the political economist, to visit Russia 'to exercise an important influence upon the mind of Nicholas I'. He spent six weeks there, in the summer of 1847, as part of a European tour, but I cannot say that his influence was more than marginal upon the development or decline of the Russian Empire. From his detailed diary comes this quotable observation: 'I discovered the beginnings of foreign business penetration in the shape of English mill managers and German officials.' He also thought the English Club in Moscow 'a very fine establishment'.

18 STOP THE WAR!

Joseph Sturge (1793-1859)

The reign of Nicholas I was not the best period for the British in Russia, since there was a reaction against the comparatively liberal regime of Alexander I. The reign started with the Decembrists' revolt, which was quickly and harshly put down. The official policy of 'narodnost' – as defined by Count Benckendorff – that 'Russia's past is admirable; her present more than magnificent; as to her future, it is beyond the grasp of the most daring imagination', was hardly calculated to encourage foreigners to Russia. But it must be admitted that, despite all the formal discouragement and petty restrictions on expression, education and travel, British involvement in Russian affairs, trade, industry, etc., continued, albeit somewhat curtailed, especially in areas where it was well established. The most difficult moment in this reign was undoubtedly the final one – the Crimean war of 1853-6, in which Great Britain was committed on the side of the Turks against the Russians. Naturally, relations between the two governments were strained, not to say broken. Sea-ports were no-go areas for foreigners, but we still see British participation inside Russia, and, what is more, as soon as the war was over, it was often British engineers and builders who were first in the field to undertake reconstruction and rehabilitation work.

When the international situation became critical, and possibility of war became marked, I led a delegation of Quakers to plead with Nicholas I to avert war. With me were Henry Pease and Robert Charleton; at St Petersburg we stayed at Benson's hotel, visited Mr

W.C.Gillibrand, who had lived in the capital for forty years and was able to give us some useful hints on approaching the Emperor. We dined with Mr A. Merrilees, a friend of Mr Gillibrand, and proprietor of the well-known store. When we were eventually able to speak to the Tsar, we, of course, flattered him with the traditional courtesies, reminding him of his elder brother's interview with William Allen, as well as Alexander's esteem for Daniel Wheeler. I have to say that we had little success with our endeavours to prevent war and all its horrors. But I must relate a curious incident which I heard later: at Sevastopol there was an outcry against the English engineers of steam vessels, who worked on during the hostilities. The Emperor therefore appointed a Russian on trial. The latter took a steamer out to sea and damaged her machinery so much that Nicholas is reported to have said that he would continue to employ the English until his own people were able to take over their duties. I seem to think you may have heard something of this kind before?!

Have you heard of Mary Seacole? She called herself 'a creole, with good Scotch blood coursing' in her veins. She was born at Kingston, Jamaica, and came to London in 1850, in search of adventure and fulfilment to her life as a widow. On the first horrifying reports from the Crimea, she attempted to get herself recruited as a nurse by Florence Nightingale, but was spectacularly unsuccessful. So she sailed out to Sevastopol on her own account (she was not poor) and opened a 'British Hotel' – a mess table and comfortable quarters for sick and convalescent officers. She is one of the few people to emerge from the Crimean war with any dignity. Her book: 'Wonderful Adventures in many Lands' is truly entertaining.

Lord Radstock (1833-1913)

I would invite the reader to decide what contribution I made or did not make towards the development of the Russian Empire. As a member of the noble Waldegrave family of Somerset, I had a conventional Christian upbringing. At Oxford I pursued the pleasures of this world with great energy, but, while visiting the battlefields of the Crimea, I caught a fever, which nearly killed me, leaving me a sick man all my life, but which led to my religious conversion.

I had met members of the Russian nobility, and from 1866 until my death I spent all my time and money on missionary and philanthropic activities in England and abroad. I was invited to visit the Russian capital in the winter of 1873-4 by a Russian noblewoman I had met in Paris. I first spoke in the American church in St Petersburg, then at soirees and salons, using French, for to begin with I knew no Russian. Fashionable ladies, such as Princess Lieven and others rallied round me and my 'new religion'. Indeed, some influential ministers, such as Count Bobrinsky and Count Pashkov, became followers. Pashkov resigned his colonel's rank and commission in the Imperial Guards to spend his life distributing his riches to the poor, establishing charitable institutions and preaching the Gospel. All classes pressed to his home to hear the Good Tidings, and the authorities, predictably, took measures to liquidate the movement, including imprisonment and exile for lower class adherents, and banishment abroad for its aristocratic leaders. I myself only escaped imprisonment for the crime of placarding the streets of Moscow by the intervention of James Brayley Hodgetts of the Diplomatic Corps, and Count Lamsdorff, a more enlightened member of the Russian aristocracy.

When I returned to England, the work I had started was carried on by Pashkov, and, strange to relate, by a German, Friedrich Wilhelm Baedeker (1823-1906), cousin to the author of the famous travel guides. After a life of travel and adventure as an army officer, he came under my influence, and was converted to Christ, and set out for Russia with his English wife and daughter. Strangely, he managed to get a hearing. He preached in English, German or French, as the occasion suited. He found some support from the Director of Prisons, who gave him free access to all prisons in the Empire, 'to supply convicts with copies of the Holy Scriptures.' (Maybe the authorities thought he could do less harm in prison than outside!) On one of his journeys in Russia, he had his wallet stolen in a crowded station; it contained his permit. The replacement permit accorded him even wider privileges.

You may think that Baedeker, being German, does not fit into our present scheme of British influence in Russia, and you may be right. But, during his travels, he recorded meeting several of our countrymen at various places, who were indeed working for Christ in this otherwise benighted land: at Sevastopol there was 'a dear Englishman, engaged in the dockyards, who is a great help in distributing the Scriptures among the men'. At Ekaterinburg he met the Wardroper family (of whom you have no doubt heard); at Tomsk the Siberian agent of the Bible society, Mr Davidson, was his host and support. At Berchneldinsk he called on a Dr Alexeiev, whose wife was English. 'They asked me to dine with them at 2. She gave me an English cake, which is a treat.'

Baedeker is easily identifiable in Tolstoy's novel 'Resurrection' as two separate and different characters: Kizevetter, a foreign preacher who discourses on redemption in the drawing-rooms of St Petersburg. He is described as a German who addresses his audience in English. (This is as near as possible.) The other character is an Englishman, an erratic traveller, who distributes New Testaments in the loathsome prisons of Siberia. Unfortunately, the author treats both these characters with disdain and distortion, whereas one would have imagined that the two men would have had some measure of common ground. But even in the report of their conversation together in Moscow, the two of them quoted Scripture at each other from differing standpoints. Each of them was convinced he was right. I know who I would have backed; but whereas Tolstoy's works have lived on, it is doubtful whether Baedeker is ever remembered. At his funeral at Weston-super-Mare, at which I delivered the address, the only wreath that his widow allowed on his grave was that 'from his grateful friends in Russia'. So maybe we did some good after all!

William T. Stead (1849-1912)

I was born in Darlington, the son of a dissenting minister. I began my career as a journalist with the Northern Echo, a local but influential newspaper. I strongly supported Gladstone, and was responsible for organising one of the very first protest meetings in Britain against the Bulgarian Atrocities of 1876. The Turkish treatment of Orthodox Christians in Bosnia and Herzegovina also incensed Liberal opinion. In 1880 I went to London to be joint editor of the Pall Mall Gazette, a very influential paper, and soon made the acquaintance of Madame Olga Novikov, a Russian of the very highest breeding and connections, who held a salon at Claridges' Hotel. She was a life-long Slavophile, embracing one of the two main philosophical and political schools of thought in 19th century Russia. It attracted Russians and others who believed in the holy destiny of Russia as the elder brother and defender of the smaller and weaker Slav peoples. To this end Madame Novikov's brother, Nicholas Kireev, had volunteered to fight on the side of the Serbs against the Turks, and had fallen in action in 1876. His death provoked an immediate and sincere reaction in Russia; in England

Madame Novikov and her circle blamed the whole business on Disraeli's pro-Turkish policy.

In 1885 I was prosecuted for allegedly abducting a 13-year-old girl; I had done it for a stunt, to highlight the loopholes in the law, but I was nevertheless imprisoned for three months. In Holloway gaol I worked on newspaper articles, daily involving myself in the issues of the day, including Home Rule for Ireland. It was in that same year that the Russian Imperial Family first subscribed to the Pall Mall Gazette, but it was not until 1888 that I had the privilege of actually meeting Alexander III face-to-face. I owed both the subscription to the paper and the interview to the good offices of Madame Novikov. The news that I, a Liberal, a supporter of Home Rule, an ex-convict, and (who knows?) even perhaps a revolutionary, was to be presented to the Tsar startled the British Ambassador, Sir Robert Morier, who in fright turned to Konstantin Pobedonostsev, Procurator of the Holy Synod. For a while it looked unlikely that the interview would succeed, and again it was only through Madame Novikov's connections in high places that I eventually managed to meet Alexander III. The interview took place at the palace of Gatchina, a few minutes before the Emperor's lunch time, but was so successful that it went on for upwards of half an hour, and would have continued but for my conscience! During the conversation I begged forgiveness for all the injuries Britain had supposedly done to Russia under the previous government; I asked the Emperor what policy he intended to pursue with regard to several questions, ranging from the Far East, through Afghanistan to the Balkans. To all my questions the Tsar gave clear, unequivocal answers, assuring me that there would be no war, that he would 'answer for peace'. As I wrote later: there were not two men in the whole wide world who more sincerely loathed war than Alexander III and Mr Gladstone.

When I got back to London, I wrote a book, entitled 'The Truth about Russia', which, I am afraid to say, displeased Madame Novikov in part, because I inveighed against Pobedonostsev's policy of religious persecution. So I was surprised to find that my book, though forbidden in Russia by the official censor, was exempt by Alexander's personal intervention, and circulated freely throughout the Russian Empire. In 1899 I went to St Petersburg again, from there travelling to Sevastopol to see Nicholas II. During the Peace Conference at The Hague, which Nicholas himself had been responsible for convening with a view 'to possible reduction of the excessive armaments which weigh upon all nations', I wrote a weekly letter to the Tsar. I must be the only

Englishman in history to have had such a privilege! I took the opportunity of enclosing a copy of my book on psychic experiences, which had been recently published.

In 1905 General Trepov, the very repressive Governor of St Petersburg, actually allowed me to hold meetings in the capital to discuss the Duma, and why, in the eyes of an English Radical, it should be welcomed as a parliament; it was I who secured the release from prison of Professor Milyukov, leader of the Constitutional Democrats in the Duma. On one occasion, a leading member of the Zemstvo Congress wrote: 'They talk about the Tsar and General Trepov, but the real Autocrat in Russia to-day is Stead!'

Back in 1888 while staying at the Hotel d'Europe in St Petersburg I met Maud Gonne (1865-1953), daughter of a British colonel living in Ireland. By profession she was an actress, by conviction she was a fervent Home Rule supporter, and experienced great difficulty getting through the Russian frontier. When she managed to smuggle secret documents, sewn into her skirt, she handed them over to Pobedonostsev, in the hope that a Russian-French pact would weaken Britain, and so help Ireland (or so she said!)

I was one of the passengers on The Titanic, travelling to America to spread the word, but that was not to be...

19 A LITERARY LOOK

Rev Charles L. Dodgson (1832-98)

You probably know me by my pseudonym – Lewis Carroll, author of Alice's Adventures in Wonderland. Well, I had some adventures in another land – Russia. In the summer of 1867 I travelled with my Oxford colleague, H.P.Liddon, overland by train to St Petersburg. In the carriage we met none other than Mr Alexander Muir, co-proprietor of the Moscow store, Muir & Merrilees. He did his best to discourage us by telling us how difficult the Russian language was! As if we needed to be told....We had to look up even the Russian words for 'bread' and 'water'. It was a great relief to be entertained by some of the English residents in the Russian capitals, such as Mr Merrilees, Mr Penny, the Moscow chaplain, Mr and Mrs Combe and their niece Miss Nathalie, and the Wares. Mr Spier took us to the New Jerusalem Monastery, and we had a kind invitation to visit Kronstadt from Fr McSwiney, the chaplain. The whole tour finished in September, just in time for the journey back to Oxford for term.

I am not the only 'Victorian' author to have recorded impressions of Russia: before we went, I had read W.H.G.Kingston's 'Fred Markham in Russia'. This account was aimed at boys, just as my fictional output tended to be girls' reading. Kingston, the author of 'The Swiss Family Robinson', 'Peter the Whaler' and other classics, says in his preface that he 'purposed to have written a book descriptive of his travels, but on second thoughts, however, remembering that many erudite works (ahem!) have already appeared about the Empire of the Czar, I came to the conclusion that my young friends, whom it is my ambition to please, would prefer an account of the adventures of Cousin Giles and the Markhams…', adding that he could corroborate all their descriptions from his own personal observations:

'The English here say that the habits of social life among the Russians have very much improved since they mixed with them: I do not know what view the Russians take of the case. Thirty years ago, palaces and public offices were alike dirty in the extreme; but the Emperor Alexander (I), after his visit to England, introduced great improvements. Now the public offices at St Petersburg, at all events, are kept fairly clean. I do not think, however, that the housemaid has got so far south as Moscow; it is too holy a place, in a Russian's idea, to make cleanliness necessary.' (? Exciting reading for boys.)

Thomas Budge Shaw

How do you do? I am a Cambridge man, who has spent much of his life in journalism. However, two things made me offer my services in Russia as a tutor: the first was reading Sir John Carr's 'Travels round the Baltic', which was published in 1810. In this he mentions openly that 'the education of the young nobility very frequently suffers from the free and unguarded manner with which they receive every needy adventurer in the capacity of domestic tutor, particularly if he be an Englishman: English tailors and servants out of livery, and travelling valets frequently become the governors of children. A fellow of this description said one day: "In summer I be clerk to a butcher at Kronstadt, and in winter I teaches English to the Russian nobility's children".

At about the same time as I arrived in Russia, an American traveller, J.L.Stephens, recorded his impressions, including his attendance at the English church in Moscow, where he noticed 'many English governesses with children, the English language being at that moment the rage among the Russians, and multitudes of cast-off chambermaids being employed to teach the rising Russian nobility the beauties of the English tongue.'

My second motive was to see how I could improve the situation, and whether it was still the same thirty years later. I went to Russia as tutor to a private family, but very soon found that life distasteful. I have to admit I was probably by nature unfitted for such a calling, so I accepted a post at the Imperial Lycee, and stayed for 21 years. I was also for 12 years a Lector at St Petersburg University. Between 1853 and 1862 I directed the studies of the sons of Alexander II, as well as of the children of Grand Duchess Maria Nicholaevna. In 1842 I married Annette, daughter of Samuel Warrand, my predecessor as Imperial Tutor, also a Lecturer at the University and the Imperial Law College, a Knight of the Orders of St Anne, St Stanislav and St Vladimir (!)

My father-in-law and I co-operated in publishing 'The St Petersburg English Review of Literature, the Arts and Sciences'. Starting in 1842, it came out on the first of each month, with a double number in December, at a cost of 13 roubles a year, post free. I do not know whether you would find the contents of any great interest to-day, but the list of subscribers is like a roll-call of the St Petersburg British: have you heard of Mr Baird, Mr Cattley, Mr Cazalet, Rev Edward Law, Mr Merrilees, Miss Muir, Sir Robert Ker Porter, Mr Whishaw, General Wilson and H.E.Sir James Wylie, Bt.? In addition, the Review was taken by The British Factory, Quarantine at Odessa, and H.I.M's library. Nor must we overlook interested Russians: Vice-Admiral Ricord, Countess Vorontsov-Dashkov, Count Tolstoy, Admiral Greig.

In addition to all this, I translated Gogol for Blackwood's Magazine, and published articles on Pushkin. I hope I made a contribution to the Russian Empire and its people, and I would have done more, had not my life ended early at the age of 49. I was buried in St Petersburg; I understand my obituary was published in 'The Nevsky Magazine', a monthly journal of Literature, Science and Art, which was first brought out a few months after my death by Charles E.Turner. Born in 1831, Turner came out to Russia in 1859, becoming in 1864 Lector in English Language at the University, a post which he apparently held until his death in 1904! He left translations of Russian authors, including Turgenev, and acquainted English readers with Tolstoy. He even included one of my poems: 'The Foam Bells'; poems by W.S.Merrilees; 'Fishing in Finland' by Charles Heath. There were reviews of the St Petersburg theatres, and a feature called 'Books of the Month', which celebrated the first issue with an article on Kinglake's 'History of the Crimean War' and Bishop Colenso's notorious criticism of the Pentateuch and the Book of Joshua.

The most interesting part of the magazine is the introduction to the first number, which states that '...Englishmen are proverbially said to hang together abroad, and we have felt that an English journal...was a want long experienced by the English community in Russia... We still hope our countrymen resident in Russia will assist us in founding an organ of their own opinion in the midst of the Russian community.' My sentiments, exactly.

Another young man who joined our ranks in 1853 was John Henry Harrison (1829-1902) He became a teacher at the High Commercial School and the Imperial Marine Corps. He was popular, and as much appreciated for his kindness as for his learning. He translated Krylov's Fables, poems by Alexei Tolstoy, edited a compendium of Russian literature, as well as writing an original work: 'Tolstoy as a Preacher'. He also founded an English Debating Society.

W.R.S.Ralston (1828-1889)

I was born in London; my father had been wealthy, but lost most of his money in litigation, so when I came down from Cambridge, I had to find a job. As an assistant in the printed book department of the British Museum, I was somehow drawn to the study of the Russian language, which was to prove beneficial to myself and to my employers. So few scholars had a knowledge of the language at that time.

When I visited Russia in 1870, I took the liberty of calling on Ivan Turgenev at Spasskoye, since I was planning to publish my translation of his novels. I felt very strongly that English readers should be aware of what was being written in Russia, one of the emerging nations of Europe, which, after all you have been reading, you must agree, had strong links with Great Britain, and needed to strengthen them. If I could do my small part towards the progress of 'democracy' in Russia, I would do so; and what better means of spreading the message than publishing literature in your own language for fellow-countrymen to read?

In 1877 I had an article in the journal 'Nineteenth Century' on 'Russian Revolutionary Literature' – something that was rather 'revolutionary' in Britain. I not only wrote, but lectured on Russian history, gave performances of my own dramatised stories, and even attended the Royal Family at Marlborough House, reading and story-telling to the young princes. Owing to ill-health I resigned my post at the British Museum, and died in 1889. My other books are: 'Songs of the Russian People' (1872), 'Russian Folk Tales' (1873), 'Early Russian History' (1874) and a work on Russian Operas (1888).

Earlier I wrote the Preface to Henry Riola's 'Manual for Students of Russian' (1878), which was an early attempt to help those who wished to master the newly-discovered tongue. It was followed a year later by a 'Graduated Russian Reader', which went from exercises on grammatical points, through reading lessons, to extracts from Karamzin, Pushkin, Lermontov, Tolstoy, Turgenev, and poetry by Zhukovski, Krylov, Pushkin and Lermontov. If you ever manage to handle this book, you may see my handiwork in it.

You may be surprised to find that in 1882 A. Ivanoff's Russian Grammar was translated, enlarged and arranged for the use of English students of the Russian language by Walter E. Gowan, a major in the Indian army, and dedicated to Maria Alexandrovna, Duchess of Edinburgh and Imperial Princess of Russia. (This may be a salutary reminder that the two royal families were at this time closely related; I can only regret that this connection did not produce the necessary flowering of relations between people of other classes of society, which so many of us had been working for.) Perhaps you will hear in due course from someone involved in changing the face of Russian Studies in Great Britain.

Edward A. Cazalet (1827-1883)

As a member of a well-established business family in Russia, I became in 1864 secretary at Odessa to the managing director of the Russian Steam Navigation and Trading Company. So when I left Russia to work in London, I realised what a dearth of knowledge and understanding there was in Britain about Russia and her problems. So, eventually, after several years of canvassing among British and Russian notables, I founded the Anglo-Russian Literary Society, the aims of which can be summarised thus:

1) to promote study of the Russian language and literature;
2) to form a library of Russian books;
3) to take in Russian periodicals and newspapers;
4) to hold monthly meetings, writing and speaking in English and Russian being alike admissible;
5) to promote friendly relations between Great Britain and Russia.

At the inaugural meeting in 1893, I was able to report that we had about 50 paid-up members. Membership was open to ladies and gentlemen, and politics were not allowed in debate. I reminded those present that many English people had spent the best years of their lives in Russia, and made lifelong friendships with warm-hearted, hospitable and generous inhabitants of that country. Too much had been said and written about Russian bribery and corruption, and far too little about the good nature and unselfishness, especially of the lower classes, who formed nine-tenths of the population.

The sort of speakers we had included Dr John Pollen, who wrote masterly translations of 'Rhymes from the Russian' and 'Russian songs set to music', and who was himself almost entirely self-taught in the language. He made reference to the fact that some officers of the British army were spending ten months in Russia learning the language, which he regarded as 'a hopeless task in a ridiculously insufficient time'. Those who failed to qualify as interpreters had to lose their furlough, and pay their own expenses and tuition fees.

We had the London correspondent of 'Novoye Vremya' address the meeting in Russian on the subject of the appreciation of English institutions and ideas in St Petersburg and Moscow. 'In Russian, the adjective 'English' has almost become a synonym for distinguished, best, excellent. To say "that came from England", "that is made in England", means that article is of sound quality, that piece of work is first class. The best store in St Petersburg for many years was known as The English Magazine. The chief clubs in St Petersburg and Moscow are both called The English Club'. (Thank-you, we did know that.)

In less than two years our membership reached over 300, and we acquired Patrons: the Duke and Duchess of Edinburgh and the Tsarevich (later Nicholas II).

One of our meetings was addressed by Rev Arthur Thompson, formerly British Chaplain at St Petersburg, on the subject of the British Embassy at St Petersburg for half a century, in which he told of the esteem in which the British community was always held by the Russian autocrats; of how 'at the beginning of the Crimean war, Nicholas I sent for Dr Law, and enjoined him to come to him direct at any time if any of the English Colony who remained required protection or help, assuring the old Doctor that the war could make no difference to the long relation of friendship which had existed between them.'

The highlight of the Society's activities in 1897 was the correspondence of several members to various newspapers on the subject of the importance of learning Russian, and the difficulties of doing so at that time. The practical result of this campaign was that the London Chamber of Commerce offered two prizes for proficiency in Russian – surely the first time such a thing had ever been known! It must be appreciated that at this time Russian was not an accepted subject of study at British universities, However, there were exceptions:

most notable being William Richard Morfill (1834-1909), who happened to have a Russian grammar book given him at Tonbridge school by a master. After Oxford, he lectured on English literature, spending his vacations travelling in Europe, especially the Slav countries. He later lectured at Oxford on Slavonic literature, eventually becoming Professor of Russian and Slavonic Languages. Equally exceptional was Bernard Pares, who admittedly had a built-in start: his godfather was Baron Dimsdale, descendant of the physician who inoculated Catherine the Great. Bernard read Classics at Cambridge, but had an especial interest in Napoleon's battlefields. This naturally led him to Russia, and he entered as a student at Moscow University in 1898 at the age of 31. He returned to Russia annually as correspondent to the Spectator, the Westminster Gazette and the Liverpool Courier, at the same time campaigning in England for recognition of Russian studies in universities. He became Professor, first of all at Liverpool, then at London University, and, I have heard, was responsible for moving the Anglo-Russian Literary Society from the Imperial Institute, where I started it, to the School of Slavonic and East European Studies in 1922. By that time there were some 1,500 volumes, as well as the Society's archives.

While in Russia, Pares did not remain on the edge of life as a commentator, but lived it to the full; his linguistic ability and general understanding of things Russian enabled him to make contacts normally denied newspaper reporters. A thing I still find difficult to believe is that when the first Duma was set up in 1906, it was Pares who was asked by the Black Rod to be Gentleman Usher, a post for which the qualifications were that the holder should be a Russian subject, have been to a Russian school and university, and should swear a special oath of loyalty to the Tsar. None of these stipulations were asked of Pares, since even the high-up officials really understood nothing about what the Duma stood for! Suffice it to say that Bernard Pares became so highly thought of, and so much sought after, by British and Russian authorities alike, that he was asked to organise the first visit by members of the Duma to England in 1909, as well as subsequent years. In his capacity as secretary of the Anglo-Russian Committee in London, he arranged for exchanges of Members of Parliament. At the outbreak of war in 1914, Pares became the official correspondent for the British Government at the Russian Front, where he earned for himself the Soldier's Cross and the medal of St George.

Like most of the British in Russia at the time, Pares regarded the oncoming Revolution with some interest and even optimism for the chance of change in a country which had reached a very low ebb both politically and socially. But like most, he found the real thing in 1917 a great disappointment, and relations with the new regime were far from easy, so he returned to England, to take up the academic post I previously mentioned.

Matthew Edwardes (- 1917)

I was brother to George Edwardes, the musical comedy impressario. I was involved in industry in Russia: I had extensive glassworks at Seversk, where my estate was, and a rope factory at Kushelevka. I learnt to speak fluent Russian, which enabled me to have a relationship within Russian society. I took on tutoring a girl called Camilla, who was sister to Alexandre Benois (1870-1960) the theatre designer. As these things do, my pupil in time became my wife. Alexandre himself had had an English governess, Miss Evans, whom he remembered in his Memoirs with great tenderness, despite describing her as 'an odd little old woman looking exactly like the bad fairies painted by Bertall and Dore.' She enriched his library with English books, and he became acquainted with the delightful style of English designers, which was going to stand him in good stead when he co-operated later with the masters of the Russian ballet.

Another who fell in love with his pupil was Felix Elston, who passed himself off as a Scotsman, but according to Prince Yussupov, (who claimed descent from Elston), he was the illegimate child of Frederick William IV, King of Prussia and Countess Tiesenhausen. It was apparently reported that the mother was so surprised at the birth of the baby, that it was stated that 'elle s'étonne', and the name Elston stuck! However, somehow he found his way into earning his living as a teacher of English, and one of his pupils was the young Countess Sumarokov. Teacher and student fell in love, and eventually married. As the young bride was a member of an ancient and distinguished noble family, she applied to the Emperor to ennoble her husband, under the title of Count Sumarokov-Elston. Their son married Princess Yussupov, probably the richest heiress in Russia, but also the sole survivor of another long and famous line. The son of that marriage (mentioned above), Prince Felix Yussupov, became famous in his own right.

I myself died at the height of the Revolution, but my coffin was borne by my loyal workmen. My widow emigrated in 1920, and lived out her days in a cottage in Lincolnshire, as the guest of my family.

Gordon Craig (1872-1966)

I was an established actor, and married, when I first met the Irish-American dancer, Isadora Duncan, in Germany in 1905. I was attracted by her personality rather than her physical attributes. After spending some time together in various parts of Europe, we parted, she to Moscow to work for Konstantin Sergeyevich Stanislavsky. I imagine they must have discussed me and my work, but he said it was as a result of reading an article of mine in the first number of my magazine 'The Mask', entitled 'The Artists of the Theatre of the Future', that Stanislavsky invited me to Moscow to discuss the possibility of producing a play together.

I arrived in Moscow in October, 1908, was made very welcome, and taken to see plays, including Chekhov's 'The Cherry Orchard' and 'Uncle Vanya'. I stayed three weeks, during which time we decided that the first play we should put on would be 'Hamlet', since I was experimenting with it at the time. So I returned in early 1909 to St Petersburg, where the Moscow Arts Theatre were performing at the time. The first night of our 'Hamlet' was an overwhelming success. The Times newspaper wrote: '.the production is a remarkable triumph for Mr Craig, and it is impossible to say how wide an effect such a completely realized success of his theories may have on the theatre of Europe.' I hope I may have had done something for the Russians, even at that late date in their history.

Incidentally, you may recall a moment in the last act of 'The Cherry Orchard', when Semeonov-Pishchik, a land-owner, comes on to announce that he has just been approached by some Englishmen, who have found 'some white clay' on his land. That is all that is said; indeed, no-one even acknowledges his statement. But it speaks volumes to the reader of this collection of 'What we did for the Russians', don't you think?

20 SPORT - OR SPORT?

Herbert Swann (1894-)

I was born at Tsarskoye Selo, the third of four sons of Alfred Swann, a clerk who later became a departmental manager at the Russo-American India Rubber Company. My aunts Ellen and Sophie were descendants of Robert Hynam, who came out to Russia in 1776 to become Court Horloger to Catherine II. My early life was that of a middle-class Russian boy: I could not speak English properly until I was sixteen. My parents were not wealthy enough to send me to England for my schooling, but we could on occasions go into St Petersburg and do some shopping at the English shop in Nevsky Prospect. I think we always regarded ourselves as English, but as for contributing to the Russian Empire, we did rather little – there was not time, because the Revolution took over, and my wife and I escaped after many narrow misses at the hands of the Soviet guards and spies. (One of my children was Donald Swann, the musician and entertainer).

However, I will tell you of some people who certainly made a hefty input into Russian life, which has lasted. I refer to the brothers Charnock: Clement and Harry. They came from Lancashire, and were engaged in the cotton industry, as you might guess. They had a large textile mill at Orekhovo-Zuevo, not far from Moscow. When it was set up in 1887, they placed an advertisement in The Times for 'engineers, mechanics and clerks capable of playing football well'. Their whole idea was to keep their employees busy out of work hours, and so forestall the industrial unrest, political agitation and vodka-drinking that would inevitably arise with large numbers of workers. Naturally, the football kit was imported from England, but, as their funds did not run to buying football boots, they had studs fitted to the employees' shoes. Their factory team, Morozovtsi, was re-named OKS Moskva in 1906, and won a series of Moscow league championships from 1910 to 1914. (It was later to achieve world-wide fame under its Soviet name, Moscow Dynamo.)

The Charnocks were well to the fore in introducing football to Russia, but they were soon followed by other firms, such as Firth-Brown of Sheffield, which had a plant at Riga; you have heard, no doubt, of the Hughesovka mining complex in Ukraine. In their team was a young man who was destined to go a long way. At the time when Nikita Sergeevich Khrushchev was First Secretary of the Soviet Communist Party and at the height of his power, a Mr Reginald Tyler, of Wembley, unearthed some photographs of his team's match against Hughesovka, and mentioned, in his article in the Daily Sketch (18 January 1958) other recollections, including a spring wire in the Russian goal, which prevented scoring, and Mr K's team won!

Most British games came into fashion in the early days of the 20th century, except cricket. Russians never understood the game, and, I suppose, never tried.

Sir Archibald Wavell (1883-1950)

I was a soldier all my life, having been trained at the Staff College, Camberley. At the age of 26, I was chosen from the course to go to Russia, as I had already passed examinations in French, Urdu and Pushtu with little difficulty. So picture me arriving in Moscow in February, 1911, not knowing a word of Russian, but under an obligation to sit for my examination as an interpreter the following January! I chose to stay with the Ertel family, in their third-floor flat overlooking the Kremlin gates. Lola Ertel was the widow of Alexander, a writer of ability, whose major work 'The Gardenins', a panoramic view of country life in late nineteenth-century Russia, had recently been re-published, with a preface by Tolstoy. Lola had set up her home as a guest-house for British officers and consular officials, with Russian language lessons. This arrangement had the added attraction of being plunged into a typical Chekhovian milieu, down to the student hanger-on, the constant visitors, and the seemingly carefree, lazy existence of the Russian middle-class household. We had a routine of heavy meals, mornings spent with my teacher, private study in the afternoon, a walk in the streets, sometimes tea at Muir & Merrilees, work until supper. I joined a football team formed by a Russian doctor.

I had a friend, Cuthbert Fuller, who had been on an earlier course, and married a Russian Princess, Sophia Shakhovskaya. In the summer, when the Ertels went to the country, Fuller, myself and an Indian Army officer, called Churchill, toured southern Russia together. In September I was attached to the Fifth Kiev Regiment of Grenadiers, played football for Russia (!), and for the English in Moscow against a German touring team. I left Moscow on Christmas day, 1911, and took my examination in January, receiving a First class Interpretership. My job at the War Office included writing a handbook on the Russian army; in 1912-3 I attended military manoeuvres in Russia, which consolidated and deepened my knowledge of the Russian army, confirmed my admiration for the Russian soldier, as well as my liking for the Russian people at large. However, while staying at the Hotel Metropole, Moscow, my belongings were searched by secret police, and I was arrested on the train home. When it was realised that a mistake had been made, I was freed and sent home. Months later I was presented in London with a gold watch and a personal message from the Tsar, ostensibly in return for translating a Russian book, but probably as an apology for the treatment I had received.

Older readers will recall that I served in both World Wars, and in 1943 became Viceroy of India. I died in 1950.

21 AN OVERALL VIEW

Sir John Foster Fraser (1868-1936)

In August, 1901, I travelled from Moscow by train to Vladivostok, then took a plunge into Manchuria. At St Petersburg on the way out, I was met by officials, all speaking English, with an honest and deep-seated liking of things English. They measured things by English standards. I was told by one Russian, in reply to my bemused enquiries: 'You must remember that my nursery governess was an Englishwoman.' No real surprise there.

I had a fascination with the Trans-Siberian railway. Obviously, it was the idea to be able to transport troops and munitions across the continent - something that Russia had been singularly unable to do. So when railways became established elsewhere in the Empire, it was thought feasible to cross this otherwise intractable stretch of land – and water – with a little help from the British, of course. I heard a legend that as far back as 1857 an Englishman, called Dull, of whom little else is known, appeared in St Petersburg with a project to build and operate a horse tramway from Nizhni Novgorod to the Pacific coast. Apparently, this met with little or no approval. Less than a year later three Englishmen: Morrison, Horn and Sleigh, offered to lay a railway from Moscow to 'the Straits of Tartary', petitioning for such privileges as would have retained the exploitation of Siberia and the ensuing profit in other than Russian hands. This scheme also came to nought. It was not until 1891 that the Russian Government took it upon itself to build the line.

On Lake Baikal there was a huge steamer/ice-breaker, called the Angara, built by Armstrong, Whitworth & Co, of Newcastle-upon-Tyne, the order having been sent in 1896, five years after the start of the building of the Trans-Siberian railway. The parts for this ice-breaker were sent to St Petersburg by ship, to be conveyed by rail as far as the line was built, and after that by sledge. I was told that between the capital and the building site several pieces got lost, even though each one had been carefully marked and numbered. The job of assembly took over two years, there being so few skilled men available. The other ice-breaker/train ferry was called the Baikal, 4,000 tons, 300 feet long, capable of carrying two goods trains fully laden. It could break through ice up to 36 inches thick, and during the winter, when conditions were at their worst, it could take a week to cross the lake.

As well as conveying convicts, soldiers and explorers, the Siberian railway soon attracted travellers from among the general public, including the British. You may come across a book, published in 1901, called 'Ribbon of Iron', by Annette M.B.Meakin, who did the whole trip across Siberia, accompanied by her sixty-year-old mother! They were the first (recorded) Englishwomen to travel the whole length of the railway. What struck them most was the convivial atmosphere amongst the passengers, which helped the time to pass quickly. The author records that at Alexandrovsk, they met a prisoner who came from Glasgow, and who had been exiled for ten years. He had been a Russian soldier, but could not return to Britain, unless he ran away. At Blagoveshchensk they met a Russian officer who was English. He told them that he had lived so long in Siberia that he found it difficult to speak English. The manager of the Grand Hotel in the same town spoke English, but was 'shaky from want of use'. The travellers found a copy of 'The Life of Tennyson' for sale in a bookshop there, and were surprised and delighted to discover that the 'Amur Gazette' had published an article about them the day before their arrival. At Vladivostok the mayor's wife was an Englishwoman, and the mayor himself was gracious enough to hand to Ms Meakin a pair of pocket scissors she had left in the train as far back as Omsk.

In 1902 Major H.G.C.Swayne, Royal Engineers, F.R.G.S., F.Z.S., learnt some Russian, and with an old friend, H.W.Seton Carr, set out for 'The Highlands of Siberia', as his book is called. He was given a private introduction to Mr J.O.Cattley, head of the only British firm at Novonikolaevsk. Mr Cattley allowed his sons to show the visitors around, giving them the benefit of their local experience. Mr P. Cattley, one of the same family, acted as interpreter for Samuel Turner,

F.R.G.S., who wrote 'Siberia' in 1905. He states that, apart from the Cattleys, there were at least three Englishwomen with their families, who had 'an intense longing for London'. Turner did not advocate investing money in Russian and Siberian firms, but 'we should try to work Russian resources with British capital, and the guidance of British managers, while utilising Russia's cheap labour and cheap land.' Have we heard that sentiment before somewhere? Is it the motto of this present collection of personal experiences?

When I was reporting in 1915, the position of English language in the Empire was suffering because of the activity of the Germans, who were clearly intent on taking over if at all possible. If Englishmen wanted their full share of trade, it was important to have representatives who could speak Russian. The way to do it was to send out young men in whom they had confidence to learn the language. I suggested the establishment of travelling scholarships for ambitious employees. It was equally noticeable that every young Russian lad and girl had the ambition to speak English. Anybody who could give lessons in English was at a premium, and many did cash in on the situation. You must understand that the government had banned the use and learning of German from the outbreak of war, and parents of school-children had petitioned the authorities to substitute English in schools.

The Russo-British Chamber of Commerce was established early in the century, specifically to resist the influx of German firms, and by the War had about 900 members, including around 100 who lived in England. I recommended the setting-up of a similar body in London, but like so much at this time it never saw daylight, and the Revolution put an end to everything.

While getting around in Russia, I came across several Anglo-Russian firms, some of which you may have heard of before. The biggest importer of cotton in Russia was Knoop, and its associated firm of Mather & Platt, who supplied many of the cotton mills with machinery. The biggest brewer in Russia was William Miller. Just outside Petrograd (as we had to call it) was the woollen mill of Thorntons, bigger than anything in the West Riding of Yorkshire. At the British Club in Moscow I made the acquaintance of Mr James Charnock, a partner and Managing Director of Vigoul Morosoff & Sons, and was invited to visit their works.

John Henry Hubback, a corn merchant, had been asked in 1910 to go to Russia to see what supplies of wheat were available. He began to learn the language from a very competent teacher, took his wife by train via Warsaw to Odessa, and from there went the rounds of the British vice-consuls: at Saratov the water engineer was John Golden, 'well named as to character and kindness'. He had lived for a long time in the region, having established the city's waterworks, and members of his family were in businesses in neighbouring provinces. He acquainted Hubback with the millers, who were so useful to him in his quest for information about grain. At Kharkov, the vice-consul, Charles Blakey, was the manager for a foreign firm of agricultural machinery. He had designed a seed-drill, which was in use all over southern Russia, and was an expert in agricultural matters. In all, Hubback made eleven visits to Russia, the last in summer 1914. He came back in a hurry in August, and did not return again!

Before I leave you, I would like to introduce Allan Monkhouse, who first visited Russia in 1911. He was engaged on the erection of the Moscow City Tramway, but during the War got himself involved in the production of munitions. His particular assignment was one million barbed-wire cutters to be attached to rifles. He had little time for recreation (!), but when not working he joined the Great Britain to Poland Relief Fund Committee, and three evenings a week he was on duty with a portable soup-kitchen at railway stations. His co-worker was a young English girl, who had been educated in Moscow and spoke fluent Russian. (I need hardly say that her situation was quite common, considering the number of tutors and governesses there had been for years among better-off Russian families.) Monkhouse was arrested on Christmas Day, 1917, and tried for sabotage, but reprieved. He got out of Russia via the Far East and America. In 1918 he took part in the British Expeditionary Force, as an interpreter. While at Archangel he met a trapper, who pointed out the tombs of British families who had lived there before the time of Peter the Great, adding that there were still families in the district bearing English names and having English blood. We seem to have gone full circle! Later, in 1921, when the New Economic Policy welcomed capitalist firms to create industry, Allan Monkhouse went again to Russia to help in the building of power stations, and was impressed by the fact that the tradition of British industry in Russia lingered on, even to the minting of new coins. In 1933 he was arrested on a charge of having knowledge of the wrecking activities of a Mr Thornton (haven't we heard that name before?)

Archibald Merrilees

I feel sure you have heard of me – and my partner in business, Andrew Muir (1817-1899). We are both Scots, who separately landed up in Russia early in the 19th century, and together set up a trading company in St Petersburg. We transferred to Moscow in the 1880's, opening up a wholesale shop for women's hats and haberdashery on Kuznetsky Most street. It was not long before we turned into a retail department store – the first in Russia. We catered for the middle class shopper – everything except food. I think I can confidently claim that our goods were of excellent quality, the sales staff were always impeccably courteous, and whenever a customer was dissatisfied, the goods would be immediately exchanged. I do not think that Russians had ever heard of such a thing! The shop was situated at the end of Petrovka Street, just adjacent to the original Kuznetsky Most, and the very fashionable Passazh. In our restaurant upstairs it was the 'done thing' to take afternoon tea.

The fame of our shop spread throughout the Russian Empire. We distributed our catalogue free of charge, and we developed a postal ordering system. One of our customers was the famous writer Anton Chekhov, who bought the furniture for his new house in Yalta. He was such an admirer of our company, that he even named his two dogs Muir and Merrilees.

One evening in November 1900 fire broke out in the shop, and by morning there was little left but the walls. We soon set about rebuilding: the new shop even had electric lifts – a great rarity at the time. After the Revolution the firm was nationalised, as was everything else in Russia. It came to be known as TsUM (Central Department Store), although Muscovites of the older generation still referred to it by its former name.

I had no desire to stay in Russia when the Revolution came, so I retired to my home in Scotland, which had been paid for with the money I had made in providing the Russians with their first department store.

Harry de Windt (1856-1933)

I hope you do not mind my inclusion in this book of what Britons did for Russia, including discovering remote parts of the Empire that the Russians might have been centuries finding out about. I refer, of course, to Siberia, that huge, unexplored vastness which belongs to Russia as it were by accident, because nobody else really wanted it! The truth is, I came from Dutch extraction, and was born in Paris, which makes me borderline for membership of this present club. But from the age of 14 I was brought up by an English country parson, so perhaps I am not so alien after all! After Cambridge, I travelled extensively in Europe and the Near East, spending, I am ashamed to say, most of my time and money on racing and gambling. I visited Australia, returning through China and Russia. In London I met the redoubtable Madame Olga Novikov, who was interested in my exploits, and sent me as an 'unbiased witness to Siberia, to draw up a plan and truthful report on the actual situation'. I was issued with an Imperial ukaz, allowing me in any place of confinement at any hour of day or night. My findings, 'Siberia as it is' came out in 1892. Madame Novikov herself agreeing reluctantly to write the preface, because she felt that her sympathies might injure the book rather than commend it to English readers. She was, after all, a 'thorough Russian, a staunch believer in Greek Orthodoxy, in Autocracy and Nationalism; convinced of the grand future of Russia…' In fact she represented all that the British people had the greatest dislike for. Whilst W.T.Stead accepted my findings, the book was attacked by those who thought they knew better: the youthful Winston Churchill seemed to know as much as I did about Siberia, only his knowledge was theoretical; another who did not accept me was the aged Lord Tennyson. In 1896, after the publication of 'The New Siberia', I chanced to meet Oscar Wilde at a dinner party: he attacked my book vehemently, saying that its author should himself be sent to Siberia! (It was only later that Wilde admitted that the Siberian prisons could not be worse than an English gaol!)

My first book on Siberia was sent to, and accepted by, the Tsarevich, later Nicholas II; my last book, 'Russia as I know it', came out in 1917, a little late to do any good!

Miss Kate Marsden (1859-1931)

I was born to middle-class parents near London, and became a nurse at an early age. I cared for the wounded during the war between Russia and Turkey in 1878, but even those wartime experiences did not prepare me for what I endured and witnessed in 1891 'On Sledge and Horseback to outcast Siberian Lepers'. The previous year I was presented to Queen Victoria, and was promised an audience with the Empress of Russia. The latter was to give me a letter requesting Russian officials to facilitate my entry to hospitals and leper colonies throughout the Empire. In the preface to my book I appealed to 'all English-speaking men and women not to find fresh cause of complaint against Russia.' I was only too aware that the conditions I would find in Russia would not pass uncriticised by British readers, always ready to find fault with things Russian. Shortly before leaving for Siberia, I received a letter of encouragement from none other than Florence Nightingale.

Thus armed, I travelled for twelve months: before Siberia I went via Jerusalem and Constantinople, to see the state of lepers in those parts, then through the Black Sea and Caucasus to Moscow, where I was received by the Governor. I went twice to St Petersburg to see the Empress, who sent me £100 towards my expenses. Countess Tolstoy did everything in her power. At Moscow, many of the resident English opened their doors to me, though I know some of them suspected me of being a political spy. I took the train to Zlatoust, where I was met by the Head of Police, and then set off across Siberia by sledge. At Ekaterinburg I met one of the Messrs Wardroper, and his son-in-law, who was agent for the Bible Society. At Tiumen, another Mr and Mrs Wardroper received me and my party, which included Miss Ada Field and a black collie with a white tail. The Wardropers treated us as if we had been their own children. We sat down travel-stained, bruised and ill, to a hot supper, and were afterwards sent off for a night's rest. Miss Field and the dog went no farther, but I visited the prisons at Omsk, Tomsk and Krasnoyarsk. At Irkutsk the Governor General formed a committee, including the Archbishop and other notables; after Yakutsk I went another two thousand miles to Viluisk – and all on horseback in the most trying conditions. I spoke hardly any Russian, and certainly no Yakut. I witnessed many, many examples of the lepers' conditions, treatment and dangerous way of life. The return journey was via the Lena to Irkutsk, then Tomsk, Tiumen (where I was pleased to rejoin Miss Field), Ufa, Samara, Moscow and St Petersburg; another audience with the Empress; another meeting with Countess Tolstoy; the Over Procurator of the Holy Synod (Pobedonostsev) had my article printed in a pamphlet, and 40,000 copies were to be distributed throughout the Empire to raise funds for leper work, and plans were made for a leper colony.

After all this adventure and danger, the extent of which I could never adequately describe, I attribute my survival to a life of abstinence from alcohol, and also to Jaeger clothing, without which it would have been quite impossible to go through all the changes of climate, and to remain for weeks without changing my clothes!

Joseph Wiggins (1832-1905)

I was born in Norwich, son of a coach proprietor. At the age of 13 I was apprenticed to a ship-owner in Sunderland, and it was not long before I was commanding sailing ships, and gaining much experience of the sea. In June 1874 I equipped a small steamer, the Diana, and left Dundee for the Kara Sea, north of Siberia, intent on discovering the mouth of the river Ob'. I also wanted to show that maps, issued as lately as 1872, showing everlasting ice between Novaya Zemlya and latitude 105 E, were wrong. The Gulf Stream kept the area ice-free for two months of the year. Unfortunately for me, we did not find the entrance to the river, and the crew were frustrated and demanded to go home.

I was determined to go on exploring, as soon as I had the means. So I collected funds wherever I could, and in 1875 I set out again, this time in a 27-ton fishing vessel, but got no farther than Kolguyev Island in the Barents Sea. Failure again. However, I obtained £1000 from Charles Gardiner, an enthusiastic yachtsman, and a further £1000 from a rich Russian, Alexei Sibiryakov, and in September, 1876, sailed the 'Thames', a screw-steamer, up the river Yenisei (farther east than the Ob') only to find that the cargo of graphite I had been commissioned to pick up, had not been delivered. So I left the ship for the winter, and undertook a sledge journey to Yeniseisk, the largest city on the river, at least 1300 kilometres from the mouth. Here was a trading centre for a huge area since the 17th century. The only ship-builder was an Anglo-German, Mr Boiling, who received me, as did the Governor-general of Siberia. You may not believe this, but I continued by sledge right across Siberia to Moscow and on to St Petersburg, where I was made a great fuss of.

The next March, accompanied by Mr H.Seebohn, an ornithologist of some distinction, I left London for St Petersburg, Moscow and Nijni-Novgorod, where we took a sledge once more, and covered the 3000 miles to Yeniseisk in less than two weeks. On leaving Yeniseisk, the steamer ran aground on a sandbank, and I was obliged to sell her to a group of merchants from Irkutsk, who happened to be on the spot at the time. With the proceeds I acquired a Russian schooner, but my men did not trust a foreign ship, preferring to get home by land! So I sold the schooner, bought a tarantass (springless carriage) and I rode across Europe to be home for Christmas! The next August, I sailed the 'Warkworth', chartered by Mr Oswald Cattley, of St Petersburg, from Liverpool to the Gulf of the Ob', with a cargo of salt, Sheffield goods, porcelain and glue; I returned to London in October with a cargo of wheat, linseed, hemp and flax. Then we formed the 'Phoenix Merchant Adventurers of Newcastle-on-Tyne', and our ship, the aptly-named 'Phoenix', left for Yeniseisk in 1887. On this occasion we visited Krasnoyarsk, a city of wide streets, where some houses even had electric light. Our party was invited to dine with some ladies who spoke fluent English (I was never sure whether they were actually English). We found a costly house, with immense rooms, parquet floors, white marble mantelpieces, with open English fire-places, an art gallery with very valuable paintings and statuary, and the furniture throughout of the best. The dinner was thoroughly English, but included splendid apples and grapes from the Crimea.

I know I was highly esteemed by Tsar Alexander III, and the Ambassador at St Petersburg, Sir Robert Morier, who even entrusted his 21-year-old son Victor to my care as a member of the crew of my next ship, the 'Labrador', which sailed from the Tyne in 1888. Unfortunately, this endeavor failed, and the Phoenix Company went into liquidation. I was not content with living on land, and 1893 saw me captaining the 'Orestes' from Middlesborough with a cargo of 1600 tons of rails for the Trans-Siberian Railway. Miss Helen Peel, daughter of the former Prime Minister, a remarkable young woman, who was determined to be the first female to sail through the icebergs of the Kara Sea and up the Yenisei, joined my colleague, Francis Leybourne-Popham on his steam yacht, the 'Blencathra', with a cargo of gold-mining machinery. We were joined at Vardoe, in Norway, by three steamers under Russian officers (though built, of course, on the Clyde). When we arrived at Yeniseisk, there was a sensational welcome, to celebrate the first time that Russian ships had completed this northern route. After the celebrations, I set off on another of my strenuous sledge journeys, stopping at Tomsk on Christmas Day, Omsk on New Year's Day. At Cheliabinsk I took the train to St Petersburg, where I was presented to Alexander III, who, as a mark of Russian official appreciation, gave me a solid silver-plate punch-bowl, salver, ladle and twenty-five mugs, each ornamented with antique Russian designs.

In the following year, I joined Mr Leybourne-Popham in a convoy, which included two paddle steamers: Pervoi and Vtoroi, (First and Second), made at Newcastle-on-Tyne by Armstrong Mitchell & Co for the Siberian Railway. Our ship ran aground in fog off the coast of northern Russia, and we finished up taking another sledge ride to Archangel, 2000 miles, where we met the very helpful British Vice-Consul, Mr Cooke. I continued to St Petersburg, where I was awarded the Murchison medal by the Russian Geographical Society. Was it worth it?

In the summer of 1896, I led a flotilla of six ships out to northern Russia, but the scheme failed, and I never went again. I died an unhappy man, but I must claim to have done much to open up Siberia. When I began my career, the majority of Britons were in entire ignorance of the natural wealth of Russia beyond the Urals. It was to become clear to all that here was a country rich and ready for exploitation.

Algernon Noble

I went to Russia in 1905 to exploit coal and copper mines near Petropavlovsk, on the Siberian railway. If you were to read my 1928 book 'Siberian Days', you would find detailed description of the terrain, the inhabitants, the wild life and climatic conditions of that relatively unexplored area. Mining rights, once minerals had been discovered, were readily granted by the Russian government, provided the natives of the district, through their chiefs, had been persuaded to sign a document agreeing to the mining taking place, and accepting compensation for any loss of grazing rights. In most cases, there was hardly a blade of grass in the place! But in Eastern Siberia there was gold in almost every rock, but not in commercial quantities, until I was approached by a family of natives, who did their own prospecting, and sold us the gold for half its value! We bribed them with lumps of sugar, to show us where they were obtaining their rich finds: it was within two hundred yards of our laboratory door! Once a group of about twenty exhausted, hungry Russian convicts bowed to the ground in begging for work.

There is no doubt, there was a large field for the prospector and geologist, and up-to-date methods would have ultimately disclosed goldfields of great value in this part of Siberia. The Soviet authorities will have found all this out, but we shall not have heard much about it!

Captain M.H.Hayes (1842-1904)

Although I spent many years as an officer in India, I had no intention, when retired, to visit Russia. It came about thus: a certain Frenchman, by name Sorel, was asked by a Russian officer to find him an Irish mare. So he came to my breeding establishment in England. The officer was so pleased with what I provided that he invited me to St Petersburg in July, 1897. Thereafter, I found myself in and out of cavalry establishments in Russia, apparently the first foreigner to be allowed to visit such places, as they were regarded as top security risks. After all, Russia had more than once been to war with Britain, and there was plenty of antagonism between the two countries, officially. However, I personally had a very warm reception, probably on account of my expertise, which was, like so much else, in demand. I never met with a trace of enmity against the English, either among Russian officials or people.

At Krasnoe Selo the Grand Duke Nicholai Nicholaevich, Inspector General of Cavalry, asked to see me quieten an unbroken horse in one hour. I was expected to give a commentary in French to allow the officers to understand me. The result of this encounter was an invitation from the Grand Duke to come again, visit the studs and write what I liked about them. So I went back home in September, chose four horses and took them to Russia along with a rough rider, called Dick. We waited three weeks in the Hotel d'Angleterre on the Nevsky Prospect before going on to Shandrovka, 150 miles north of the Crimea. I was fascinated to discover that my hotel had a reading-room with English, French, German as well as Russian daily and weekly newspapers, and was consequently frequented by foreigners, large numbers of English and American tourists as well as Anglo-Russian residents. Russia was a happy hunting-ground for Englishmen of commerce; I rarely saw one of them without the "materials" in front of him. Those gentlemen told me that to do business with Russians, one must drink. All I can say is, they were lucky in having an occupation that combined duty with pleasure.

On later visits, I was joined by my wife, Alice, who worked on a bright and interesting review of Russian history.

In the course of four years no fewer than eight young English jockeys and trainers died in Russia owing to the climate. All rather unfortunate, and not typical!

Dr Howard Kennard (1872-1916)

In 1905 I went in attendance on a traveller to Russia. When that engagement came to an end, I found myself alone out there, so decided to travel into various parts of the Russian Empire. As a result of my experiences, I published a book, entitled 'The Russian Peasant', which concerns us little at present... You may be more interested in my 1911 'Russian Year Book', which starts with facts and figures about the administration of the Russian Empire; its population; then comes business information, commercial law, and such account of the military organisation as was available. Under the heading 'General Information for Travellers' I wrote:

'From a social point of view the traveller should take such clothing as he would if he were going to any other civilised country - including frock-coat and evening dress.' The 1914 and subsequent editions add: 'a black morning coat is absolutely necessary. Dress suits are much less worn than with us. A lady should take no thick underclothing except a pair of warm knickerbockers to wear out of doors, a fur or fur-lined hat, a golf jersey (very useful to wear under a fur coat, or else an undercoat of wadded material), a small fur toque, a motor veil to wear on cold days to protect the ears, snowboots, fur gloves and goloshes. Travellers to Russia are especially warned that in the matter of wearing furs and keeping their coats buttoned up, 'Discretion is the better part of valour'. Britishers are apt to imagine that they can play with the climate, and disregard the native's advice born of experience, with the result that many of our countrymen have met their death here prematurely. There is no more treacherous climate in the world than one meets with in St Petersburg.

The first edition of my book had 388 pages; one year later I had gained so much experience that it ran to 822 pages! It was, of course, suspended after 1917. In any case, nobody visited Russia after the Revolution, or wanted to!

My rival was Baedeker, who in 1914 was offering a slightly different angle on what to wear in Russia:

'Clothing should not be too light, for even in summer the nights are often chilly, and changes of temperature are frequent and extreme. Woollen underwear is recommended. The traveller should be provided with a pillow or an air-cushion, linen sheets (useful on long railway journeys and in provincial hotels), towels, a coverlet or rug, a small india-rubber bath, and some insect powder. Visitors to Southern Russia should have a light summer suit; the Russians themselves often wear suits of linen. For winter journeys warm furs and well-lined rubber boots (best obtained in Russia) are indispensable. In spring a spell of warm weather is often succeeded by a sudden frost; it is therefore safer not to discard winter clothing until summer has actually arrived. Unboiled water should be avoided. Tea is a good substitute.

'In making purchases in Russia the traveller should not rely quite so implicitly on the *bona fides* of the shopkeeper as he does at home. It is quite customary, especially in the less fashionable shops, to accept 10-20 per cent less than the price originally demanded.'

? Another case of 'what the Russians did for us'?

After centuries of visitors from overseas, especially from Britain, now came a spate of guide-books like mine. We were all a bit late in the day, but the one which purported to give the most direct and quickest route between England and Russia was 'The Tourist's Russia' (1911) by an American, Ruth Kedzie Wood:

'The Wilson Line: Hull to St Petersburg – a weekly service of new steamers, all of 2000 tons: S.S.Borodino, S.S.Gourko, S.S.Tosno and S.S.Kovno do the passage in an average of four and a half days. Messrs Thomas Wilson & Co Ltd are the sole agents for goods traffic for the Nicholai Railway between St Petersburg and Moscow. The tourist who is also a businessman is strongly advised to take advantage of Messrs Gerhard and Het's fifty years of experience of doing business with the Russians.'

The alternative method of travel was detailed in the Official Guide to the South Eastern & Chatham Railway:

St Petersburg:	1727 miles from London via Calais
	1636 miles from London via Flushing

Approximate express service from London via Calais – 51 hours

Fares from London

via Calais:	1st	219/2d	2nd	137/7d
Return:	1st	422/6d	2nd	282/2d
Ostend:	1st	207/6d	2nd	145/7d
Return:	1st	403/5d	2nd	267/2d
Flushing:	1st	192/4d	2nd	126/11d
Return:	1st	347/3d	2nd	246/4d

22 LINGUISTS AND AUTHORS

William Gerhardi (1895-1977)

I came of a family that had originally emigrated to England during Napoleonic times, but by the time I was born could be considered English enough for inclusion in this study. My paternal grandfather took his wife and children to Russia, with no knowledge of the language and little business acumen, but soon prospered from a small cotton spinning mill he set up on the right bank of the Neva. It was at St Petersburg that my father and mother met and married – she was a member of the Wadsworth family from Yorkshire, who had been in Russia for several years managing another cotton mill.

I grew up in the Russian capital, in a house on the river bank, with many servants, German and French governesses, speaking four languages, English least of all. With my sisters I attended the English Sunday School, at which the teacher had to explain to the other children, sons and daughters of foremen in local cotton mills, who hailed from Lancashire and whose knowledge of languages was confined to that of their county, that if we seemed to cut a poor figure at the Sunday School it should be remembered that we were at home in three other languages.

My father was loved by the workmen at his mill, but in 1905, when Revolution emboldened some of them, they tied him up in a sack, which they then put into a barrel and wheeled him along to tilt him in the Neva. They were stopped on their way by an elderly workman, who put them to shame by asking them what they meant by thus treating the English Socialist Keir Hardie. They then asked my father whether he was indeed the English Socialist Keir Hardie, to which he replied that he certainly was. After that they released him with apologies!

On leaving school in St Petersburg, I was sent to a secretarial college in London for a year, returning home in July, 1914. It was decided that I should go back to England to work, perhaps in a bank, and I grasped the opportunity of trying to get my play 'The Haunting Roubles' accepted by agents in London. It was rejected by three of them, so I joined the British army, and applied for an interpretership. At the end of 1916 the shortage of Bulgarian-speaking officers caused the War Office to lay its hands on everyone knowing Russian, and a Bulgarian prisoner-of-war was instructed to teach his language to us. However, I never used my new acquisition, as later that year I was posted to the British Embassy in Petrograd, which had apparently applied for my services. This assignment saw me through the October, 1917, Revolution, after which I advised my family to leave Russia. In the following March, the remnants of the British Embassy left, but by June I was a member of the British Military Mission, which left via America for Siberia, remaining there for two years. During this tedious, phoney-war period, I wrote a novel "Futility", and for my services was awarded the Russian Order of Stanislav from the White authorities, and the O.B.E. from the British government.

It was all a bit too late for me to contribute much to the development or decline of the Russian Empire, which is what you were looking for. But it was not my fault that I was born when I was!

William Barnes Steveni (1859-)

At my home, Normanby Grange, Lincolnshire, I had a governess, who was descended from Mikipher Alphery, whom I think you have met, and my family had in their possession the history of the Alphery family. I was therefore always interested in Russia, and was not happy until I obtained the post of Professor of English in the College of Peter the Great, and for ten years was correspondent for the *Daily Chronicle* and other English papers.

I resided upwards of twenty-seven years in various parts of the Russian Empire, and can safely say that I got a balanced view of society and business. I was lost in astonishment at the perfect English spoken by members of the Russian aristocracy. There is not the least doubt that the Russians have a peculiar aptitude for languages. Add to this the fact that many had English governesses and tutors; when they eventually emigrated, they were served well by their knowledge and skill in English, as testified by the number of autobiographies and books of reminiscence which I hear have been written by Russian emigres during the twentieth century.

Take, for example, Vladimir Nabokov, who needs no introduction. The author of 'Lolita', recalls in his autobiography that his mother took 'The Times' newspaper, and his governess, Miss Norcott, an English illustrated weekly (which?). Vladimir and his brother could write English and not Russian, and so had to have the village schoolmaster in to teach them. Nabokov mentions no less than eight other family tutors (all English): Miss Greenwood, Miss Rachel, Miss Clayton, Miss Hunt, Miss Robinson, Mr Burness, Mr Cummings and Miss Lavington (could this latter be the same lady who turns up in the book 'I, Anastasia', as governess to the Duke of Leuchtenberg?).

Galina von Meck, in 'As I remember them' (1973) had a governess, Miss Bennett, known to all as 'Missie', but she is more explicit on Miss Eastwood, who had been governess to the Davydov family, and gave English lessons for a time to none other than Petr Ilyich Tchaikovski. "She was a great character, became a real member of the Davydov family, and very often bossed them all, looking upon them as her own. As she grew older, however, poor dear, she became fantastically ugly. I remember her well, because she once came to stay with us in the country, when I was about 10. She spoke very good English, and taught the children perfect English. At the end of her life she fell in love... But dear Miss Eastwood must not be remembered for her foolishness, but for what she had done for the family before that."

In a similar book 'The Autobiography of a Princess' (1968) Sofka Skipwith (nee Dolgoruky) had a Miss Lewis come every afternoon to teach her English when she was about 4 years old. Later she came under the control of Miss King, who stayed with them until the family emigrated. She sounds a typical governess, deciding the day's programme, what clothes to wear, the times for meals and for bed. She read aloud and played games, such as draughts and snakes and ladders. When Miss King caught typhoid, Sofka came under the stricter regime of Miss New, whose typical advice was: 'Masticate it well, dear'.

As long ago as 1891, at the suggestion of W.T.Stead, a prominent journalist, and author of the book 'The Truth about Russia' (1888), I made a tour of famine-stricken Russia with Count Bobrinsky and Count Lev Lvovich Tolstoy, the novelist's son. (I met the great man himself at Moscow).

My book 'Petrograd Past and Present' came out in 1915, and affords information about the British population in and around the Russian capital. I also contributed to C.E.W.Petersson's 'How to do business with Russia', which, unfortunately, did not appear until February, 1917, a little too late to do any good! We dedicated the volume to my brother Oscar Steveni, 'first guild merchant of Petrograd and Cronstadt'. The foreword by Charles E.Musgrave, of the London Chamber of Commerce, contains the classic line: 'If Russia is to prove an Eldorado for British trade, it will only be so on the basis of reciprocal advantage.' If you care to take a look in this handbook, you will read of firms that you have already heard of, like Muir & Merrilees, Knoops, and some less well-known, such as Bouton & Co, 6, Admiralty Quay; the Russian and English Bank, 28, Nevsky Prospect; Hopper & Son; Toulmain & Smith. At Kharkov one of the best and oldest firms for agricultural machinery was Messrs Hume & Lister. I could add the Thorntons, who employed some 3000 men in their cotton mills at Alexandrovsk, half a day's journey up the Neva. Other mills were run by the Becks and the Hubbards. In the timber trade were my brother, Oscar, Charles Stewart and Edward Reynolds; in shipping, commerce and engineering were the Johnstones, Maxwells, Wylies, Whishaws, Andersons, Howards, Merryweathers and Tamplins of Brighton.

Speaking of the Hubbards, it reminds me of a family I met, by the name of Birse. Mr Birse, senior, was a member of the Hubbard company, spinning and weaving cotton. He had three sons, and at least one daughter. They lived the comparatively comfortable life of the colonial trader. They, like others in their position, had a dacha, sent their sons to Realschule, were members of the British Club. Of the sons, Edward was to become commercial assistant to Robert Bruce Lockhart, British Consul in Moscow from 1912. He is described by the diplomat as 'a Moscow businessman, who had talked Russian from birth'. George became an opera singer. Margaret Birse married Rev Frank North, chaplain to the Moscow Britons, in 1915. Arthur married a British girl, engaged, like many others, in teaching English. Like most people with any sense, they escaped Russia at the Revolution. Arthur eventually became prominent during the Second World War as interpreter for Churchill at the great conferences with Stalin. No doubt he had the odd hour off to go and look up his old neighbours in and around Moscow?

Stephen Graham (1884-1975)

If helping to interpret the Russians for the British has any part to play in the development and eventual decline of the Empire, then I think I can claim to have played a modest role, even if a little late!

It was from a barrow that I bought my first tattered copy of Dostoevski's 'Crime and Punishment', a book which was to change the course of my life. Fired with enthusiasm for Russia, I began to learn the language, first from a grammar book, then from Berlitz, later and more significantly from a Russian consul, aged twenty, Nicholai Lebedev, who was working for Vickers Maxim in England, constructing a warship for the Tsar. It suited us to exchange lessons, and before long Nicholai and I became great friends. I took a month's holiday in Russia in 1905, during which I visited the fair at Nizhni Novgorod. During the Revolution that was sweeping Russia that year, I was twice arrested as a foreign agent. Nicholai returned home to Ukraine, I to London, where one Sunday I heard a sermon by Canon Scott Holland, who said: "No one has achieved much in life who has not at one time or other staked everything upon an act of faith." So I resolved to give up my safe job at Somerset House, and go back to Russia. I saved up £20, and set off for Nicholai's home, where I was received as a child of the family, and eked out a living as an *au pair*, teaching English.

In the spring of 1910, I went to the Caucasus and started what was to become a feature of my life for the next few years – tramping. I wrote and published all my experiences - including my adventures with Russian pilgrims to Jerusalem, and with poor Russian emigrants to America. In November, 1913, I was commissioned by Lord Northcliffe to report on Russia for The Times newspaper; when war broke out I went to the Russian front to provide my stories. Nor did hostilities prevent me travelling via Egypt to study the Copts, that unusual branch of Christians to be found in Arabic lands. If I am proud of any of my six books, it would be 'The Way of Martha and the Way of Mary', which came out at Christmas, 1915. In order to understand it even in a small way, it is necessary to read the whole of it, and perhaps re-read it. It is an organic unity, and reflects in its form something of the Russian idea.

I was in London when the 1917 Revolution took place, and my life thereafter was very different. But I must mention my brief visit to Russia in the spring of 1916 to arrange for the publication of "The Way of Martha and the Way of Mary", translated into Russian by Lola Ertel, daughter of Alexander Ertel, a friend of Tolstoy. On this occasion I stayed at Ertolovo, the family estate near Voronezh. Owing to the war, I was obliged to reach Russia via Murmansk and Archangel. I have written several more books during the 20th century, but if I have done anything lasting, it will be my interpretation for British readers of the essentially spiritual nature of the Russians, despite their age-old and continuing appearance to the contrary. I hope I have helped to erase the sketches of the Russians which we have seen so many times, even in this brief study.

Arthur Ransome (1884-1967)

I was already an established writer when I visited Russia in 1913 for two purposes: I was wishing to go anywhere to escape from my tiresome wife, and, having an interest in folk tales, which had been stimulated by reading Ralston's "Russian Folk Tales", I made up my mind to learn enough Russian to be able to read folk-lore in the original. So I sailed to St Petersburg, and was received with hospitality by an Anglo-Russian family. I made the acquaintance of Norman Whishaw, an English flax merchant, who gave me a lot of help learning the language. Whishaw had himself translated works by Korolenko, which I undertook to get published on my return to London, but I failed to find a publisher. This was strange, considering the interest in things Russian at that time. However, I returned in May, 1914, with a commission to write a guide to St Petersburg, and a book of fairy tales. The former was written, but never published, owing to the war and the Revolution. Englishmen were unusually popular in the Russian capital in the summer of 1914, and there was much good will in the air on the brink of the war, in which the two countries were to be allies. I carried with me a letter with an impressive crest and signature, which acted as a passport in Russia!

I was introduced to Harold Williams, a lifelong pacifist, who came originally from New Zealand (where I was born) and who had fulfilled an ambition to make a pilgrimage to Tolstoy. Employed as the correspondent in Russia for the *Manchester Guardian* since 1904, he had managed to visit Yasnaya Polyana, home of the legendary writer and thinker. Tolstoy is reported to have spoken in English, but was pleased to meet an Englishman who spoke Russian. He forced the modest Williams to confess how many languages he knew (which was said to be 42), and asked him why he had learnt Russian. Williams's answer came without hesitation: to read 'Anna Karenina' in the original. Harold Williams attended congresses of the Zemstvo (local council), talked to Russians of all classes, and thoroughly endeared himself to all and sundry. His wife, Ariadna Vladimirovna Tyrkova, was later to become known as a literary critic and writer. The couple were in England when the 1914 war started; they stayed part of the time at H.G.Wells's country home at Dunmow, Essex. During that year Harold's book "Russia of the Russians" was published. It is a mine of information and opinion on every subject: the history, governmental system, arts and religion of Russia, not forgetting a chapter on trade and industry:

"Many English families have been established in the Russian capital for generations, and although some have become through lapse of time Russian subjects, and it occasionally happens that the members of families originally English are unable to speak the language of their ancestors, the persistence with which the greater part of the colony retain their English traits, maintain their connections with the mother country, and send their children to England to be educated is remarkable... When Germans settle to carry on business they more readily become assimilated than the English do, although, on the other hand, the Englishman seems as a rule to be much more successful than the German in acquiring a good Russian accent." I think you have heard such sentiments before...

Harold longed to get back to his beloved Russia, so went as war correspondent for the *Daily Chronicle* and reported from the Russian front. After the Peace of Brest-Litovsk in 1918, Mr and Mrs Williams returned via Murmansk and Newcastle to settle in England for good. His biography 'Cheerful Giver', written by his wife, and published in 1935, gives much information on early 20th century Russia, as well as on those who, like me, visited the Williamses at their estate.

At the start of the War, I became an unofficial newspaper correspondent. I was advised to visit Moscow while there was still time, and it was there that I met Hugh Walpole, about whom you have yet to hear. He and I discovered that by pure coincidence we were both born in New Zealand of Cornish mothers. We became good friends. Later I became correspondent for The Daily News, but managed to find time to collect folk material. For safety's sake, I sent my collection, entitled 'Old Peter's Russian Tales', with illustrations by Mitrokhin, in the diplomatic bag from the British Embassy to London, where it was published. I married a Russian, Evgenia Petrovna Shelepina, whom I first met at the Smolny Institute, where she worked as secretary to Trotsky. We came to England after the Revolution, but not before I had a conversation with Lenin, who disapproved of my book "Six Weeks in Russia". Be that as it may, after Lenin's death in 1924 the book was translated into Russian, but, strange to tell, in lieu of royalties, the State publishing House presented me with – the complete works of Lenin!

Paul Dukes (1889-1968)

I ran away from home when my father remarried at the age of 60: I was eager to study music, and pictured Russia as the right country in which to achieve my ambition. So I worked my way across Europe, starting by teaching English at Rotterdam, thence to Germany, Poland and finally Riga, where I became acting Director of the Institute. It was 1909, and I managed to save enough of my earnings to be able at least to apply to the Conservatoire for piano lessons. It was while I was in St Petersburg that I met perhaps the greatest conductor at the time in Russia: Albert Coates – an Englishman, of course! He was born in St Petersburg in 1882 of a well-known industrial family. He seems to have been one of the few British in Russia to have any sympathy with the Soviets: he conducted a series of symphony concerts in Petrograd in October, 1917, along with A. Ziloti and A. Glazunov. (He was to return to conduct the Leningrad Symphony Orchestra in 1937.) I attended the rehearsals of Coates's performances, and in time met the conductor and his wife, eventually being asked to stand in as a music copyist. This led to my attending the concerts and operas, sometimes in the orchestra pit, sometimes in Mrs Coates's box. I met such composers as Glazunov, Rachmaninov, Arensky, Scriabin and Stravinsky, as well as performers like Chaliapin. When the Anglo-Russian Commission, under Hugh Walpole, sent out to liaise with the Russians in 1915, wanted assistants who knew Russian, I joined them: my job was to make a daily digest of the Russian press for the Ambassador, Sir George Buchanan, and ultimately therefore the Foreign Office in London. (I happened to be in London when the Revolution took place, but was soon sent on a roving commission to report on the new conditions prevailing under the Soviet regime.).

Hugh Walpole (1884-1941) was born in New Zealand, but was educated in Britain. A life-long pacifist, he offered his services as a stretcher-bearer in the Russian 9th Army during the First World War. His experiences gave birth to his novel "The Dark Forest" (1916) The main character of the book is a man called Trenchard, who can safely be taken as the novelist himself. He is described as 'just the figure for high romantic pictures. He had doubtless seen Russia in the colours of the pleasant, superficial books of travel that have, of late, in England, been so popular, books that see in the Russian a blessed sort of Idiot unable to read or write, but vitally conscious of God, and in Russia a land of snow, ikons, mushrooms and pilgrims.' (Could he have been referring to Stephen Graham's works, by any chance?) The sequel to 'The Dark Forest' was 'The Secret City', set exclusively in Petrograd before and during the 1917 Revolution. I think it is the most illuminating prose about Russia and the Russians to come from an English pen for centuries. I recommend you to read it. He even writes like a Russian; the book could easily be a translation from Russian.

We must not overlook the fact that Walpole was himself Head of the Military Mission. He calls it 'the noble but uphill task of enlightening the Russian public as to the righteousness of the war, the British character, and the Anglo-Russian alliance.'

William John Birkbeck (1859-1916)

I was the son of a Quaker, but, strange to relate, I went to school at Eton, where I soon acquired a taste for High Anglican doctrine and practice, visiting Clewer church for the festivals, and installing my own private oratory in my bedroom. At Oxford (home of the Anglo-Catholic revival) I found my spiritual home. During my undergraduate years (1877-1881) I witnessed Turgenev receiving an honorary degree, although I knew nothing of his work up till then. But it opened up an interest in Russia, and the more I learnt about the country, the more I was struck with the honour given to the national religion there. After graduation I attended the Royal College of Music, where I had organ lessons from Sir Walter Parratt, and made a study of plainsong – an unusual subject for those days – but one which brought me into contact with the Russian church chant.

Being somewhat smitten with the peculiar charm of the country, but knowing nothing about Russia or its language, I made my first visit in 1882. After that nothing could stop me reading about this fascinating place. In London I moved in influential musical and ecclesiastical circles, sufficiently to be asked to attend in 1888, as the Archbishop of Canterbury's envoy, the celebrations to mark the 900th anniversary of the baptism of Vladimir at Kiev, the first recorded appearance of

Christianity in Russia. I was fortunate enough to have a friend from Oxford days, Sir Arthur Hardinge, who was now Secretary at the Embassy in St Petersburg, and who was able to open various doors, which might have otherwise been difficult of access. This was but the beginning of a career involving many a visit to Russia. I like to think that my contact with people in high places in Church and State helped somewhat in the process of maintaining and improving the lot of the Russian people through exposure to Western influence. I was ever receptive to the influence of Russians on us.

In 1894 I, along with Mandell Creighton, Bishop of Peterborough, represented the Church of England at the Coronation of Nicholas II, after a considerable tour of Siberia, inspecting the Orthodox missionary work, and the degree of success (or otherwise) the Russians were having in converting Mohammedans in places like Kazan'. Three years later I accompanied Archbishop Maclagan of York on a delegation from the Church of England, during which tour I was privileged to be interviewed by the Emperor. I heard later that he had told his closest adviser: "We are always glad to hear that Mr Birkbeck is coming to Russia, and when he brings a bishop with him it is all the better."! The tsar expressed to me his wish that Russia and England should be drawn nearer to one another, and 'this might be done by our churches'. An invitation was issued for a Russian bishop to attend Queen Victoria's Diamond jubilee. I myself contributed slightly to British understanding of Russia by publishing several small works on Russian church doctrine and practice, including published lectures; I was also responsible for the editing of The English Hymnal (1906), and the inclusion in it of the Russian Contakion for the Departed, the Kiev melody of which was edited by my old teacher and friend, Sir Walter Parratt.

Back home, in 1910, I was appointed High Sheriff of Norfolk; I presented to Norwich cathedral a cope, made of Russian cloth-of-gold, fastened with a morse set with jewels which I had obtained in Russia. In 1912 I was part of the Speaker's delegation to the Russian Duma; during our stay we visited the field of Borodino on the day of the centenary of the famous battle. My last visit to Russia took place during the war, in 1916, shortly before my death. I understand that J.Athelstan Riley, who had collaborated with me and others on The English Hymnal, wrote a study entitled 'Birkbeck and the Russian Church'(1917). I am grateful to him.

Another churchman who did much to make the Russian point of view understood in Britain was Walter H.Frere (1863-1938). His first introduction to Russia came in 1909, when he went with his sister to represent the University of Cambridge at the Gogol' Centenary celebrations. This whetted his appetite for the Russian people and the Orthodox faith, and he returned the next summer, mainly to the Baltic and Finnish parts of the Empire. In early 1914 Frere made a tour of the main centres – Moscow, Riga, Polotsk, Petrograd, where he delivered addresses on the English church, and, had time allowed, his influence might have been felt in places where it mattered

I must leave the reader to judge whether I did anything to forward the Russian cause, and so merit inclusion in this present book of worthies, such as the next gentleman!

Robert Bruce Lockhart (1887-1970)

When I was posted to Moscow as Vice-Consul, I was surprised to find that people had heard of my prowess as a footballer. So immediately I was enlisted to play for the Morozov textile factory team, 30 miles east of Moscow. We won the League in the 1912 season. (My medal is still, as far as I am aware, in the National Library of Scotland). It was only afterwards that I realised that it was my brother John who played rugby for Scotland, and the Russians did not know the difference between the two games! We were not the only Scots playing football in Russia: in the 1890's, I am told, there was a team called Nevka, which consisted entirely of Scots workers.

Someone I greatly admired was Maurice Baring (1874-1945). After an unpromising educational start, he joined the diplomatic service in 1898, and after assignments in Denmark and Rome, where he met a good many Russians, and continued Russian lessons, he visited the Benckendorff estate at Sosnovka, south of Moscow, for three weeks in 1902. On return to London he suggested to a publisher that he could translate all the works of Dostoevski or Gogol, only to receive the reply that there would be no market for such books in England. Suitably disappointed but not defeated, Baring decided to ask for six months' leave from his Foreign Office post, and went to Russia at Christmas, 1904. At Moscow he stayed at the house of Maria Karlovna von Kotz, who took in English pupils, mostly British army officers and consular officials to teach them Russian. At the outbreak of the Japanese war, Baring got himself appointed correspondent in Manchuria for The Morning Post, and travelled out east by the Siberian

Railway, with two other correspondents. Back in Moscow, he continued to report for his paper, until taking over at St Petersburg in 1907 from Harold Munro (known to the literary world as 'Saki'). Baring was interpreter to the Parliamentary Delegation visiting Russia in 1912, and then went to cover the Balkan war, after which he returned to Russia, continuing to write books on Russian life and literature. Russia so badly needed men like Baring, who could appreciate those qualities of spirituality which escaped most visitors, and, indeed, resident foreigners. You know, from what you have read in this collection, that the majority of Britons who lived and stayed long in Russia did so because it suited them economically.

I myself was Acting Consul-General at the first Revolution in March, 1917, but left before the October Revolution. However, I was sent back as Envoy to the Bolsheviks in January, 1918, to counter German influence - and the rest is history.

Denis Norman Garstin (1890-1916)

After public school and Cambridge, I took a tutorship in the Crimea, arriving in 1912. While in Russia I contributed articles to the London press, some of which I published in book form under the title 'Friendly Russia' in 1915. I was fortunate enough to enlist none other than H.G.Wells to write the Introduction. He wrote:

"Happily the knowledge of the real Russia is no longer the secret of a few travellers. A new unbiassed literature grows up to set us right. We have Dr Williams's admirable 'Russia of the Russians' if we want an ordered statement of facts; we have Mr Maurice Baring, Mr Stephen Graham, and now, a welcome recruit – Mr Garstin, if we want aspects and atmospheres."

I must say I was taken aback, being linked with such august writers. One such that I met personally at the Embassy in Petrograd was Hugh Walpole – an honour indeed. No one could have been more helpful and sympathetic: after my death during the Onega expedition (I was buried in the cemetery at Archangel) my only work of fiction 'The Shilling Soldiers', about my experiences in wartime France, bears a preface by Hugh Walpole.

Another colleague, whom you have already met, was Paul Dukes, who went out to Russia with the best of intentions, but who, like the rest of us, was limited in what he could do for the Empire: it was all a bit too late! If only I had been born thirty years ealier! Like John Baddeley, whose father was a British army officer serving in the Crimean War, and died young, leaving a widow and child. Through a not fully explained connection, Count Peter Shuvalov, the Russian Ambassador in London, befriended the boy and took him on a visit to Russia. John was full of curiosity, and thrilled at the thought of the opportunity of shooting a bear. On the long train journey he swotted up Russian vocabulary. At St Petersburg he did the sights, including a visit by sleigh to Mourino, twelve miles north of the city, the estate of Prince Vorontsov. In Baddeley's book 'Russian in the Eighties', which was published in 1921, he describes the houses of many of the English colony, and the first and only golf-links in Russia. He so fell in love with Russia and the Russians, that he outstayed the Count, only returning home when his money ran out. But when Shuvalov was recalled to Russia soon after, he invited John to go with him again. He had to earn a living, so hit on the idea of being a newspaper correspondent. He landed a job with *The Standard* on the understanding that the paper should be first to report any news of consequence. His connections among the Russian aristocracy often enabled him to gather very valuable items of exclusive information.

Someone whose modesty is in danger of depriving him of a place in this collection of Britons who did something for the Russians is Charles Heath, M.A.(Oxon), who was tutor to the young prince Nicholas, and companion to his father, Alexander III. He was a burly Englishman, beloved by all who knew him. He was made an honorary general in the Russian army, was a first-rate sportsman, and accompanied the Emperor on hunting excursions in Finland. On these occasions all formality vanished: they had picnics in the forest, for which Mr Heath cooked the meat, the Empress the potatoes and the Tsar managed the fire. He appears to have been on such terms with the Imperial family that he even allowed himself to remonstrate with Grand Duke Nicholas for wishing to drink the water of the Neva on the occasion of the annual Blessing of the Waters, on the grounds that the river was contaminated. Heath was a talented water-colour artist, whose work, naturally, fetched high prices. One can imagine this gentleman in his apartments in the grounds of the Anitchkov Palace, just as one can imagine the Grand Duke George's green parrot, Popka, who mimicked Mr Heath in an exaggerated English accent! Heath had married in 1861 at the English church in St Petersburg, where his funeral also took place. Among the mourners was the Dowager Empress; other members of the Imperial family bore the coffin from the hearse to the grave. You cannot live like that without having an influence where it is most needed!

Colonel the Hon. Fred H. Cripps (1889-)

I have been asked to contribute to this study the other side of the coin. The majority of the people you have been meeting put at least as much into Russia as they got out of it. I am the exception that proves the rule!

My childhood and youth were spent in plenty and even waste, and in adult life I made and lost money on a very large scale. I happened to meet Mr Robert Boulton, who had started a firm of merchant bankers under the name of Bouton Brothers, and I was induced to join them in St Petersburg. The firm I was with gave me three months' leave of absence to go to Russia, with no knowledge of the language, but with letters of introduction to the Ambassador, Sir George Buchanan. In the capital I wasted no time fixing a brass plate to a suitable house on Admiralty Quay, enlisted the services of a lawyer, Vladimir Robertovich Idleson, and Miss Pinkerton, another half-Russian, as my housekeeper. I made a contract with the chief steward of the Winter Palace to supply me with food, and, if I was entertaining, with catering staff, too. (The steward asked me for an English medal to add to his numerous foreign ones; I gave him a very nice tie-pin).

Bouton Brothers joined up with a Russian firm to form the Russian and English Joint Stock Bank, with offices on Nevsky Prospect. As joint managing director, I worked hard, both at the task of extending business, and acquiring the language. With my unmarried sister, who was staying with me, I had great fun with all the well-off and highly placed, not entirely oblivious to the discontent of the masses. We had shooting parties with large banquets and champagne. Once, our host, apologising for the lack of game, got his servants to toss the china up into the air for us to shoot at. Pity it was priceless Sèvres! Once when I had to travel overnight to Moscow by train, at the last minute I was forced to share my sleeping compartment with a large Russian gentleman and his crate of champagne. On arrival in Moscow, the stranger invited me to be his guest at the Opera House that evening. It tuned out to be none other than Fedor Chaliapin, who asked me to join him after the performance for a champagne supper.

I kept away from Russia for the period of the First World War, but I returned afterwards to a country changed by the Revolution. Much of my wealth had been seized, but I explained to Kamenev, Mayor of Moscow, that I was not interested in politics, but would like to do something useful for Russia. So I was allowed to help rebuild houses for the Soviet authorities, and to remain on good terms with several leading figures in the government. I lived for a long time in Moscow in a house overlooking the river and the Kremlin. Curious coincidence: my younger brother, Sir Stafford Cripps, was Ambassador in Moscow during the Second World War, and 'my' house was now the Embassy, complete with the same hall porter who had served me those years ago!

23 THE TUTOR

Sidney Gibbes (1876-1963)

I was born in Rotherham, the son of a bank manager, and studied at Aberystwyth and St John's College, Cambridge, where I graduated in 1899. I planned to become ordained, but without success. As I had a longing to do something different, I decided to visit Russia, which at the time was becoming known as an unusual but challenging country. 1901 saw me tutoring two boys in the Shidlovski family. My journey from the station to their country house was not encouraging, as the horses broke into an uncontrollable bolt. When I was asked if I was not too shaken by the experience, I felt I had to exhibit the traditional English cool, declaring that I was not surprised, having been told before leaving England that all Russian drivers went at that rate! Another feature of travel was the fact that cabbies were always excessively fat!

I did not approve of the social conditions of the peasant classes, nor, I must admit, of the Russian Orthodox church services and rituals. Nor was I very happy in my post as tutor – boys and their mother were very difficult. In 1908 I was fortunate enough to succeed a Mr Epps as tutor to the Imperial family: my brief being to teach each of the children English, which at the time was considered essential along with French, which was taught by M.Pierre Gilliard, a Swiss. Continuing my work as an usher at the Imperial School of Law, and at a girls' finishing school in St Petersburg, I started to commute 15 miles to Tsarskoe Selo by train. I was first commissioned to teach the two eldest princesses,

Olga and Tatiana, then Anastasia, and eventually, in 1913, the Tsarevich Alexei himself, for up to sixteen lessons a week.

When the War broke out in 1914, I was on holiday in England to be near my father, who was approaching his death. But I was ordered back to Russia, and accommodated in the Tsarskoe palace, although I was allowed to continue working as a Director of Studies at the Pritchard School for modern languages. Wherever the tsar went on his military duties, he took his son with him, and wherever his son went, I had to go, including the military headquarters at Mogilev. It was during one of my days off in 1917 that the Imperial family were put under arrest, and I was locked out of my apartment in the palace. In August of that year, after I had been allowed to collect my things, I was given permission to make the lengthy journey across Russia to Tobolsk, where for a time I resumed lessons with the Imperial children, along with Gilliard, who had accompanied them at the outset. Later on, life at the House of Special Purpose at Ekaterinburg was anything but pleasant, though we had some lighter moments. We had been allowed to go to church in Tobolsk, but even that was later forbidden.

I cannot bear to go into the details of the assassination of the Imperial family, much of which has become well known to everybody; suffice it to say that I was heart-broken, and longed to return to England. The only safe way was eastwards across Siberia to China and eventually home. Several years later I became a member of the Russian Orthodox church, and eventually took orders as Father Nicholas, in honour of the late Tsar, ministering to the White Russian communities in London and Oxford, where I died in 1963.

Postscript

What is there left to say? All through this collection characters have appeared from nowhere, mere names picked up from odd places in reading, who do not seem to be important, and of whom little more is heard. All we know is: they contributed something, however small, to the development and eventual destiny of the Russian Empire.

Would it not be interesting to know more about Harry Best, who in the 16th century was involved in a trial by combat? His opponent, a Moscovite, immediately petitioned Ivan the Terrible to forbid foreigners engaging in the lists with citizens. And what of William Barnsley, of Worcester, who was exiled to Siberia for allegedly familiar behaviour towards Ivan's wife?

Who were Morton Bydlar and Jack Starkey, actors, and Thomas Shelley, a musician, who were included in a troupe taken to Moscow by J.Kunst (?German) in 1702?

Cottrell, in his 'Recollections of Siberia' (1842), recalls a Mr Adams, attached to the Imperial Academy of Sciences, who accompanied Count Golovin on his embassy to China in 1805. It surely could not be the same Mr Adams, who turns up in Moscow in 1808 as a harp teacher.

Who was the young English clergyman, 'a curate attached to the British church', mentioned by Fred J.Whishaw in 'Out of Doors in Tsarland' (1893)? The reverend gentleman knew no Russian, but being of an inquiring disposition, visited the terminus of the Moscow railway in St Petersburg, and sat in the third class waiting room to look and listen. On the third occasion he was accosted by the station police. Being ignorant of the language, he was arrested and locked up. Unfortunately, we are not told the end of the story, but we may safely assume that he did not contribute much to the development of the Russian Empire.

A few miscellaneous people make a fleeting appearance in biographies. Take, for example, the carpenter Adamson, who lived in one wing of Alexander Benois' house, when the future stage designer was a boy. Adamson made a special model stage for the young Benois in 1878, and was instrumental in setting him up on the road to his brilliant career.

Or what of Mr Tweedy, of the Russian Petroleum and Liquid Fuel Company, who had wells at Baku as early as 1902? Do we know any more about Mr Bligh, who was 'a young brewer sent out from England to teach a big Russian firm how to brew 'Imperial Stout' in bottles as impressive as those of champagne, as recorded by Arthur Ransome in his 'Six Weeks in Russia' (1919)?

More substantially perhaps, we hear of a Mr Septimus Beardmore, a civil engineer, who provided material for the 1871 book on 'Russian Sheet-iron' by John Percy. The process was communicated to him by Mr W.Yates, a mechanical engineer, in charge of an engine-manufactory at Nizhni-Sergha in the Urals. In the same area, at Vyksa, the director of the estate and iron-works was Mr Herbert Barry, who wrote in 1870 'Russian Metallurgical works, iron, copper, gold, concisely described'.

No doubt, there are scores, if not hundreds, of other brave Britons who spent their lives in the service of the Russians, and whose names and exploits have been lost for ever.

Bibliography

Alcock, T.	Travels in Russia	1831
Anderson, M.S.	Britain's Discovery of Russia	1958
Anderson, Rev W.	Sketches of the History and Present State of the Russian Empire	1815
Armstrong, T.B.	Journal of Travels	1831
Arnold, R.A.	From the Levant, the Black Sea and the Danube	1868
Atkinson, G.F.	Pictures from the North	1848
Atkiinson, J.A.	Foreign Field Sports	1814
Atkinson, J.B.	Art Tour of Northern Capitals	1873
Atkinson, T.W.	Oriental and Western Siberia	1858
Atkinson & Walker	Picturesque Representation of the Russian People	1812
Baedeker	Russia	1914
Baldwin, M.A	Schoolgirl of Moscow	1911
Bantuish-Kamensky, D.N.	Slovar' Russkoi Zemli	1836
Bantuish-Kamensky, D.N.	Age of Peter	1851
Baring, M.	Puppet Show of Memory	1922
Barrett, W. A.	Balfe: His Life and Work	1882
Barrow, J.	Excursions in the North of Europe	1834
Barry, H.	Russian Metallurgical Works	1870
Bates, E.S.	Touring in 1600	1911
Bax, A.	Farewell, my Youth	1943
Bax, A.	The Cruise of the Dwarf	1875
Bell, S.F.	Annals of Thomas Banks	1938
Bell, J.	Travels from St Petersburg	1788
Bellows, J.	Letters and memoirs	1904
Benois, A.	Memoirs	1960
Bentham, Sir S.	Life	1862
Berdmore, S.	Scratch team of essays	1883
Billings, J.	An Account of a Geographical and Astronomical Expedition to The Northern parts of Russia, 1785-94	1802
Birkbeck, W.J.	Life and Letters	1922
Birse, A.H.	Memoirs of an Interpreter	1967
Blunt, W.	Lady Muriel	1962
Boddy, A.A.	With Russian Pilgrims	1893
Borrow, G	Letters to the British & Foreign Bible Society	1911
Borrow, G.	Talisman	1835
Borrow, G.	Targum	1835
Bowring, J.	Autobiography	1877
Brabazon, E.J.	Russia and her Czars	1855
Bremner, R.	Excursions into the Interior of Russia	1839

Brown, C.A.	Letters	1937
Brown, C.A.	Narensky	1814
Brown, J.C.	Forests of Russia	1884
Bruce, P.H.	Memoirs	1782
Buchanan, M.	Victorian Gallery	1956
Bulmer, J.	A Note of such Arts & Mysteries	1649
Bury, H.	Russian Life To-day	1915
Cameron, G.P.	Personal Adventures and Excursions in Georgia, Circassia & Russia	1845
Cardozo, N.	Lucky Eyes and a High Heart	1979
Carr, Sir J.	Northern Summer	1805
Carr,Sir J.	Travels round the Baltic	1810
Carr, James	Russia as it is	1855
Carrington, G.	Behind the Scenes in Russia	1874
Carroll, L.	Russian Journal	1867
Cathcart, G.	Commentaries on the War in Russia, 1812-13	1850
Cazalet, E.A.	Znachenie Dzhona Govarda	1892
Chown, J.L.	Sir S.M.Peto	1943
Clarke, E.D.	Travels in Various Countries	1810
Cochrane, J.D.	Narrative of a Pedestrian Tour	1829
Coglan, F.	Guide to St Petersburg and Moscow	1836
Connell, J.	Wavell, Scholar and Soldier	1964
Consett, T.	Present State and Regulations of the Church of Russia	1729
Cook, J.	Voyages and Travels	1770
Cottrell, C.H.	Recollections of Siberia	1842
Coxe, W.	Travels into Russia	1784
Craig, E.G.	Gordon Craig – the Story of his Life	1968
Craven, Lady E.	A Journey through the Crimea to Constantinople	1789
Creighton, M.	Life and Letters	1904
Cripps, F.H.	Life's a Gamble	1957
Cyril, Grand Duke	My Life in Russia's Service, Then and Now	1939
Dashkov, Princess	Memoirs, ed. K.Fitzlyon	1958
Davies, R.C.H.	Hugh Walpole	1952
Dalyell, Sir J.B.W.	Binns Papers	1938
Deacon, J.	Vladimir and Catherine	1864
Deane, J.	Letter from Moscow to the Marquess of Carmarthen	1699
Dee, J.	Private Diary	1842
Dicey, E.J.S.	A Month in Russia	1867
Disbrowe, C.A.A.	Original Letters from Russia	1878
Dixon, H.	John Howard	1854
Dobell, P.	Russia as it is	1833
Dobson, A.	18th Century Vignettes	1911
Dobson, G.	St Petersburg	1910
Dobson, G.	Russia's Railway Advance	1890

Dukes, P.	The Unending Quest	1950
Eagar, M.	Six years at the Russian Court	1906
Edwards, H.S.	Russians at Home and Abroad	1861
Elliott, C.B.	North of Europe	1832
Elliott, C.B.	Travels in Three Great Empires	1838
Eyre, S.	Sketches of Russian Life	1878
Farmborough, F.	Nurse at the Russian Front	1974
Farmborough, F.	Russian Album	1979
Fenton, R.	Photographer of the Crimean War	1954
Flood, W.H.C.	John Field	1921
Forster, G.	Journey from Bengal to England	1798
Forster, J.	Free Protestant People	1746
Frankland	Narrative of a visit	1832
Fraser, J.F.	The real Siberia	1902
Fraser, J.F.	Russia of To-day	1915
Fulford, R.T.B.	Samuel Whitbread	1967
Gadsby, J.	Trip to Sebastopol	1858
Gallenga, A.C.N.	Summer Tour in Russia	1882
Garnett, D.	The Golden Echo	1953
Garstin, D.	Friendly Russia	1915
Gazley, J.G.	Rev. Arthur Young , 1741-1820	1956
Gerhardi, W.	Memoirs of a Polyglot	1931
Glen, W.	Journal of a Tour from Astrachan	1823
Glover, M.	A very Slippery Fellow	1977
Gordon, A.	History of Peter the Great	1755
Gordon, P.	Passages from the Diary	1859
Gowing, L.F.	5000 miles in a sledge	1889
Graham, S.	Changing Russia	1913
Graham, S.	A tramp's sketches	1912
Graham, S.	Undiscovered Russia	1912
Graham, S.	Vagabond in the Caucasus	1911
Granville, A.B.	Autobiography	1874
Granville, A.B.	St Petersburg	1828
Green, G.	An Original Journey	1813
Grylls, M.R.G.	Journal of Claire Clairmont	1939
Guthrie, Mrs M.	A Tour through the Crimea	1802
Guthrie, Mrs K.	Through Russia	1874
Hakluyt, R.	Voyages of the English Nation	1972
Hamel, J.	England and Russia	1854
Hamel, J.	Anglichane v Rossii	1865
Hamel, J.	Opisanie Tul'skago Zavoda	1826
Hamilton, E.H.	English Governess in Russia	1861
Hamilton	Life of Rear-Admiral Jones	1845
Hamilton, F.S.	Vanished Pomps of Yesterday	1919
Hannah, I.C.	Capitals of the Northlands	1914

Hanway, J.	British Trade over the Caspian	1753
Hanway, J.	Remarkable Occurrences	1798
Hapgood, I.	Russian Rambles	1895
Hare, A.J.C.	Studies in Russia	1885
Harrison, R.	Notes of a 9-years' Residence in Russia	1855
Harleian Collection:	Voyages and Travels	1752
Hayes, M.H.	Among Horses in Russia	1900
Heber, R.	Life	1830
Henderson, E.	Biblical Researches	1826
Henderson, E.	Extracts of Letters	1817
Henderson, E.	Travels in Russia	1826
Henderson, P.	Life of Laurence Oliphant	1956
Hill, A.	The Northern Star	1724
Hill, S.S.	Travels in Siberia	1854
Hill, S.S.	Travels on the Shores of the Baltic	1854
Hodgetts, E.A.B.	Moss from a Rolling Stone	1924
Howe, B.	A Galaxy of Governesses	1954
Holderness, M.	New Russia	1823
Holman, J.	Travels	1825
Hubback, J.	Cross-currents in a Long Life	1934
Hume, G.	Thirty-five Years in Russia	1914
Ikonnikov, V.S.	Graf N.S. Mordvinov	1873
James, J.T.	Journal of a Tour	1816
James, J.T.	Views in Russia	1826
Jane, F.T.	Imperial Russian Navy	1904
Jenkins, H.	The Life of George Borrow	1912
Jesse	Notes of a Half-pay in Search of health	1841
Johnson, H.	Life of Joseph Wiggins	1907
Johnson, J.	Journey from India to England	1818
Johnston, R.	Travels in Russia	1815
Johnstone, C.L.	British Colony in Russia	1898
Johnstone, H.A.	Trip up the Volga to Nijni Fair	1875
Jones, G.M.	Travels in Norway etc	1827
Joyneville, C.	Life and Times of Alexander I	1875
Justice, Mrs E.	Voyage to Russia	1746
Keppel, G.T.	Personal Narrative of a Journey from India to England	1827
King, J.G.	Letter to the Bishop of Durham	1778
Kingston, W.	Fred Markham in Russia	1858
Knill, R.	Memoir of Walter Venning	1822
Konovalov, S.	Oxford and Russia	1947
Krol, A.E.	Angliiskie Portrety	1939
Lansdell, H.	Chinese Central Asia	1893
Lansdell, H.	Through Siberia	1882
Latimer, R.S.	Dr Baedeker and his Apostolic Work in Russia	1907

Latimer, R.S.	Under Three Tsars	1909
Latimer, R.S.	With Christ in Russia	1910
Law, E.	Sermon	1827
Lee, F.	Proposals given to Peter the Great	1752
Lee, R.	The Last Days of Alexander I and the First Days of Nicholas I	1854
Lefevre, Sir G.	Life of a Travelling Physician	1843
Leigh, M.S.	Memoirs of James Whishaw	1935
Leigh, M.S.	A History of the Whishaw Family	1935
Lethbridge, A.	The New Russia	1915
Lloyd, H.E.	Alexander I	1826
Longworth, J.A.	A Year among Circassians	1840
Lowth, G.T.	Around the Kremlin	1868
Lumsden, T.	Journey from Merut to London 1819-20	
Luppov, S.P.	Istoria Stroitel'stva Sankt-Peterburga	1957
Lyall, R.	The Character of the Russians	1823
Lyall, R.	Travels in Russia	1825
Lyall, R.	Military Colonies in Russia	1824
Macartney, G.	Account of Russia	1768
Macgill, T.	Travels in Turkey, Italy, Russia, etc	1808
Marsden, K.	On Sledge and Horseback to outcast Siberian lepers	1893
Marshall, J.	Travels through Holland, etc	1772
Martuinov, A.	Nazvanya Mskovskikh Ulits	1881
Marvin, C.	Region of the Eternal Fire	1884
Marvin, C.	Railway race to Heart	1885
Masson, C.F.P.	Secret Memoirs	1800
Maude, A.	Tsar's Coronation	1896
Maughan, W.S.	A Writer's Notebook	1949
Mavor, E.	The Virgin Mistress	1964
Meakin, A.M.B.	Ribbon of Iron	1901
Meakin, A.M.B.	Russia – Travels and Studies	1906
Meck, G.von	As I remember them	1973
Merry, W.M.	Two Months in Russia	1916
Michell, T.	Handbook for Travellers in Russia	1864
Michell, T.	Russian Pictures	1889
Middleton, K.W.	Britain and Russia	1947
Mignan, R.	A Winter Journey through Russia	1839
Mikhankova,V.	N. Ya. Marr	1949
Moore, J.	Journey from London to Odessa	1833
Morell, J.R.	Russia as it is	1854
Morison, T & Hutchinson, G.	Life of Sir Edward F.Law	1911
Morley, H.	Sketches of Russian Life	1866
Morton, E.	Travels in Russia	1830
Murchison, R.I.	Geology of Russia and the Ural Mountains	1845
Murphy, J.	Russia at the Time of the Coronation of Alexander II	1856

Napier, E.H.	Life of Admiral Sir C. Napier	1862
Nevinson, H.W.	The Dawn in Russia	1906
Nikiforov, L.A.	Russko-angliiskie otnoshenia pri Petre I	1950
Noble, A.	Siberian Days	1928
Norman, Sir H.	All the Russias	1902
Oliphant, L.	Russian Shores of the Black Sea	1854
Oliphant, M.	Memoir of the Life of L. Oliphant	1891
Page, W.S.	Russia Company	1912
Paley, Princess	Memories of Russia 1916-19	1924
Pares, B.	My Russian Memoirs	1931
Parkinson, J.	A Tour of Russia, Siberia and Crimea, 1792-4	ed.1971
Parry, A.	Whistler's Father	1939
Paterson, J.	The Book for Every Land	1858
Paul, R.B.	Journal of a Tour to Moscow	1836
Peacock, N.	Russian Year Book	1911
Pearson, C.H.	Russia, by a recent Traveller	1859
Peel, A.H.	Polar Gleams	1894
Pemberton, M.	Cronstadt	1898
Percy, J.	Russian Sheet-iron	1871
Perry, J.	The State of Russia under the Present Czar	1716
Pinkerton, R.	Russia	1833
Porter, Sir R.	Travelling Sketches	1809
Prelooker, J.	Heroes and heroines of Russia	
Prelooker, J.	Russian Flashlights	1911
Prelooker, J.	Under Czar and Queen Victoria	
Price, M.P.	My Three Revolutions	1969
Price, M.P.	Siberia	1912
Pridham, F.	Close of a Dynasty	1956
Prothero	Life of Dean Stanley	1893
Puilyaev, M.I.	Zabytoye proshloye Sankt-Peterburga	1889
Puilyaev, M.I.	Staraya Moskva	1891
Raeff, M.	Michael Speransky	1957
Raikes, T.	Visit to St Petersburg in the Winter of 1829-30	1838
Ramble, R.	Travelling Opinions	1836
Ransome, A.	Six Weeks in Russia	1919
Ravenstein, E.G.	The Russians on the Amur	1861
Reed, E.J.	Letters from Russia	1876
Reid, A.	From Peking to Petersburg	1899
Rennie, Sir J.	Autobiography	1875
Richard, H.	Memoirs of Joseph Sturge	1864
Richardson, W.	Anecdotes of the Russian Empire	1784
Ridley, J.C.	Reminiscences of Russia	1898
Rigby, E.	Letters from the Shores of the Baltic	1842
Riola, H.	How to learn Russian	1878
Riola, H.	Graduated Russian Reader	1879

Ritchie, L.	A Journey to St Petersburg	1836
Rose, E.	Gordon Craig	1931
Royer, A.	The English Prisoners in Russia	1854
Russell, W.H.	The Great War with Russia	1895
Sala, G.A.	A Journey due North	1859
Sala, G.A.	Life and Adventures	1896
Scott, R.C.	Quakers in Russia	1964
Scott, C.H.	The Baltic, the Black Sea and the Crimea	1854
Seacole, M.	Wonderful Adventures in Many Lands	1857
Seebohm, H.	Siberia in Europe	1880
Semeonov, Y.	Siberia	1963
Seymour, H.D.	Russia on the Black Sea	1855
Shaw, T.B.	St Petersburg English Review	1842-3
Sherley, Sir T	The Sherley Brothers	1848
Sherman, J.	Memoir of William Allen	1851
Shoemaker, M.M.	Great Siberian Railway	1903
Simmons, E.	English Literature in Russia	1935
Simpson, J.Y.	Sidelights on Siberia	1898
Smirnoi, N.	Zhizn' I Podvigi Grafa Platova	1821
Smith, Mrs M.	Six Years' Travel in Russia	1859
Stanley, A.P.	Life and Correspondence	1893
Stead, W.T.	The Truth about Russia	1888
Steuart, A.F.	Scottish Influences in Russian History	1913
Steven, C.	Catalogue des Plantes Rares	1811
Steven, C.	Nastavlenie o shelkovodstve	1827
Steveni, W.B.	The Russian Army from Within	1915
Steveni, W.B.	Petrograd Past and Present	1915
Steveni, W.B.	Things seen in Russia	1912
Swann, H.	Home on the Neva	1968
Swayne, H.G	Through the Highlands of Siberia	1904
Swinton, A.	Travels in Norway, Russia, etc	1792
Thompson, A.S.	Home Words	1875
Tolstoy, I.	Tolstoy, my Father	1971
Tolstoy, S.	Tolstoy remembered by his Son	1961
Tolstoy, Y.	The First Forty years of Anglo-Russian Relations	1875
Tooke, W.	View of the Russian Empire	1799
Trevor-Battye, A.	Ice-bound on Kolguev	1895
Trevor-Battye, A.	A Northern Highway of the Tsar	1898
Troyat, H.	Daily Life in Russia	1961
Tuirkova, A.V.	Cheerful Giver – the Biography of Harold Williams	1935
Tupper, H.	To the Great Ocean	1965
Turner, C.E.	The Nevsky Magazine	1863
Turner, S.	Siberia	1905
Turnor,R.	James Wyatt	1950

Venables, R.L.	Domestic Scenes in Russia	1839
Wahl, O.W.	The Land of the Czar	
Wallace, Sir D.	Russia	1877
Wallace, Sir D.	Interpretation of the Russian People	1915
Wallace, Sir D.	The Times Book of Russia	1916
Ware, J.R & Mann, R.K.	Life and times of Col. Fred Burnaby	1885
Wenyon, C.	4000 miles across Siberia	1914
Wheeler, D.	Memoirs	1842
Whishaw, F.J.	Out of Doors in Tsarland	1893
Whitworth, C.	An Account of Russia as it was in the Year 1710	1758
Wilbraham, R.	Travels in the Transcaucasian Provinces	1839
Wilkinson, S.	In the Land of the North	1905
Willan, T.S.	Muscovy Merchants in 1555	1953
Williams, A.R.	Through the Russian Revolution	1923
Wilmot, M.& C.	Russian Journals	1803-8
Wilson, W.R.	Travels in Russia etc	1828
Wilson, F.	Muscovy: Russia through Foreign Eyes, 1553-1900	1970
Windt, H. de	My Restless Life	1908
Windt, H. de	Russia as I knew it	1917
Wolff, J.	Travels and Adventures	1861
Wood, R.K.	The Tourist's Russia	1912
Youssoupoff, F.	Lost Splendour	1953
	Anglo-Russian Literary Society Proceedings	1893-1920
	British & Foreign Bible Society, History of	1904-10
	British & Foreign Medical Review	1836
	Description of Muscovy	1698
	The Englishwoman in Russia, by a Lady ten years Resident in That Country	1855
	Guide to Moscow	1835
	Murray's Handbook for Travellers in Russia	1893
	A New and Exact Description of Muscovy	1698
	YMCA in Moscow	1915

Index of Characters

2022806R00108

Printed in Great Britain
by Amazon.co.uk, Ltd.,
Marston Gate.